TERRORIST
LIVES

TERRORIST LIVES

Maxwell Taylor

and

Ethel Quayle

Brassey's
London • Washington

First English edition 1994

UK editorial offices: Brassey's, 33 John Street, London WC1N 2AT
UK orders: Marston Book Services, PO Box 87, Oxford OX2 ODT
USA orders: Order Department, Macmillan Publishing Company,
201 West 103rd Street, Indianapolis, IN 46290

Distributed in North America to booksellers and wholesalers by the
Macmillan Publishing Company, NY 10022

Maxwell Taylor and Ethel Quayle have asserted their moral right to be identified
as authors of this work.

Library of Congress Cataloging in Publication Data
available

British Library Cataloging in Publication Data
A catalogue record for this book is
available from the British Library

Hardcover 0-08-041327-7

Typeset by M Rules
Printed in Great Britain by
Bookcraft (Bath) Limited

Contents

Acknowledgements

The work presented here is in many ways the 'data' from which the first author's other books have been drawn. This consists of interview material, documents, press material, and other sources. Many people have contributed by participating in interviews, or allowing the authors to discuss matters with them. For obvious reasons, a number cannot be identified, but for others we may not know their true identity. The best policy seems to be not to name any individuals or organisations, but to make a collective acknowledgement here of the authors' debts to them.

Others can be clearly acknowledged. Jim Cusack has shared with us his enormous knowledge of this area, and participated in some of the interviews reported – perhaps more importantly, his friendship and common sense has greatly contributed to the book's development. Alison Jamieson gave her time and help, making possible one important element of the book. Members of the *Centrale Recherche Informatiedienst*, The Hague, and *Gemeetepolitie* Amsterdam provided invaluable assistance both making possible and contributing to some of the interview material. The use of previously published material from Associated Press and News International is acknowledged.

Working with the earlier material used in this book brought back memories of the late Bill Wilson. It is difficult to over-estimate how valuable his influence was both in terms of his knowledge and friendship.

Our thanks are due to Helen Ryan who gave invaluable help in reading early versions of the manuscript, and as ever, the authors acknowledge the sensitive and helpful editing of Bryan Watkins. Noreen Moynihan coped with tantrums and typing and sometimes made tea (or coffee) to help things along! Fouad Alaaragi translated Appendix 1. Alice and Cathy generally helped, but Joshua didn't always.

1

Introduction

Acts of terrorism have become so commonplace throughout the world that, despite the suffering and loss of life they cause, all too frequently they pass almost unnoticed, with the exception of a few that dominate the world's media – primarily because that is just what they were intended to do. Terrorism has become an ineradicable feature of the international scene. The political and ideological reasons behind most terrorist movements are not the principal subject of this book but rather the nature of the men and women who perpetrate the appalling crimes with which those movements are associated. To set the scene, seven brief reports of terrorist incidents in Algeria, India, Italy, France, Egypt, Germany and Turkey, all of which took place between late July 1993 and September of that year, are given below.

Algeria

In September 1993, two French surveyors working in Algeria were kidnapped and later killed. A government source said that François Bertelet, aged 32, and Emmanuel Didion, aged 25, were found dead on a Tuesday morning outside Sidi bel Abbes, some 150 miles southwest of Algiers. The two had been kidnapped a day earlier whilst driving to work near the city of Tlelat, where they were involved in a high-tension line project for the French company Herkiq. They were both killed by gunshot wounds to the head. The men had been driven about 60 miles to the southwest of Tlelat, in the Sidi bel Abbes area, where they were executed. There was no claim of responsibility, but the killings bore the marks of previous fundamentalist guerrilla actions.

These two Frenchmen were the first foreigners to be killed in a 20-month-old Muslim fundamentalist insurgency in Algeria. The slayings came as fundamentalists appear to have stepped up attacks over the past month in a region previously free of violence. An estimated 2,000 people have died in Algeria since January 1992 when the government cancelled elections in which candidates associated with Islamic fundamentalist groups were expected to win. These killings were particularly embarrassing for the Algerian Government, who are seeking to establish closer ties with the West in an effort to attract investment from abroad for the country's depressed economy. A government spokesman said that the killings of the two Frenchmen 'mark a higher degree of barbarism by the guerrillas. In the face of this tragic terrorist attack, which targeted foreign workers for the first time, the Algerian Government will deploy all its means to safeguard the property and people of foreign nationality'. In Paris, the French Foreign Ministry said it vigorously condemned 'this criminal act.' It said that France's ambassador in Algiers had expressed 'deep worry' to the Algerian Government and asked that 'all light be shed on this drama'.

India

While searching for guerrillas who had planted a car bomb outside the youth wing of the governing Congress Party in New Delhi in September 1993, the police arrested about 150 people in Punjab State. The attack was apparently aimed at the President of the Youth Congress, Maninder Singh Bitta, who had been targeted by Sikh extremists from Punjab twice before. In fact, Bitta still walks on crutches because a terrorist attack in the previous year destroyed one of his ankles. He is himself a Sikh who served as a police informer in the 1980s, later joining the Congress Party and becoming one of its most vocal opponents of Punjab's war of independence. Eight people died in the car bomb attack – three of Bitta's bodyguards and five civilians. At least 35 people were injured.

India's police and soldiers have defeated many guerrilla groups in Punjab, but they are still seeking some of the various groups' leaders and skirmishing nearly every day with terrorists. At least 17,000 people have been killed during the 10-year-old insurgency. In the same week as the car bomb, police killed seven suspected Sikh militants in several confrontations around the state.

If Sikh guerrillas had managed to sneak the explosives into the city, their move could challenge claims by the government that the insurgency has nearly ended. The Khalistan Liberation Force, the Khalistan Commando Force, and the Bhindranwale Tiger Force of

Khalistan – terrorist groups that Punjab police had claimed to have wiped out – all claimed responsibility for the car bombing. These groups are among a dozen that have been fighting in Punjab for an independent state of Khalistan for Sikhs, who form two per cent of 880 million people in predominantly Hindu India. Police have offered a 500,000 rupee reward for information about the car bomb. Squads of policemen and paramilitary soldiers raided suspected terrorist hideouts across Punjab, arresting about 150 people, United News of India News Agency reported later. They were looking for Kuldeep Singh Keepa and Navdeep Singh Khalsa, two militants who reportedly specialise in assembling and exploding such devices. The police believe that Navdeep Singh Khalsa, a former teacher in an engineering college in the Punjabi town of Ludhiana, had assembled car bombs used in two previous attacks. They are also looking for one of the injured in the car bombing who escaped from a hospital. Dayal Singh, believed to be a cigarette vendor, is thought by the police to have been the person who pressed the remote control button that set off the two bombs in the car.

Italy

Gunmen in a car fired shots and threw a small explosive device at a US military barracks near an air base used by American fighter planes patrolling Bosnian airspace in September 1993. The base is some 60 miles northeast of Venice at the town of Aviano. Guards at the base noticed a black Saab pull up slowly near the gate of the barracks, about 3 miles from the base, at about 11:30 pm. A man got out of the Saab and, seconds later, another man inside the car fired 'a rapid series of shots' from the sunroof. A 'grenade-like bomb' went off inside the grounds of the barracks, apparently thrown by one of the men before the car sped away. US military police gave chase but failed to catch the vehicle. No one was hurt in this apparent terrorist attack, but bullets struck a dormitory and a window was shattered. The attack was the first against the facilities of the base since **Operation Deny Flight** began over Bosnia on April 12, but it prompted no new security measures. More than 30 fighter jets and 2,600 personnel are stationed at the base. A spokesman for the base said that 'We were already in a heightened state of alert' since the operation patrolling Bosnian airspace began. The dormitory where the attack took place houses about 200 military personnel and is one of nine support installations in and around Aviano.

France

Four suspected Basque terrorists were arrested in August 1993 in the Paris area. Prosecutors later ordered the four people – including two Spaniards and a Mexican – to be held on charges that they were linked to Basque militant activity. This arrest was the result of the increased co-operation between French and Spanish authorities, who have increasingly worked together to combat terrorists in the Basque region that straddles the border between France and Spain. The two Spanish nationals – Carlos Almorza-Arrietta and Jose-Maria Dorronsoro-Malaxetxebarria – were charged with criminal association in a terrorist operation, falsification of documents and weapons possession. The two are further accused of running an extortion racket that imposed 'revolutionary taxes' on businesses. Almorza is an alleged top-ranking member of the Basque revolutionary group ETA. Two others who were lodging them, Philippe Roblin and Virginia de las Nieves Avellana, a Mexican national, were also charged with criminal association and aiding illegal aliens. Four other men were arrested in Spain on Friday in a crackdown on extortion operations by ETA. On Saturday, a small bomb planted by Basque separatists injured a young Italian tourist and a policeman at a hotel in the popular southern resort area of La Manga del Mar Menor.

Egypt

In mid-August 1993, an Afghan trained bomb expert died of injuries from a blast which he helped to engineer in an attempt by Islamic extremists to kill the Egyptian Minister of the Interior, Hassan el-Alfy in Cairo. The minister was in charge of the Government's security response against the Islamic militants' anti-government campaign. The bomber, Nazih Rashed, who was aged 35, lost a leg in the bombing attempt. Rashed was admitted to hospital with forged documents, but he was later identified by his fingerprints and a picture. Four people were killed in the bomb blast, but el-Alfy escaped with a broken arm and other minor injuries.

Rashed was a member of a group of Islamic extremists called 'Vanguards of Conquest' who are fighting to remove Egypt's secular government and install Islamic rule. In the campaign to date, more than 190 people have been killed. Nazih Rashed was among seven members of the group, who, police sources say, planned and carried out the attack. He was already wanted on charges of murder, belonging to an illegal group and trying to bring down the government through terrorism. The Interior Ministry said Rashed was trained to use explosives and weapons in Afghanistan. The Egyptian government has frequently suggested that leaders of the Islamic anti-government campaign fought with Muslim radicals in Afghanistan against the Soviet backed Communist régime in the 1980s, before returning to Egypt. The Vanguards faction is believed to be a revival of the Jihad movement that killed President Anwar Sadat in 1981. During June and July, more than 700 Vanguards members were reportedly charged for a series of attacks and anti-government activities. The attack against el-Alfy came after threats by Muslim radicals to avenge the executions of 15 of their colleagues by the government since June.

Germany

In July 1993, the German Red Army Faction (RAF) Terrorist group threatened to avenge the killing on June 27th 1993 of one of its members, Wolfgang Grams, by shooting top politicians in the knees. Grams was killed during a shootout with the police, but witnesses have testified that he was only injured in the shootout, and was later executed with a bullet to the head as he lay wounded. Red Army supporters are circulating pamphlets threatening 'kneecapping action' against important German figures. 'Kneecapping' is a method used by a number of terrorist groups, and is designed to cause severe pain and permanent injuries. It has been used before by German and Italian terrorists, and the threat was taken seriously by the German Government.

Turkey

In late July, 1993, a bomb exploded in a garbage bin in the popular Aegean resort town of Kusadasi. The bomb wounded 17 people, none seriously; five foreigners were among the injured. This was the third bombing in Turkey in that month, and the second involving foreigners. The explosion occurred at about 7:15 pm, and the police were reportedly searching for a man and a woman who were seen driving off in a car after the explosion. The car was eventually found by the police; 17 suspects were detained. The motive of the attack was unclear, but a few days before, a statement on behalf of the Kurdish People's Liberation Army warned tourists of attacks. 'The war will be spread to the touristic regions and major cities of Turkey,' said the statement signed by the ERNK, or the Kurdish People's Liberation Army, the military wing of the Kurdistan Workers' Party (PKK).The PKK has been waging a guerrilla war in southeastern Turkey since 1984 for Kurdish self-rule, and at that time held six foreigners

hostage after abductions earlier in July. The statement warned
tourists against going to Turkey, saying its tourist spots, agencies,
boats, and other facilities, would be sabotaged. In earlier attacks,
bombs thrown at hotels in the Mediterranean resort city of Antalya
had killed one Turk and injured 26 people, including 12 foreigners.
PKK militants had been blamed for the attacks which followed a similar warning in late May by the rebel leader Abdullah Ocalan. These
attacks complement an apparently parallel strategy of kidnapping
Western tourists in southeastern Turkey.

* * *

None of the seven incidents described were particularly noteworthy,
and none received media coverage outside of the country in which
they occurred, except where nationals from another country were
involved, when there may have been some modest coverage. Even in
the countries where they happened, they did not attract much attention. The listing is far from exhaustive, and excludes the almost
routine daily accounts of shootings or bombings in Northern
Ireland, or the numerous atrocities committed in Bosnia-
Hercegovina. The incidents were presumably thought newsworthy
enough at a national level by Associated Press (from whom the
accounts were taken), but in the scale of international events none
were of great significance. In the same period, Associated Press
made reference to other incidents in Italy, Algeria, Germany, Russia.
They represent the typical incidence of terrorist incidents, the background of continuing and largely unnoticed terrorist activity in the
world.

In these limited examples a total of 15 people were killed, and
somewhere in the region of 100 injured. They refer to bombings,
shootings, kidnapping, extortion, and threats to injure – the stock in
trade of terrorist methods the world over. Excluding the attacks
aimed at Bitta in Delhi, Hassan el-Alfi in Cairo and the threatened
knee-capping of politicians in Germany, most victims, or intended victims, were primarily people uninvolved in any direct sense in the
conflict that gave rise to the particular incident. Whilst the incidents
can, to a large extent, be dismissed as almost routine events by the
observer distanced from them, they of course represent major
trauma for those involved, and the sanitised newspaper accounts protect us from the reality of shattered limbs and lives. The extensive
geographical distribution of even this small sample, the almost routine way in which the media treats these events, despite the personal
tragedies each incident involves, gives some clues to the ubiquity of
terrorism, its potential to wreck the lives of those subjected to it but
paradoxically the insensitivity of those not directly involved in it. The

characteristic that distinguishes these crimes (for that is what they are) from other kinds of crime is their *political* quality, where violence is used to further some form of political demand. On the basis of the small sample described above, we can see that, at the very least, terrorism is a popular and probably universal form of political dissent.

One reason for the popularity of terrorism as a tool of political dissent is that it offers the disenfranchised the opportunity to attract and address an audience. In doing this, it inflicts a political and psychological short-term cost on the communities involved, through the killing and maiming of innocents. But in the longer term, terrorism creates conditions in which the values of the liberal state become eroded and compromised by the social effects of terrorism, and the response to it. However, whatever else terrorism might be, it is a highly effective means of gaining attention in the media; indeed, the amount of attention is positively correlated with the severity of a terrorist attack. We can best see terrorist incidents as a psychological element of informal war, much as battles and attacks are elements of conventional warfare. Effective terrorist groups recognise this, and use terrorism in that way. The more sophisticated a terrorist organisation is, the more violence is integrated into the organisation's broader political programme, complementing and extending its impact through propaganda and choice of targets. Recognition of the psychological qualities of terrorism is important in our understanding of the political and social processes of terrorism. Given this, how then can we begin to understand in psychological terms why terrorism has the effect it does?

An important contextual factor in understanding the effectiveness and ubiquity of terrorism is how we understand the concept of justice in psychological terms. By justice in this psychological context we mean a concept which has important elements in common with the legal usage of 'justice', but which has essentially personal and social reference points, rather than being grounded in 'the law', or sets of universal juridical principles. In the sense in which we will use it here, it is a general quality of people where we have a tendency to believe that the world is just, that there is a sense of order and rightness governing our lives so that people get what they deserve and, conversely, deserve what they get. This may not, of course, objectively be the case, and we are all aware of many examples of when this is clearly not so. Nevertheless there is a strong tendency for us to feel it *should* be the case. There is clearly a sense in which the legal system seeks to achieve the same end in a relatively limited array of areas. In the psychological sense used here, the notion of 'psychological justice' extends to most facets of our lives.

Social Psychologists call this the 'just-world phenomenon', and this is a widely recognised feature of our interpretation of the world as it impinges on us. We like to think that virtue is rewarded, that a hard working life should result in a comfortable retirement, that those who cheat or steal to our disadvantage are ultimately caught. There clearly is a sense of order in the world as we experience it, and we tend to feel that fairness and reasonableness should characterise that order. Equally, of course, we recognise that sometimes the world is not fair. Perhaps we work hard, but fail to get promotion and we then have to stand by and see someone else who seems less deserving (in our eyes) receive promotion. Or perhaps, when a young parent dies from accident or illness, we feel sorrow not only at a death, but at a death of one so young with responsibilities, because it seems undeserved, and therefore unfair. An element of the sorrow, anger or envy we might feel in these circumstances is often *because* they seem to offend against a sense of fairness or just deserts.

The sense of offence against the idea of a just world lies at the heart of many peoples' feelings about terrorism and the terrorist. In one way, many terrorists and their supporters would claim that what they do is a response to an *unjust* world. They have been the victims of unfair discrimination, of injustice, of repression. On the other hand, an important element in the horror of terrorist violence, as experienced by the victim or relative of a victim, and by society in general, is the *unjust* quality of random non-specific violence which characterises terrorism – the sense in which a terrorist bombing produces victims who might be incidental, people in the wrong place at the wrong time who had no way of knowing that they were about to be killed or injured.

The sense of a 'just world' seems to lie at the very heart of the social and psychological response to political violence of both terrorists and their victims. But of course, whilst we can identify such a measure of commonality at that level, the reality of these two responses is that they are necessarily opposed to one another. The sense of remedying injustice which might lead to terrorism *creates* the injustice to the innocent bystander, such as the child caught in an explosion. Often the injustice which initiates terrorism (legitimate or otherwise) becomes lost under layers and layers of later affronts and perceived injustices, such that the starting point no longer has relevance other than through mythology. But whatever might be the starting point of terrorism, its central quality seems to be that it creates a self-sustaining cycle of injustice which once established, experience suggests is very difficult to break. Many of our confusions about terrorism relate to our failure to recognise the important difference in the meaning of 'justice' in the psychological sense used here, in contrast to a limited and narrow legal sense. This failing, of course, provides rich material for the propagandist.

What is terrorism?

A core element in any account of terrorism is that it involves the use of violence to achieve political ends. Terrorism seems to begin where political dissent stops being peaceful, and where violence starts to be used as a political tool. Terrorism in the sense we will use it here is never the use of violence for its own ends (to satisfy some personal vendetta, to eliminate an opponent), but always has some ulterior aim focused ultimately on the political process. The ancient Chinese proverb 'Kill one, frighten ten thousand' captures the emotional and essentially psychological effect that the terrorist seeks to achieve. That of course is not to say that from time to time individual terrorists do not indulge personal grievances, or engage in more general forms of criminality. But an essential quality of terrorism is its political agenda, in which acts undertaken for personal gain may well be likely to be significant, but incidental, factors.

A terrorist incident is always a crime, although criminality does not characterise terrorism. This may seem a strange thing to say, but often the terrorist says and believes that he or she acts for the highest of motives. Personal benefit rarely figures in the terrorist's own objectives as they might articulate them, and the benefits of terrorism are almost always expressed in altruistic terms of communal rather than personal benefits. Indeed, what greater altruistic motive could there be than seeking justice for your community and traditions or beliefs through exposing yourself to danger and possible death? Attempts to denigrate terrorists by describing them as madmen or psychopaths simply serves to deflect attention from the unpalatable truth that in their own eyes and those of their supporters, terrorists are often moral, even responsible, people.

At a personal level, I suspect that we would all have no great difficulty in recognising what *we* would regard as terrorism. For the supporter of terrorism, for the adherent to a political ideology that condones violence, it is the use of political violence to overthrow an illegitimate and oppressive régime. For those who do not support terrorism, or who are the victim of it, it is the use of violence to intimidate and force political change without reference to democratic social rights. When we see it, we probably have no great difficulty in deciding for ourselves what we mean by terrorism. But it is very difficult to move beyond that essentially personal perspective, to the development of a suitable objective definition for use, for example, in the courts.

There are many ways in which we can illustrate the ambiguities of the concept of terrorism. What if a state is acknowledged to be unjust? Would we not want to condone violence which seemed to be the only way of forcing change or overthrowing an oppressive régime? What if a state practised discrimination? As members of a liberal democracy, would we not want to support those who tried to establish similar liberal values in their own state? At the level of international law, it is broadly agreed that if oppression is so harsh, perhaps the only response people have is the violent overthrow of a régime; such attempts at overthrow may well appear to the supporters of that régime, or even to sympathetic observers, to be terrorism when the violence extends to uninvolved civilians. For many people in the West who hold liberal views, the situation in South Africa graphically illustrated until recently the problem of feeling sympathy with efforts to overthrow the manifestly unjust apartheid régime, combined with unease at the increasing use of what, in other contexts, would be described as terrorist violence to achieve that end.

Many writers abhor the clichéd adage that one man's terrorist is another man's freedom fighter. But regrettably it is to a large extent true, because one of the difficulties in trying to identify an objective definition of terrorism is that our views about it do contain large subjective elements. How *we* experience the violence of terrorism, how *we* view the rightness of the cause, how much *we* are prepared to see the ends justify the means are critical qualities to how *we* approach the use of violence in the political process.

We can move a little beyond this apparent impasse, however. There seems to be broad agreement at a moral level that the involvement of third parties unconnected to a dispute is illegitimate, and somehow offends against our sense of justice. For example, most people would have no difficulty in recognising the wrongness of bombing an airliner containing passengers from a variety of countries, as a means of drawing attention to a particular cause. However just a cause might appear, there is probably broad agreement that deliberately targeting children is wrong and deserving of condemnation. Unless we feel that the ends always justify the means, from a comfortable distance we can label such acts as terrorism without much difficulty.

But what if, as part of a civil war, civilians, including children, are deliberately targeted as a means of forcing a political outcome? Is this terrorism or is it an unfortunate consequence of warfare (and therefore in some sense more 'legitimate'), given that the principal antagonists are recognisably State elements? During 1992–93, some 1600 children were killed in the siege of Sarajevo both through shrapnel damage from shells and through sniping. Whilst it might be claimed that shell fire is indiscriminate, and that the deaths of children are regrettable but inevitable consequences of a siege of this kind, sniping requires a deliberate choice on the part of the sniper to target a child in his sights, and to squeeze the trigger. Estimates are difficult to come by, but perhaps between a quarter and a half of child deaths in Sarajevo have been the result of sniper fire. Members of the Serbian Army have been responsible for these atrocities. Are they terrorists? Or are they members of an army acting under orders? Their behaviour is abhorrent to most people, and might justly be described as 'evil'. Yet to label them as soldiers diminishes the sense of personal responsibility for the deaths that we might assume to be the case if we labelled them as terrorists. In the circumstances, it is difficult to regard the actions of Serbian snipers as anything other than examples of terrorist behaviour designed to frighten, intimidate and demoralise the civilian population. The events in Sarajevo have been widely repeated across Bosnia-Hercegovina, and it is quite clear that Sarajevo does not represent some kind of aberrant example – indeed, there may well be many worse examples of atrocities.

In situations such as Sarajevo, there are clearly difficulties in understanding the relationship between terrorism and warfare. Yet it is clearly the case that terrorism sometimes constitutes a *form* of warfare. Some authors have emphasised the covert warfare nature of terrorism, and others have referred to it as surrogate warfare. To confuse matters further, terrorist organisations often adopt the term 'Army' in their title (such as the Provisional Irish Republican Army (PIRA)), and members of such 'armies' may even adopt military styles and ranks, (such as Brigadier,). There is propaganda value in doing this, of course, but there is also a sense in which the concept of an army and its structure are useful to a terrorist group (obedience to authority, hierarchical relationships, and so forth). What, of course, is different is that armies tend to be very much larger than terrorist organisations, and armies tend to belong to states, rather than to dissident movements, within states. But even this simple distinction breaks down; if a dissident group is victorious, it may well then become the legitimate army of the state displacing its former enemies. Events over the past few years in Ethiopia illustrate this process, where the EPRDF made the transition from a rebellious guerrilla army to the official army of the State on their victory over the Dergue régime.

Terrorism is clearly a complex set of activities, and if we are to have any kind of sensible view on it, it must encompass those complexities. We can try to draw together elements of a definition of terrorism, but inevitably what we will have is a list of attributes, rather than a water-tight definition. Ambiguities are bound to arise, because not all of these attributes need necessarily always be present for us to view something as terrorism.

In what follows, we will attempt a discursive account of the qualities of terrorism. The value of such an exercise is not to create a spurious consistency where none exists, but rather to illustrate and emphasise the complexity of the subject. At the heart of any approach to terrorism we can say that a terrorist act involves *violence* or *force* or *threat* of force directed towards some political end. This seems to be the core quality of terrorism, but we can extend this further by saying that the political end of terrorism is normally (but not necessarily) expressed as the action of a *non-state* group or organisation, and may be achieved through *coercion, extortion, intimidation,* or *induction of compliance* in some area of political policy. A further important element of a definition is that terrorism is essentially *criminal* in character, and uses the *publicity* generated by the act of violence as a potent weapon. To a great extent, it is because terrorism involves non-sanctioned damage to persons or property that we notice it. By the use of publicity, future *fear, apprehension* or *terror* is emphasised, through actual or potential threat. The threat intended is the result of *purposive, planned, systematic,* and *organised* action, where the threat is expressed in terms of *extranormality,* and is *in breach of accepted rules without humanitarian constraints.*

Victim qualities are central features of the effects of terrorism and a critical element in the choice of terrorist action, and a central element of the effectiveness of terrorism, is the *lack of direct relationship* between victims and the political agenda of the terrorist organisation. Civilians, noncombatants, nonresisting, neutrals or outsiders are therefore the principal victims. Allied to this, terrorist actions show an impersonal, arbitrary and random character, where the *indiscriminate* choice of innocent victims is again a central quality. However, it must be stressed that the quality of indiscriminateness lies only in the absence of the expected *psychological just* relationship (in the sense we have discussed earlier) between victim and event. This emphasises the fact that terrorist action is invariably planned to a purpose, even if the purpose may be simply to generate fear. Through its *clandestine* or *covert* nature, incalculability, unpredictability and the unexpectedness of occurrence of violence constitute important features.

One thing is clear, however: if we label something as terrorism, we can be pretty sure that we do not like it. In the main, terrorism is a pejorative term, implying disapproval. Like many words used widely but poorly understood, it has also become a word that from time to time is used in circumstances quite unrelated to the political arena from which it has emerged. We might speak of a child 'terrorising the neighbourhood' for example, or even of a dog 'terrorising' other dogs. In these circumstances, we presumably mean someone acting aggressively, rather than someone acting with a political purpose in mind using violence as a means towards achieving political change. Such are the vagaries of a living language, of course!

Who are the terrorists?

Terrorists perform acts of terrorism, and this book is about the terrorist and his or her acts, rather than terrorism as an element in the political process. This is not a clear distinction, but it does serve to emphasise its psychological, rather than social or political agenda. It is not a technical book which labours psychological theories to help to explain away terrorist behaviour, although some psychological concepts are used from time to time to help place the discussion into context. Where possible, it uses either the actual or paraphrased words of terrorists to describe their own world and actions as they see them. Hearing the voices described here and seeing the individuals concerned leads to some uncomfortable conclusions. Whilst many of the people who have been interviewed are violent, and most have committed horrific and sometimes barbaric crimes, few if any fit the image in any technical sense of an abnormal individual.

This might seem to be a disturbing assertion contrary to commonsense, and perhaps needs to be qualified. To be specific, in the sense used here, abnormal means in need of some form of clinical treatment. There is no doubt that a life of terrorism, or indeed even limited contact with terrorist organisations changes people. There is no doubt either that continuing exposure to violence brutalises and desensitises people. There is also no doubt that the clandestine lifestyle of an active terrorist takes a substantial psychological toll on the individual, and it is equally the case that the immediate community in which the terrorist lives is often itself brutalised and distorted. But most active terrorists show few if any of the attributes of clinical abnormality. In a statistical sense, terrorists are not 'normal', by virtue of the lives they lead and the things they do. But there seems to be no discernible pathological qualities of terrorists that can identify them in any clinical sense as different from others in the community from which they come. The stresses of the terrorist lifestyle doubtlessly take their toll, but other occupations and lifestyles also take their toll on individuals. The habitual criminal, for example, probably adapts to continuing involvement in criminality in ways similar to the way the terrorist adapts to his or her lifestyle. Violence and brutality, may characterise the criminal, yet, as with the terrorist, we would be unlikely to place the criminal within the category of clinical abnormality.

Our image of the terrorist is as confused as our image of terrorism. Our view of the terrorist is largely derived, either from news journalism or contemporary fiction. Both present partial, often sensationalised accounts. Just as we use the term terrorism as a label implying condemnation, so we tend to use the term terrorist to describe people who do violent things which we disapprove of. In addition, however, we often also include within our view of the terrorist notions such as mental illness and psychopathy. The acts of terrorism we read about are often so horrific that we seem to need to explain them by making reference to abnormality – after all if individual terrorists are 'normal', how can they do the dreadful things they do?

The image of the terrorist as a psychopathic killer planting bombs, or compulsively injuring people is simply inaccurate. It is probably true that terrorist organisations from time to time make use of extreme and overtly violent people. But when this arises, such people are most likely to be used in disciplining their own people, rather than as part of a political terrorist campaign. The leaders of contemporary terrorist organisations are well aware of the need to control and focus their violence. The unreliable psychopath, incapable of the controlled and 'sensitive' directed actions of the modern terrorist, has little to offer the political causes. Nor is the criminal, with a police record and an extravagant and perhaps expensive self-centred lifestyle, attractive to the terrorist organisation. Such organisations need discrete, almost invisible activists, who can undertake bombing campaigns without drawing attention to themselves, and who can merge back into the society they have damaged without drawing attention to themselves. The reality of the terrorist is that they are essentially unremarkable people, in psychological terms disturbingly similar to their victims. The voices reported in this book are essentially ordinary voices. They belong to, and come from, the communities they seek to defend.

A prominent activist once asked me why I as a psychologist should be interested in terrorism. Was it because I thought I could identify the terrorist personality? Rather in the way that assumptions are made that the terrorist *must* be abnormal, so assumptions are sometimes made that there is a terrorist 'personality' that somehow goes with the violence of terrorism, supporting and enabling violence as an inherent part of the individual.

Psychologists often use the term personality to mean an individual's characteristic patterns of behaviour. In one sense, by attempting to understand the terrorist and why he becomes involved in political violence, you are trying to put some order into an individual's account of his life, seeking for consistencies and logical relationships. In psychological usage, the term personality structure is used to describe the basic elements of personality and how they fit together. By asking individuals questions about themselves and their actions, you are in one sense identifying that person's personality structure and dynamics. One tradition in psychology seeks formally to do this by identifying personality traits. This approach tries to make people's behaviour more understandable by reducing the complex observations we might make of people to more simple prominent characteristics. These characteristics are also often associated with attempts to classify people into types. At a commonsense level, these may be based on temperament, or at a more technical level, they may be based on psychometrically measurable qualities of individuals.

Are there identifiable personality qualities of terrorists? At one level, the simple answer to this question is that because of practical problems it is impossible to know! To answer the question in a way that would satisfy the strict scientific evidential demands of modern psychology, it would be necessary to have access to active terrorists in order systematically to undertake psychometric measurement of their personality qualities. No one has done this on any useful scale, nor are they likely to. It is of course possible, under some circumstances, to access captive terrorists, and there have been a number of studies that have done this. But studies of this kind give rise to substantial methodological difficulty in interpreting any results. It may well be the case that those terrorists who are captured are not typical of active terrorists – the process of capture may change people, perhaps captured terrorists are those who are not very good at evading capture. But a more substantive problem is that those who consent to participate in this kind of research (for consent would be necessary) are likely to be those who no longer, for whatever reason, subscribe to the use of violence in politics. However, even given all these limitations, such sparse research evidence that does exist suggests that there are no discernible personality consistencies amongst terrorists. As in the case of abnormality, the research conclusions lead to the view that terrorists are not discernibly different from other people from the communities from which the terrorists come.

The activist who asked about terrorist personality also added something to that question that merits consideration. Was my interest in terrorists based on the thought that what I found might help the police to catch them more easily, or perhaps to understand their tactics better? This raises a very important issue at a more general level – what is the purpose of research on terrorism? Because terrorism is by definition illegal, and because the crimes committed by terrorists are often horrific in the extreme, the researcher may well be thought to have a moral obligation to assist the security services in their work.

Is work on terrorism undertaken therefore to help understand the phenomenon, and thereby make it more easy to control? This is an entirely legitimate view, but it gives rise to an immediate practical problem – no active terrorist, or for that matter no past terrorist who has committed crimes for which he or she has not been charged, is likely to co-operate with anyone who appears to be an agent of the security services. To gain the confidence of activists, it is necessary to maintain a degree of impartiality and distance from the security services, otherwise the necessary trust to enable meaningful interviews to take place can never develop. Equally, of course, distance and impartiality from the terrorist must be maintained, otherwise the investigator can become an agent of the terrorist, perhaps conniving with him in hiding information, or even in aiding and abetting terrorist activity.

The central dilemma of work in this area is the maintenance of a balance between respect for the law and its values, and closeness to terrorist organisations and their values. As with much journalistic coverage of terrorism, there are undoubtedly examples in the academic and popular literature on terrorism that fall into both these camps. Some works are little more than disguised propaganda for either the security services or the terrorist organisation.

When looking at the state's response to terrorism, there is often a peculiar sense of symmetry and reciprocity in the way terrorist organisations relate to the security services. This is evident in a number of ways, but is most obvious in the interplay of initiative and counter-initiative in the use of the media, where both recognise the value of propaganda. The former British Prime Minister, Margaret Thatcher, referred to 'the oxygen of publicity' as being a vital requirement for the sustenance of a terrorist organisation, and there is a clear recognition on the part of all sides that terrorism is a war largely fought in the media. Thus organisations like the Provisional IRA and Sinn Fein have very well-developed press sections, who have developed complex long-term strategies for the use of the media to project the central messages of the organisation. In most terrorist organisations that have any degree of complexity, media managers are located amongst the highest decision-making elements of the organisation, helping to shape and direct the terrorist campaign. The press sections can respond immediately to events, feeding material to sympathetic journalists and presented in ways to emphasise the current propaganda issues, and diminish any negative effects. The security services operate in the same way, and media management and propaganda feature as important policy considerations in determining the state's response.

Hence, the independent researcher has to tread a careful path between the security services and the terrorist organisation. Whilst television and newspaper journalism are the principal targets for manipulation by both sides, the academic researcher is also often seen as fair game, to be used to propagate one or other view. For the academic, it is of course tempting to be given special information denied to others, or to be given access to a particularly interesting set of data. The sense of conspiracy may give added piquancy to the work, and in the case of state sponsorship of research, the availability of large grants might tempt the hungry researcher in these days of intense academic competition.

It probably is not possible to conduct truly and totally independent 'hands on' research into terrorists. The subject of the research (the individual terrorist, or the terrorist organisation) must give consent to interviews, and they are well aware of both the dangers of revelation and the virtue of manipulation. Reliance on sources from the security services carries similar dangers, in that any material given may well be distorted to present a particular view. The material presented in this book, therefore, must be interpreted with this in mind. Individuals when interviewed have their own agenda, (or their organisation will have formulated an agenda) and in the formal interviews detailed, the influence of such contaminating factors cannot be dismissed. Furthermore, in any interview there are certain demand characteristics that implicitly shape and pressure the respondent to meet expectations. Doubtless this is also the case in the interviews conducted for this book. However, whilst in many situations demand characteristics are often seen as negative influences, leading respondents to say what they think the interviewer wants to hear, in the cases described here, it is likely that those demand characteristics actually helped focus the interviews away from propaganda onto more psychologically appropriate areas. In the formal interviews undertaken, respondents were all aware that they were talking to an independent academic researcher who had some standing in the area, and whose principal aim was to understand them and why they did what they did without any further external agenda.

Terrorists are not mindless automatons, sub-normal psychopaths or evil and heartless killers. They are generally undistinguished in appearance and manner. They come from backgrounds that are like others in their community, and they often give the impression of being alert to their condition. Above all, they often have well developed rationales that justify what they do. As we will see later these rationales are sometimes little more than means of protecting themselves from the recognition of the awfulness and wrongness of what they do. But there is usually behind a terrorist's actions a sense of political direction, a justification and reason. What is striking, is that these reasons are not in themselves unique. They draw upon well understood psychological processes that operate on most people. Indeed, the more the interview material in this book has been analysed, the greater is an emergent sense of the 'ordinariness' of the terrorist, in terms of the processes that have made him or her into an active terrorist, which are the same kind of processes that characterise most life choices that people make.

In thinking about terrorism, and in trying to understand why individuals become involved in a terrorist lifestyle, it is important not to lose sight of the reality of the subject. Terrorism is about injuring and killing people who have no role in the issues that the terrorist is addressing. No amount of political rationale and rhetoric can remove that inescapable and powerful fact. Terrorism is the systematic victimisation of innocent people, where the victim's rights are overwhelmed by the terrorist's own perception of the situation. The ends of terrorism are used to justify the means, even when those means involve death and injury. Plausible political rhetoric, strength of feeling and a determined sense of righteousness do not take away from its awfulness and wrongness.

Violence and aggression

There are a number of reasons why we should be interested in understanding the terrorist and terrorism. From a social and political perspective, terrorism is clearly a major political factor affecting society, and in some cases producing political change. As such, it of course merits investigation. From a psychological point of view, however, terrorism is of interest because people involved in terrorism indulge in extreme forms of violent behaviour. It is reasonable to suppose that the study of the terrorist may throw some light on the more general nature of violence and aggression, and the factors that lead people to become violent and aggressive within a social context.

In the aftermath of the Second World War, many academics and statesmen felt that the greatest problem facing mankind was the control of the extreme violence that had emerged in both Nazi Germany and Stalinist Russia. The Second World War of course saw heavy fighting between the armies of the opposing states, but it gave rise to something else which was in its way far more frightening and worrying – the deliberate attempts at genocide of civilian populations. Hannah Arendt writes of the sense of despair felt by many when faced with the evidence of horror and evil in, for example, the concentration camps or the efforts of doctors to exterminate 'socially undesirable' patients. But above all, what gave rise to that sense of despair was the broad tolerance of these activities by the general public. This sense of despair undoubtedly diminished as the century progressed, and social and economic optimism returned. But towards the end of the twentieth century we again seem to have been brought face to face with the harsh realities of extreme violence. The significance of the study of terrorism and the terrorist to the modern world is that it offers one way of trying to understand these issues.

Psychologists define aggression as physical or verbal behaviour intended to hurt or damage someone or something. Two forms of aggression can be identified, hostile and instrumental. Hostile aggression is related to heightened emotional responses, particularly anger, and its goal is to injure someone. The emotional quality of hostile aggression means that it is most typically an impulsive, emotional outburst. Instrumental aggression, in contrast, intends to hurt, but only as a means towards attaining some other end. It is typically cool and calculating and deliberately embarked upon as a means to attain a specific goal.

This distinction is not always straightforward, but quite clearly most if not all forms of terrorist violence are examples of instrumental aggression. Terrorist violence may be undertaken in a general way as a response to emotions, but it is usually so distanced from any emotional events as to be separate, and in any event, the particular terrorist action is generally subsidiary to some greater political end. We can think of any particular act of aggression as being located along a conceptual dimension extending from *inborn* aggression through *frustration* related aggression to *learned* aggression. Specific examples of terrorist violence, whilst they might have their origins in a sense of frustration or even hatred, seem predominantly to show qualities of learning, principally because of their calculating and premeditated nature. The motivation behind planting a bomb, for example, may be hatred of an ethnic group or an attempt to punish a politician or military official, but the act of planting the bomb for the terrorist implies calculation of the merits of the target, detailed logistical planning to construct and place the bomb, and consideration of the relationship between planting the bomb, the mechanism of detonation, and the time period for the terrorist to escape before its detonation.

In the above we have made an important distinction between contextual and general motivational factors, and motivational factors related to a specific act. We will see later in this book that this distinction emerges in the way people talk about their involvement with terrorism. When asked, the reasons individual terrorists give for their involvement in terrorism are both varied and often diffuse. But whilst individuals may be able to identify events that they associate with involvement, it is generally a *process* rather than a single or simple precipitant event that they describe. There are no simple explanations of why a particular individual becomes involved in terrorism, as distinct from his or her friends who have shared similar backgrounds and experiences. Poverty, discrimination, family traditions, and ideology are often all elements in an individual's story, but the overt political reasons emphasised by terrorist rhetoric are rarely evident in psychological terms. These reasons rarely if ever relate to any specific terrorist act, and the process of terrorism generally bears little relationship to the particular events in an individual's account.

In contrast, the reasons for the choice of a particular act of terrorism are often readily articulated, both in terms of the logic of the incident and in terms of its political or propaganda value. But these specific reasons often have little or no relationship to the kinds of general factors people draw upon to explain their involvement with terrorism. We can, therefore, think of the process of becoming a terrorist as something different from, and probably unrelated in any psychological sense, to the factors that give rise to a particular example of terrorist behaviour. Individual terrorist acts are not emotional and are not characterised by anger, for example, in the sense of being engaged in an act of terrorism in some form of spontaneous outburst. Particular terrorist attacks are usually planned to achieve a purpose, taking advantage of opportunities such as lapses in security force coverage of an area, specific presence of individuals, and so on. In psychological terms, the reasons for such behaviour can be best seen in terms of how the individual, and those members of the terrorist organisation's hierarchy who make decisions, have learnt to practise terrorism both as a means of gaining attention from the media, as a form of communication and as a means of reinforcing intimidation and a sense of social unease.

Aggressive behaviour, just like any other kind of behaviour, can be learned. We know that aggression is related to its consequences, and that specifically, when aggression is rewarded, it occurs more often and more frequently. Research evidence has shown this in a wide variety of settings. One of the most powerful rewards for all sorts of behaviour is attention, and it is of course precisely attention, in the form of media coverage, that the terrorist seeks to achieve. Media attention to acts of terrorism, the 'oxygen of publicity', is the product of terrorism, and also its own reward – thus we see how a very strong self-sustaining cycle can be established. Furthermore, we not only learn as a result of consequences, however, but we also learn by seeing others. Observational learning also plays a significant role in the development of aggression, a fact well supported by research evidence. In the context of terrorism, this is particularly significant when we consider its social environment. Violent subcultures, through the provision of role models, provide many opportunities for the young to become initiated into violence. This applies as readily to a drug dealing gang as it does to a terrorist group.

We can see, therefore, that thinking of aggression as a learned response helps us to place terrorist violence within its situational context, and specifically draws our attention to the importance of the consequences of a particular violent action for the terrorist. Whether we like it or not, the reality of the situation is that terrorist violence, like other kinds of violence, yields rewards. At one level, the reward of media attention is easily attained. This is significant, because, as we noted above, it is this attention that is very often the principal short-term objective of a terrorist campaign. But terrorist violence also gains other rewards. At the political level, it does affect the political process and, as can be seen in Northern Ireland, enables a small minority republican movement effectively to dominate the political agenda, despite its inability to gain significant public representation. At the personal level for the individual terrorist, involvement in violence enables that individual to meet cultural stereotypes and to gain kudos through association with violence. In situations like those in many parts of Northern Ireland or the Basque country, a rich cultural heritage of dissent and violence finds renewed expression in involvement in terrorist organisations. The terrorist lives up to and emulates his or her cultural stereotypes and role models, and, in turn, provides role models for other younger members of the community to follow. Such involvement might almost act as a right of passage for the individual, confirming membership of his community, linking present behaviour to past generations.

Furthermore, we know from research that involvement in a group represents an additional factor facilitating the expression of violence. Groups in themselves can act to facilitate violence by giving opportunity for imitation, and through the effects of group dynamics which facilitate obedience and compliance. Membership of a group can also result in a diffusion of responsibility for violence, weakening moral prohibitions against the use of violence. There are many studies which have demonstrated that when the decision to undertake violence is removed from those who actually commit violence, there is an increase in the severity of violence through a lack of a sense of responsibility for the actual violent act on the part of those committing it.

We can see, therefore, that there is a systematic psychological context from which we can understand terrorism. That context, emphasising situational rather than personal factors, helps us to understand how terrorist behaviour might develop, and how the individual terrorist remains engaged in terrorism. It offers an alternative perspective to approaches based on social processes.

Looking ahead

This book presents accounts of terrorist lives mainly by using the words and concepts of terrorists. In some respects, it is the psychological data base from which two other books have been drawn[1]. The material used has been collected over a period of some 15 years or so. It comes from a variety of sources and individuals were accessed in a range of ways. The most extensively quoted material comes from a series of interviews undertaken in the period 1989–93. These were highly structured, and explored a range of issues related to such things as lifestyle and background. They were modelled on the kind of interview which might be undertaken for a clinical assessment. This form of interview focuses on the collection of information about the individuals psychological and social background.

Interviewees for these extended interviews were sometimes accessed through terrorist organisations, or organisations that had links with terrorist groups; on other occasions, more informal means of approaching people were used, based on personal contacts. Most interviews were given on a strict understanding of anonymity, and that wish has been respected in all cases. Sometimes this has meant that obvious distinguishing qualities of the interviews have had to be amended or deleted. Some respondents made it a condition of an interview that materials (tape recordings and notes) should be destroyed after use. This has been complied with, and all material relating to the interviews published in this book has been destroyed. Other interview and background material comes from less well-defined access to individuals and organisations. This material is in many ways more significant in terms of conceptual development, but is more diffuse and complex than the relatively straightforward interviews. The material is taken verbatim from tape recordings and notes and, in order to preserve its integrity and value, no attempt has been made to edit it in any way. For this reason, it has been presented in italic. No apology is offered for the repetition of words or phrases or, indeed, for distortions for they are all part of the fabric of the interviews.

It is important to stress that this is not a book about Irish terrorism, although Irish examples are often used to illustrate points. In part this is because the author is most familiar with Irish terrorism, and it has therefore often proved easy to illustrate a more general point with an Irish example. It is also regrettably the case, however, that

Ireland has probably the longest history of terrorism of any country in the world. Ireland has seen examples of most kinds of terrorist activity, including the very worst of atrocities. Children in the heartland of Republican and Loyalist terrorism in Northern Ireland have grown up never knowing peace; the whole structure of Northern Irish society (and in many ways substantial elements of life in the Republic of Ireland) have effectively absorbed the stresses of continuing terrorism, and have learned to live with them creating an uneasy compromise of gross social abnormality alongside familiar domestic normality. Some authors have asserted that the situation in Northern Ireland is unique and unlike other terrorist arenas. It is beyond the capacity of this book to explore that issue, but if the assertion has any truth, it lies at the level of political, rather than psychological analysis. The Irish examples used may from time to time be specific to Ireland, but generally they serve to establish a broader picture of terrorist lives from a psychological perspective. Shorn of their local content, these examples reflect on broader psychological processes.

Can we understand the terrorist? The basic thrust of this book, as has already emerged is that the terrorist is like everyone. Therefore, to the extent that we can understand anyone, we can presumably understand the terrorist. But we must always remember that terrorists are individuals; even if members of an organisation all come from similar backgrounds, each person's particular life story is different and unique. In one interview with an active terrorist, whilst not regretting his involvement with terrorism, he posed the rhetorical question 'Why did this happen to me, rather than someone else?' We could all ask that rhetorical question about our life choices. To the extent that we can answer for ourselves, so we can begin to have some understanding of the terrorist.

2

Becoming and Remaining Involved:
a general overview

If you are to gain any understanding of the psychological qualities of those involved in political violence, it requires meetings, interviews and discussions with people involved in it. In most parts of the world, gaining access to members of paramilitary organisations is, generally speaking, not too difficult. Contacts can usually be established with the various groups, and once you are accepted, they are usually co-operative and facilitative in so far as you have the capacity to meet some of their objectives of gaining a broader hearing and publicity. There are invariably limits to what can be asked, or what they will divulge – this is hardly surprising, given the illegal activities in which these organisations are involved. Most groups engaged in political violence have also learned to take charge of interviews, and become skilled media performers to ensure that their perspective is made clear. In the contemporary world, terrorist organisations appreciate the importance of publicity in the development and propagation of their aims. The only reason for which an organisation is willing to allow a meeting is because they feel they have something to gain from it. In the particular circumstances of the concerns of this book, they may not fully understand why an academic psychologist might have an interest in their activities, but they certainly fully recognise the importance of providing a wide public with access to their infor-mation and perspectives on events.

As part of a more extensive series of interviews and discussions in 1989 to 1992, I sought agreement to undertake an interview with a currently active terrorist from a particular Northern Ireland para-military group[1]. An account of this interview is given here to introduce some of the issues which are relevant to our gaining insights into why individuals become involved in political violence, as well as serving to introduce some of the qualities of a psychological analysis of those engaged in political violence.

The negotiation with the organisation had lasted for weeks, with a number of false starts and failed meetings. I had asked to meet some-one who was actively and currently involved in paramilitary violence, and this, from the terrorist organisation's point of view, of course pre-sented difficulties of security. But at last a date and time were agreed, and I was taken to meet the man. I was escorted down a corridor, and led into a dimly lit room. As I entered, he rose from behind the big table, and held out his hand to shake mine. The room was dingy. The paint work was faded and dirty, and there were old upright metal chairs around the table, and against the wall. It could have been a back room in an old workingmen's club or a pub, but there was no smell of beer, no beer mats on the table, no overflowing ashtray.

The man was friendly; there was almost warmth in his welcome. We shook hands, and he asked me to sit down in the chair immediately in front of the table. He wore a black leather jacket, with a white shirt underneath; the impression given was a man who was careful about what he wore. His hands were smooth, and he had a firm grip. The most striking impression of his face was his bright eyes, but the black mask he wore gave a distorted prominence to his mouth, for only his eyes and mouth were visible. He was probably clean shaven, but the mask made it difficult to tell. Throughout the interview, he seemed to find the mask uncomfortable, and perhaps that and some nervous-ness led him often to finger and adjust the hole in the mask around his mouth.

He asked me if I minded the three men who had entered the room behind me remaining present throughout the interview. I answered 'No, of course I don't mind', and I turned to look at them. Two of them sat side by side against the wall with folded arms, look-ing forward, but not particularly at me. The third, nearest the door, looked deliberately at me, and whilst he looked, moved his chair round to block the door in the corner. These men were 'heavies', and looked well capable of beating me up if need arose. If their purpose was to intimidate, they achieved it. Throughout the interview, I heard occasional noises of these men behind me, as they changed posi-tion, or coughed or shuffled their feet. It took a considerable effort to disregard their looming presence. They were the dramatic 'extras' of the meeting, a chorus to the drama of the interview.

I asked the man in the mask if he minded if I tape recorded the interview. He shook his head, and said '*No I don't mind. But I will be less frank with you if you do record it.*' I straight away turned the tape machine off, and put it back into my briefcase. '*You're a psychologist aren't you?'* he asked, smiling as he spoke. I replied that I was. *'Does this mean that you will use what I say to make it easier to catch people? Why are you doing this?'* I explained that I was involved in research into terrorism for my own interest, and that whilst I certainly would write about our interview, I didn't think what I said would lead to anyone being caught. 'I hope it will help people to understand you better' I added. There was a moment's pause, and then the man shrugged his shoulders and said *'OK, let's get started. I have about an hour before I must go, is that enough?'* I answered that it was, and we began the interview.

* * *

This man was a self-acknowledged terrorist. The interview had been organised by an illegal Irish terrorist organisation, and the man was presented to me as having been recently involved in a major and dramatic terrorist incident. When asked outright if he was a member of that terrorist organisation, he denied it; when asked explicitly for details of the events he had been involved in, he refused to give any. Indeed, when necessary he skilfully deflected the conversation, or evaded issues that he thought were sensitive. Yet in his account of his life, and in the course of the interview, he gave information in considerable detail sufficient to identify what he had done, and what his status was. He was clearly and unashamedly an active terrorist responsible for the recent deaths of several people.

To say that I felt at ease with the man as the interview progressed is rather strange and unbelievable. To suggest that it is possible to establish any sense of rapport with a man in a mask, or to ignore the presence of three intimidating onlookers behind you strains credulity. Yet he did not produce in me any sense of fear, or repulsion. The circumstances in which the interview took place most certainly gave rise to some sense of apprehension, and the knowledge of what he had done most definitely coloured how I felt about him. But at the level of the impression he made on me, he did not give rise to fear or loathing. He talked quietly; he answered my questions thoughtfully, and coherently. He was articulate, and well able to place his activities into a broader context. That the way he described that broader political context often seemed cliché ridden, and dependent on stock phrases which substituted for analysis, did not reduce the impression of a capable and thoughtful person. His mannerism of fingering the mouth hole in the mask, and pulling the mask away from his nose, did however suggest some nervousness and he shuffled and moved around in his chair quite a lot. But throughout the interview, he looked directly at me, and seemed better able to ignore his colleagues behind than I was!

He said he was in his mid to late 20's, born and brought up in

Belfast. His father had been a tradesman, who had been involved in the troubles from the very beginning. He described his childhood as 'happy' and when asked could not identify any particular events that caused him great upset or concern. But quite clearly, right from his early childhood, he had been aware of the tensions and problems his community faced. He was clearly proud of his father and the fact that he had been involved in the troubles, of his family, and of the sense of tradition which he saw himself belonging to. His family was large, and they had '. . . *become closer to each other as they had grown older.*' He was married, but declined to answer questions about his family life – '*You'll understand*' he said '*that I have to be careful about that.*' That he did have children, however, emerged later in the interview, when he said he wanted them to '. . . *have contact with the church to learn. . . .*' his community's traditions.

School life had been '*OK*' and his memories of his early life were in general positive. The school he attended only had children from one religious denomination (the normal state of affairs in Northern Ireland) but he did not recognise that as a sectarian background. As in his family life, he could not recall any particular, significant events in his school career that might relate to his later political or terrorist activity. School was strict, and he left at 15 without much regret. Sectarianism was clearly a fundamental, almost unspoken element of his childhood, but mainly present in the background of life and only occasionally surfacing. Indeed, the only event that he said he remembered vividly as a significant event related to his later view of life was a sectarian attack on his community which took place close to where he lived. They '. . . *took over a place near the chapel*' he said '*and I saw blue flashes coming from it. They came down then, and I saw someone shot. They were just shooting at us.*' The children had to be moved away, because they were interested in what was happening and had not recognised the danger they were in. He did not think this had had any immediate effect upon him, but he said that later, it became clear to him that the lesson that this taught was the need to defend your community; that there were forces 'out there' that were out to destroy what he had grown up in, and what he valued.

Whilst there may not have been any single significant event that he could draw attention to, what did become clear during the interview was that his experiences at school seemed to sustain and develop his sense of identity. This came not so much from the formal school curriculum, but from the general atmosphere of the school and from his interaction with his school friends and acquaintances. He had no recollection as a child of meeting people from other religions so he had no opportunity to experience directly their positive or negative qualities. But he was aware that a number of his friends and classmates had family who were involved in 'the troubles', just as his parents and family were. He gained status from this '. . . *It marked you out . . . yeah it made me feel something . . .*' are expressions of these positive qualities of family and peer endorsement to engagement in political violence.

On leaving school he had wanted to be a tradesman like his father, and had even started an apprenticeship, but then left it. He gave no clear reason for this, but it seems likely that his principal interests were even at this stage not on developing a career, but on his growing involvement with paramilitaries. In the course of his career he had a variety of jobs such as a petrol pump attendant and as a delivery man, but none had lasted long and he was not in employment now.

He had become involved with the terrorist organisation whilst at school. He was '. . . *pushing to do these sort of things . . .*' and his family had tolerated, if not encouraged him. Why he had been anxious to join was rather less clear. He made reference to '*threatened identity*' and '*nationality*' as factors, but these seem unlikely reasons for a working class adolescent in his circumstances. Undoubtedly, the frequent reference to family values played a role, in that he knew his father was involved. But the specific reasons for his involvement can probably be inferred from the clues contained in his references to his early participation in riots and civil disorder, and the excitement and comradeship that they produced. There is no doubt that he was also aware of the traditions to which his behaviour belonged, and even at this relatively early age, it seems that in an almost intuitive way he could recognise the continuity of his present behaviour with the past. But as he experienced it, it seems that the excitement of protest interacted with his family and social background to produce the young activist. In contrast, his legitimisation of his behaviour in terms of social values seems to be an important element in his own justification for violence, and in some measure served to limit and diminish any moral doubts that might have arisen for him.

Psychological reflections: two themes

Identity, community, threat; these words littered the conversation, recurring over and over again as we discussed his life. '*We must organise to defend . . .*' and '*Violence is a reaction . . .*' were phrases that he used whenever we talked about the reasons for his involvement. Yet throughout the interview, there was also a constant reference to the evil of violence, how violence was undesirable and that other ways were preferable. In the light of his involvement in violence, this paradoxical sensitivity to the moral issues, and the awareness it suggests is resolved in a way common to many terrorists by locating the cause of violence away from the individual. Violent responses are forced by circumstance, by conspiracy, by the State's inaction, but never by deliberate intent; these are the rationalisations of violence from terrorists the world over.

For the individual above, in his discussion with me two themes can be discerned that seem to offer clues about his psychological motivation to become engaged in violence. These themes are worth elaborating here to establish a background against which other accounts in later chapters can be viewed. They serve to illustrate to us more general processes which might be lost sight of, and although they are presented here with reference to that one interview, these themes are generally present in some sense in all of the interviews reported here.

The first theme is the sense of legitimacy and appropriateness of violence, despite its horror. This is derived from what in the above interview he clearly saw as the right to engage in violence *as a defence* against threats to his community. This appears to have its primary origins in the past through family, cultural, historical and religious traditions. But the influence of immediate family members or close family friends also seems to be very important, providing models for the child that illustrate and legitimise violence.

How does this sense of legitimacy emerge in the individual? The psychological concept of 'role model' as a form of social learning is a useful way of thinking about some of the psychological processes that might be involved. In early childhood, we learn from other people about our feelings, our beliefs, attitudes and behavioural tendencies. During this time, the most powerful teachers are our parents, but as we grow older and our circle of friends and acquaintances grows, so the influence of parents wane somewhat, and teachers, friends and others become more important. The traditions of a community, relayed through stories about 'olden times' and family and community anecdotes, reminiscences and straightforward moral homilies can also serve as models, that for this specific example in the narrow sectarian communities of Northern Ireland may serve to reinforce and amplify the more tangible effects of family and community example. Also, as we will again briefly note in Chapter 3, the distinctive community based songs which are popular in both communities in Northern Ireland may play an important role in this. In his particular case, his father's involvement was a source of pride, and undoubtedly facilitated and legitimised a way of looking at the world in which violence became an acceptable, appropriate and community-sanctioned response to social strains.

The second theme that emerges from his discussion is violence as a *forced* response to circumstances, expressed either as a regrettable but entirely reasonable response to past violence against the community, a legitimate response to conspiracies to disadvantage the community, or in a reactive way as a response to current aggression. Dialogue as a way of solving problems is impossible because 'you can't trust them', because they deceive, or because they 'only understand force'. But the recurrent theme is that force is always justified as a response to some external event, a threat of violence or an actual attack. The violence he has been involved in is never the initiator of a cycle of violence, it is never seen as primarily proactive, but a response to the violence of others. The effect of this is to deny his own contribution to the violence by focusing attention on external causes.

This raises an important issue. In the interview discussed here, the individual concerned was clearly well aware of the moral context of his behaviour. He recognised a need to justify his actions in moral terms, not only to others, but more importantly to himself. Furthermore, he was sensitive to the potential difficulties to which his behaviour might give rise in this respect. He solved the problem in the way that many individuals in similar circumstances do – he sought moral refuge by seeing his behaviour as a response to the actions of others. But the important point in furthering our psychological understanding of him is his sensitivity to the need to justify his behaviour in moral terms. His actions may appear immoral or amoral or abnormal to society, but to the individual concerned, they are an appropriate and defensible *moral* act. Contrary to the popular view, both the recognition of a moral problem, and the solution discussed here, is not at all uncommon amongst those involved in political violence.

We can throw some psychological light on this. The processes that result in this external focus as a justification for violence may have origins in the psychological concept of attribution, and in particular in what are known as 'the fundamental attribution error' and the 'actor-observer effect'. Psychologists use the term attribution to refer to our efforts to understand the actions of people around us. The fundamental attribution error refers to a bias which we tend to show in thinking that people do things because 'they are that kind of person', rather than because of the circumstances in which they find themselves. We tend to explain the behaviour of *other* people in terms of disposition, especially pejorative explanations such as 'they are bad', 'they deliberately did something' – explanations drawing on sectarian qualities also clearly fall into this category. Even when such explanations are unwarranted we still show this tendency. In contrast, we tend to explain our *own* behaviour in terms of the situation in which we find ourselves, instead of the dispositional explanations we tend to use for other people. This is what is known as the 'actor-observer' effect.

A simple example will illustrate these pervasive tendencies. If, when walking down a road, your companion trips and falls, you are quite likely to think this is because *he* is clumsy (a dispositional explanation); if you trip and fall, *you* are likely to blame the uneven pavement (an environmental explanation). The more you dislike or feel negative about your companion, the more you are likely to attribute dispositional rather than environmental causes to behaviour. Lady Bracknell in Wilde's play *The Importance of Being Earnest* makes a similar attributional error to good humorous effect – 'To lose one parent, Mr Worthing, may be regarded as a misfortune; to lose both looks like carelessness.' Wilde had a good, if intuitive, understanding of the ambiguities of social relationships, and the processes that give rise to them!

Both the Fundamental Attribution Error and the 'Actor-Observer' effect complement each other, and provide a powerful bias towards explaining our own behaviour in terms of responding to events and explaining the behaviour of others in terms of some quality of the individual involved. This can help us to understand how the terrorist can in a sense evade the responsibility for his actions by locating the causes of his or her behaviour in the actions of others

Added to this, however, is another powerful sub-theme which might exaggerate and interact with the external focus of justification. This is a sense of conspiracy. When people are intensely committed to particular views, defeats are difficult to deal with. Rather than acknowledge our own inadequacies, they are often interpreted as the result of traitorous actions – '. . . *we were let down by them* . . .' – or by traitors and informers (in Ireland known as touts) within the organisation. A volunteer had been arrested and charged with a serious offence because '. . . *there was a tout you see . . . that's what did for him.*' Recourse to conspiracy theories is, of course, sometimes appropriate, especially in the labyrinthine world of paramilitary organisations. But reference to a conspiracy is also a way of helping to make sense of the world when you cannot understand what is happening.

In fact, we are particularly prone to take refuge in conspiracy theories when something happens that we feel is not deserved. This becomes especially significant in circumstances where community values become exaggerated through real or perceived threat. If you feel you are right, if your view of history confirms that, if your family, friends and community support your view in the face of what to you is oppression, then when the world fails to meet your expectations, it *must* be because of some unreasonable interference. For it to be otherwise offends against our sense of a just world. The most likely

sources of such interference are, of course, the agents of authority –
the police, the army and the state in general. In Northern Ireland,
the British Government fills that role, and is often seen as deliberately 'letting down' reasonable expectations, or hindering legitimate
aspirations. The British Government therefore necessarily acquires
the role as the agent of conspiracy, secretly subverting, plotting and
tricking people into submission. The particular occasions when this
seems actually to be the case serves to confirm the more general
view. In this respect if no other, the conflict in Northern Ireland has
a great deal in common with the Islamic fundamentalist's perception
of his world, as we will see in Chapter 6.

Because conspiracies are necessarily covert, explanations in terms
of conspiracy can rarely be disproved once the accusation is made.
But we can see a further quality to them, related to our discussion
above of the significance of external justifications – they have a comforting external quality to them, moving attention away from yourself
or your community, to an outside agency or force.

In the interview discussed above, the heady mixture of history,
community, family and situational variables that contribute to the
development of the terrorist all emerge. The factors we have identified all contribute to a justification of violence through creating an
enemy with diabolical qualities. This serves an important purpose –
we might feel guilty when we are aggressive towards a reasonable
person *like ourselves*; but conspiratorial and cheating enemies are fair
game!

These forces also create the world in which the young terrorist can
develop. But, of course, not everyone from those communities,
although subject to those same or similar influences, becomes a terrorist. In the interview discussed here, probing about the specific
factors that led to involvement with terrorism does not yield any
clear cut evidence. Rather, a complex of issues related to excitement
and belonging emerge as specific local influences. Perhaps in this
case, a facilitating context combined with opportunity, and the influence of particular friends and relatives is sufficient to give us
psychological understanding.

How typical is this account presented above? What measure of
generality can we attribute to the issues that emerged? It would
clearly be wrong to represent the person interviewed above as a typical example of a terrorist. His motivations are undoubtedly different
from others, and his array of experiences are probably idiosyncratic
and unique; but then of course so are everyone's! The fact that he
was chosen by a paramilitary organisation to speak to me is probably
also a measure of their confidence in him to present a reasonable
image, as much as he might have been chosen to give information.

This might suggest that he is atypical, or at least has more attractive qualities than others similarly engaged. Certainly, he was more articulate than many other paramilitary activists I have met in Ireland in a variety of situations, many less formal than this.

Yet many of the themes that emerge from his account recur in other discussions drawn on for this book. His particular sectarian affiliations and the references to obvious sectarian issues have been deliberately obscured in the account presented. This is not particularly to protect him in any way, but to draw attention to the fact that at a psychological level, the kinds of issues that emerge as relevant are shared by terrorists from a variety of backgrounds. Interviews with active terrorists from other sectarian backgrounds in Northern Ireland, or others from more explicitly political rather than nationalistic backgrounds, yield material emphasising similar themes.

It is important to note, however, that this is in no sense an argument for a 'terrorist personality'. Concepts such as this lend a deceptive sense of order to what is a profoundly difficult issue. Explanations of terrorism in terms of 'personality' serve to push the explanations inside the individual – they offer accounts in terms of essentially unobservable and unmeasurable qualities of people. But the issue of concern to us is not an unspecifiable tendency to behave, but actual terrorist behaviour. The violence and damage the terrorist inflicts is the result not of a personality trait or disposition, but of an act of some form – a behaviour. What we might observe in the voices and accounts presented throughout this book are responses to circumstances and forces that have a measure of commonality – what we hear are individuals coming to terms with their environment (historical as much as contemporary) and making sense of that environment in similar ways. The processes we see are those which in some measure affect all of us.

Violence as a response to violence, violence forced upon a community (and that individual seeing himself as a victim of circumstance, or more positively as a defender of that community) and conspiracy provide the psychological link between terrorists of different persuasions and aspirations. In the above, the only further factor missing to complete the account is reference to the organisational dependence and pressure the active terrorist feels which arises out of his membership of a paramilitary organisation. The particular interview outlined above did not identify this as a factor, but that was because of the nature and direction of the interview.

Structurally, politically and organisationally there are important differences between terrorist groups. At one level, size and complexity is one obvious difference, and kinds of political aims are another. If we follow through that latter theme, broadly speaking, two classes of groups can be identified – nationalist terrorist organisations and political terrorist organisations. Nationalist organisations, of course, have political ends, and the simple division this implies, in reality is often more complex. One important dimension of difference relates to the kinds of people who become involved in the organisation. Radical political movements (of the left and right) tend to have members who are children of professionals, and who have had some form of extended education, often to university level. Nationalist movements, on the other hand, tend to have a much larger working class membership, who tend to have lower than university level educational qualifications, if any at all.

It is important to note, however, that these differences can obscure psychological analysis, and may lead us to exaggerate the extent of psychological dissimilarity between individual terrorists. Whilst educational attainment may be a dimension of difference between people, we cannot necessarily assume that it reflects differences in intellectual ability, of course. In many circumstances, educational level attained may relate more to opportunity than ability. From this point of view, we can see that some of the differences we notice may be of context rather than of substance. Indeed, we can infer that the processes of adjustment, of accommodating to the world, that we can identify that result in the terrorist, and that sustain his involvement once initiated, may have surprisingly wide currency.

We can identify a variety of influences that seem to relate to a potential terrorist's engagement with a paramilitary organisation, and involvement with violence. A problem in analysis, however, is that attempts to reduce these factors to provide simple explanations necessarily fail. Becoming a terrorist is a complex process that usually extends over a considerable period of time. Many factors influence the individual, and answers lie in a complex combination of circumstances, rather than a simple linear account. Recognition of the complex pressures, our appreciation of which can only reveal the shadows of the reality experienced by the individual, is probably all that the observer can hope for to aid understanding. However, that is still sufficient for us to develop our analysis.

Of course, terrorism is in this respect no different from any of the other things people do. In one sense, embarking on a life of terrorism is like any other life choice. We are not surprised to be told that the factors that influence career choice, for example, are complex and relate to opportunity, ability and sometimes simply sheer chance. To ask why an individual occupies a particular social, career or even family role is probably a deceptively easy but essentially unanswerable question. What we can do, however, is identify the factors in any particular situation that help to understand why particular life choices have been made. This same analysis applies to the development of the terrorist.

Understanding Terrorist Lives

How the terrorist sees the world

'*The only way to avoid the trauma of killing is to go on doing it . . . If you stepped to one side, I don't think you could tolerate it and I don't think you could live with yourself. . . . After a time you don't really think too much about it, and at the beginning I was too frightened for myself to think about it anyway . . . I have to believe in myself, I have to have confidence and certainty that my contribution is worthwhile and important . . . my self-respect is important to me . . . yes we are achieving something, we have to be.*'

This is a comment by a social science graduate who was involved in European terrorism. He had participated in a number of terrorist bombings, and was charged at the time with attempted murder. He was able to articulate more clearly than many the themes that recur in many discussions with terrorists, European or Irish. Once embarked on a terrorist lifestyle, and once engaged in violence, it is very difficult to question it and to renounce it, or to even admit of doubts. The truly awful acts that the terrorist commits have to be justified in terms of a greater goal, and that greater goal in turn is intimately related to the individual's own self-worth. The certainty and confidence in the rightness of the cause, necessary to become involved in and to sustain violence, necessarily limits the capacity for self-reflection. In a sense, the demonstration of commitment which engaging in a terrorist act might initially represent also binds the individual to further violence. It initiates a self-sustaining cycle which is very difficult to break.

The individual terrorist's justification for terrorism is therefore related at a fundamental psychological level to a sense of purpose and self-worth, in the same way that most people's major life choices are. It is, at least initially, a means to achieve something which is intrinsically desirable and important to the person involved. That desirability may relate to nationalist or political aspirations, but as far as the person is concerned, its attainment will result in a better world, either for the individual or for his community. Seeking for '. . . *a place in the sun . . .*' or some similar phrase has occurred more than once in interviews about this subject, and it captures the sense of aspiration and commitment that characterises the active terrorist in the initial stages of involvement. Later, however, that idealism may well be tempered both by reality and experience.

To understand how someone becomes involved in terrorism, we first of all have to have some appreciation of *how the terrorist sees his world*. In any empirical sense this is difficult, if not impossible to achieve. It is morally and legally inappropriate to identify people in the initial stages of involvement and follow them through their terrorist career, making some form of psychological assessment of them from time to time. The only evidence that is available is usually from the more mature (in terms of length of involvement) terrorist, who is willing to reflect upon the conditions that led to his or her engagement with terrorism. The difficulty with this is that the present state of the individual (whether he remains active, is in prison, or has renounced terrorism) influences the colours in which he might paint his early career. Furthermore, there are a lot of pressures on the individual to rationalise motivations to fit in with subsequent events, or to try to project an image of a particular kind of person.

The discussion of the interview which started this chapter gives some indication, however, of the kinds of theme to which terrorists themselves make reference – notably the sense of legitimacy and appropriateness of violence, both as a defence against threat and as a response to threat. These themes derive from that individual's particular 'world view' that gives structure and meaning to the individual. 'World view' is a dangerous phrase; it suggests something that sounds concrete, but it is an amorphous term, lacking specificity and meaning when examined in detail. It will serve our purpose, however, to illustrate an important quality of the terrorist.

In a sense we all have a 'world view', or perhaps more accurately a variety of world views. Furthermore, because we generally live in complex social environments, the elements which go to make up our 'world view' may well be inconsistent. In the case of the terrorist, however, one thing that emerges in discussions is a consistency of view for the individual about significant political or national issues, which is shared in some detail by others. When we encounter this degree of consistency, we term this embracing world view *ideology*. '. . . ideology is an organisation of beliefs and attitudes – religious, political or philosophical in nature – that is more or less institutionalised or shared with others, deriving from external authority. . . .'

To say that an individual is influenced by ideology may be saying little more than that his behaviour is consistent with others who share the same beliefs (as distinct from behaviour which may appear idiosyncratic or random). Crucially, however, that individual also gives the same reasons for doing something as do others of the same persuasion. Those reasons are derived from an authority, who has invariably written down injunctions to guide behaviour, and explanations of the world. Mohammed, Marx, Lenin, Hitler; all can be identified as founders, or developers, of particular kinds of ideology which command belief. We can recognise belief by the extent to which an individual's behaviour is influenced by a particular ideology. Attitudes can also be influenced by ideology, but in the case of terrorism, the critical issue is the extent to which behaviour rather than attitude is influenced. The propensity for behaviour to be influenced by a belief in this sense may have its origins in a variety of forces, including historical, psychological, and perhaps cultural. But for our purposes, we might note the self-confirming nature of the value system that emerges. An ideological interpretation of the world gives meaning and structure to an individual, and through helping to understand events, confirms the bases of belief. This self-confirming circularity is an important factor in sustaining belief and involvement in terrorism.

The most striking feature of discussions with terrorists, or for that matter most political activists, is the sense in which they use their ideology to interpret the world. By reference to *their* ideology, the world becomes knowable; values emerge that are consistent with the world as they see it. But it is of central importance to recognise that it may not be necessary for the individual to understand fully the detail of what is espoused – hence the extensive use of clichés as substitutes for analysis. Of course we all use clichés, sometimes because we lack the vocabulary or capacity to articulate a concept, but more often to avoid or slip over an issue. Terrorists fight for 'freedom', 'justice', 'anti-imperialism', 'our people' . . . but probe beneath these terms, and there is often very little substance. Pointing out the inconsistencies in killing people to achieve freedom, for example, or trying to explore the sense is which justice is progressed by the death of a bystander rarely evokes much concern or illumination. In a sense, the clichéd ideological phrase substitutes for analysis; it offers a way of justifying an action by reference to some broadly desirable end without the need to appreciate or explain what has been done. It masks raw sectarianism, and gives a sense of legitimacy to what would otherwise be illegitimate. Such is the power of cliché derived from ideology.

The political theorist Hannah Arendt was well aware of the role that clichés play in the justification of extreme violence. In her discussion of the trial in Israel of the Nazi war criminal, Adolf Eichmann, she notes his extensive use of clichés in his own justification for his behaviour. Whilst being cross-examined by one of the Presiding Judges at his trial, Eichmann found himself unable to explain what he wanted to say other than by the use of clichés. He was aware of this, and apologised, saying '*Officialese [Amtssprahe] is my only language.*' His trial judges criticised Eichmann for this, and saw it as a strategy used by him deliberately to evade or diminish his responsibility for the atrocities with which he was associated. The judges told him that all that he had said was 'empty talk', which they thought was feigned and used to cover up other thoughts which were 'hideous' and far from empty.

But Arendt perceptively comments that his use of cliché reflected not deliberate evasion, but his own inability to move beyond his own ideological constraints. She felt that despite his bad memory, '. . . he repeated word for word the same stock phrases and self-invented cliché . . . each time he referred to an incident or event of importance to him. . . . The longer one listened to him, the more obvious it became that his inability to speak was closely connected with an inability to *think*, namely, to think from the standpoint of somebody else. No communication was possible with him, not because he lied, but because he was surrounded by the most reliable of all safeguards against the words and presence of others, and hence against reality as such.[2] His use of cliché was a reflection of the strength of his absorption of Nazi ideology, rather than an evasion of responsibility.

When speaking to terrorists, or their politically sophisticated leaders, the quality of evasion through cliché is very apparent. But as in the case of Eichmann, it would be a mistake to assume that the use of clichés indicates something to hide; it seems much more likely that clichés reflect the extent to which the individual is under the influence of an underlying ideology that limits his capacity to appreciate positions other than his own. It is of course to this quality of an ideology that we must look when we try to understand why political violence occurs. The individual terrorist, therefore, is not necessarily able to articulate a coherent and sophisticated ideological position. He most likely makes reference to ideology through stock phrases and clichés which serve to provide a structure for justifications which are in reality poorly understood.

Northern Irish terrorists frequently lack a sophisticated understanding of their own ideological position, at least initially. Indeed, it is often only after a period of imprisonment that the capacity that characterises the European terrorist to articulate a relatively sophisticated political position emerges. Imprisonment in this context acts very much as a learning environment giving prisoners the opportunity and facilities to develop their own understanding of their particular movement. Indeed, one of the paradoxical effects of the extensive use of imprisonment as a response to terrorism in Northern Ireland is the extent to which that presumed punishment actively facilitates the ideological development and commitment of prisoners from both republican and loyalist backgrounds. Comments from imprisoned European terrorists also indicate the extent to which prison provides the opportunity for ideological and political discussion and exploration.

The experiences of Christof Wackernagel and Gert Schneider[3] illustrate the significance of prison experience. In their case, that influence was benign, because it led to their eventual renunciation of terrorism – but this is far from the normal situation. Wackernagel and Schneider were members of the Red Army Faction, a West German terrorist organisation. They were both arrested after a shoot out with the police in Amsterdam in 1977, and both received long prison sentences. In 1981, they were moved to the same prison, and allowed to associate with each other. '*That was the start of our critical thinking. Together we could examine whether we had done anything wrong.*' They read and explored the work of Lenin and Marx '. . . *on which our fight was allegedly based*' and concluded that '. . . *the more we read, the more difficult it became to justify our armed struggle. It just didn't work.*' For Wackernagel and Schneider, therefore, prison provided the environment in which they could reflect on their activities and beliefs.

The experience of prisoners in Northern Ireland is generally less benign. There are many examples of convicted terrorists gaining increased sophistication and knowledge, and indeed renewed commitment. '*It was when I went inside that I began to see more clearly the nature of our struggle . . .*' is a telling comment on the power of prison to provide an opportunity for education and development. Not only does prison act as an educational experience, however. There is evidence to suggest that meetings in prison cement trusted friendships and relationships that last even outside prison, and even between republican and loyalist prisoners. Indeed, such meetings may have played a role in the development of the extensive paramilitary involvement in extortion during the 1980's, facilitating the allocation of territories between different paramilitary groups and developing contacts between loyalists and republicans.

The acquisition of a shared all embracing world view is one element in becoming a terrorist. But in itself it is not sufficient. The terrorist also *does* terrorism – he engages in violence. It is of course this central quality that distinguishes the terrorist from others who share his or her views. The acquisition of violence as part of an individual's repertoire usually (but not always) occurs over a period of time. It takes place in a very complex situation, where the overt political aim of the activities is less important for the individual in psychological terms than the setting and context in which it occurs. Participation in riots or demonstrations is often the beginning point

on the road to engagement with violence. In part, this is because such
events can readily lead to violence, especially where police handling
of the event is insensitive. But also because participation in such
activities begins the development of the sense of camaraderie and
friendship, the sense of solidarity with others that is so important in
sustaining involvement. In Northern Ireland this is enhanced by
involvement in youth movements which all major paramilitary organisations control.

Shared experience, shared excitement, and a shared sense of purpose. These are the roots from which terrorism may flower. But of
course, in themselves they do not necessarily lead to violence. Rather
the sense of illegality, of being outside and above the law (because
your ideology gives insights into more important factors than the
transitory present) and the gradual confirmation of this through
increased experience initiates the cycle that can lead to violence and
terrorism. '*I felt a sense of pride . . . we stood up to them*' '*. . . this Pig*[4] *came
round the corner, and one of the boys threw a petrol bomb. I don't think it did
much damage, but they turned round quick enough . . . we ran off then . . .
it was great, really great.* '*. . . we were all together, all my mates . . .*'

'*None of us had a sense of what the so-called "new society" should have
been. Looking back, I think that was our greatest weakness. The simple fact
that we weren't able to imagine a new society was a decisive factor in our
defeat . . .*' '*I think we substituted our own way of living for the aims we were
trying to achieve. That was a confusion, an error . . .*'

'*We never thought we would arrive at the end of the revolution. We thought
we were the beginners of something, and that afterwards others would come
and take our place. There was a great sense of shared purpose*'. '*Perhaps we
were too involved in the details . . . we could see a strategy, but somehow it
became lost . . . partly because you have to do something, partly because it's
exciting and there is a great sense of achievement in a successful event.*' '*We
certainly thought we knew where we were going . . . there is great strength in
that certainty, you know, and we all shared it . . .*'

The sense of shared commitment, and of belonging to a worthwhile cause is an important theme emerging from discussions and
interviews. In the case of nationalist organisations which can claim
long traditions, the sense of belonging can acquire almost mystical
qualities, confirming membership of the community. Some authors
have referred to membership of such organisations as 'a rite of passage' which the young member of a community must experience to
claim full membership. Certainly, the paramilitary organisations in
Northern Ireland can claim a wide degree of contact and influence
with young people, often in school. This also seems to be the case for
the Basque terrorist organisation, ETA. Undoubtedly, to be involved
can confer status amongst peers, and can seem to many like the

fulfilment of traditional cultural stereotypes and role models. '*I was pushing to be involved . . .*' '*I think my parents knew, alright. I think they were quite proud . . . at least my mother was. She worried about me, like, but I think she was really proud of me. That mattered to me a lot.*' '*I joined in school, sort of. Well, I hung around with some mates, and we all like joined. It was against the law like, but it was no harm . . .*'

More politically orientated organisations can't make such claims, but can substitute other kinds of traditions, emphasising, for example in radical left groups, the continuity of the class struggle. Important figures in revolutionary activity acquire almost mythical properties, and serve to act as role models for aspirant revolutionaries. One very powerful figure who occupied this role was Che Guevara. '*. . . the . . . important thing to us was the South American movements of the 'Guerilla'. It was all the experience of Cuba, Che Guevara . . . and all those things . . . they were revolutionary communists as well.*' '*. . . there was the realisation that there were a whole lot of communist movements in the world which are revolutionary, which use violence not peace . . . this is what we saw for ourselves*'

A role model is someone who exemplifies to others desirable behaviour. People in positions of authority are often seen as role models, and we are probably most familiar with this concept as it applies to the classroom – the teacher providing the role model for his or her pupils, for example. In a technical sense, it is a form of learning based on observation of others, and the example set by the role model can provide a powerful force to facilitate behaviour change and direction. This is undoubtedly a central factor in the development of the terrorist.

Being a terrorist

Life for the active terrorist is, in a sense, very extraordinary. It is adventurous, it is purposeful and it is busy. The member of a terrorist group not only participates in violence, but also becomes involved in other qualities of political activism – meetings and discussions. In contrast to the mundane world of work, a terrorist lifestyle has structure and purpose. Indeed, the sense of purpose which membership gives serves to substitute for many of the qualities of ordinary living, or perhaps more accurately serves to intensify those attributes. Most notably, the sense of friendship and comradeship is frequently referred to as critical in developing and sustaining membership, and is often described in intense ways. Shared danger, a sense of conspiracy, and the sense of rightness contributes to this. The terrorist is the custodian of secrets, he moves in a shadow world where he can exercise great power and destruction.

At a more ordinary level, however, the terrorist lifestyle can have its attractions, especially when contrasted to the mundane world of low incomes, the routine of marginal employment or unemployment. Michael Baumann, founder of the West German terrorist group 'The 2nd of June Movement', makes the point that '*he. . . had an exceptionally good time . . .*' as a terrorist. '. . . *If you had long hair, there were always an incredible number of chicks hanging onto you. They thought it was great, a guy like that. . . .*'

It is a world that values action. Demonstrated prowess in placing bombs or daring in shooting increases status amongst the group. Such success also demonstrates talent, and leads to greater involvement, and more central roles in action. In this world, individual acts of violence acquire the status of heroism dissociated from the victim, with the corollary that death or failure attracts some of the attributes of martyrdom. In the pub in the evening, or when chatting amongst friends, the spectacular escape and the dramatic incidents are retold, with the characters involved acquiring saga-like heroic qualities of courage or humour.

The interview which started this chapter also reveals another critical quality of nationalist terrorism – the influence of family membership. Certainly within Northern Ireland, the family connections that emerge when discussing terrorist organisations are considerable. Brothers, brothers-in-law, cousins and sometimes sons, are often referred to as co-terrorists, either as direct participants or as people who provide moral and material support such as safe houses. In particular, leaders often have cousins or brothers-in-law as their juniors, and some certainly select their critical members on the basis of family connection as much as talent. This is important in two senses. The first is that family ties provide the facilitating context which legitimises terrorism. Current involvement is often a mirror of past involvement, and many terrorist families can give a litany of past events where they have played a role, and where individual family members have been injured, killed or imprisoned. The present therefore has continuity with the past, and the young person growing in this environment absorbs the ethos of terrorism as part of his early socialisation.

A second sense in which family is important is that family links give confidence and dependence. Family members are known to each other, and are bound by common links of loyalty. There are shared reciprocal obligations within a family, and in a sense, therefore, family members might be thought to be more trustworthy than non-family. Even if family members are not necessarily more trustworthy, the closeness of family relationships can offer a means of gaining knowledge about such matters as movements and friendships.

It is, in fact, hard to judge whether family relationships are more secure or more reliable, for there are many examples of family members informing on each other or of usurping roles. Nevertheless, family provides a basis on which trust can develop. Above all, however, the family provides opportunity for the non-threatening authoritative experience of extreme political views, legitimising politically violent behaviour.

It is less clear whether these same factors influence membership of the other important nationalist terrorist organisation in Europe, the Basque group ETA, where previous family membership or involvement seems to be less evident. A reason for this may be that the Basque organisation cannot draw on the complex historical background available to the Irish terrorists, where periodic violent dissent has frequently occurred. The support of friends or job associates, for example, does however, seem to be of critical importance in the Basque situation.

This then is the world the young activist sees. It is one he hears about from friends, or in the case of Northern Ireland and other areas where nationalist terrorist movements exist, hears about from family and relatives. Membership of such movements brings its own rewards that are, in a psychological sense, much greater than those of regular employment, or apprenticeship; thus the young person is drawn in.

In the early stages of involvement, it is most likely that only small and unimportant tasks are given at first, both to test the individual, and to train him in the 'work' of terrorism. '*The first time, I was standing lookout . . . I had to warn if a car came down the street. I was terrified of getting it wrong.*' '*I was given this package, wrapped in plastic, and told to take it to a certain house, and leave it with whoever opened the door. No-one stopped me, and I did it OK. I didn't know what had happened, although afterwards I could guess.*'

'*The first time I fired one [. . . a pistol . . .], it was only a practice, I was terrified. I was covered in sweat, but in the end it was no big deal*'

The first major terrorist action an individual is involved in figures in many accounts as a significant confirmatory experience. Up to that point, involvement has usually been minor and undemanding. Whilst even low level involvement, if provable, can command very stiff prison sentences in Northern Ireland for example, there is little sense in which the risk of apprehension seems to influence the behaviour of the young person, loyalist or nationalist, on the fringes of terrorism. But to take part in a major event such as a bombing or shooting crosses a line, and places that person into the category of illegal in their own eyes. At this point, the organisation assumes even greater importance, offering advice, structure and support; it also, of

course, confers and confirms status. This seems to be a general quality of terrorists of many different persuasions.

'*You reach a point when there's really no turning back.*' The significance
of this may escape the individual at the time, because life is full of
excitement. But on reflection, there seems to be a boundary in many
terrorist careers that marks a movement away from normal society.
Being wanted by the police, and having to lead a clandestine life is
one indicator of this change. But for most it occurs well before that
point. It is a critical *psychological* boundary, rather than a legal or
moral point of reference.

A marker of that important boundary may be a personal event,
such as the death of a friend or acquaintance, or an incident of significance to the community or party, such as an atrocity. A recurrent
theme is some kind of security force excess – these may range from
gratuitous insult to physical abuse – it may even extend to third parties.

Michael Baumann describes the critical point that turned him
from a left-wing activist to an active terrorist as the shooting of his
friend, Bruno Ohnesary, by a policeman during a protest against the
visit to West Germany of the Shah of Iran in 1967. '*That gave me a
tremendous flash, one cannot really describe it. It really shook me to the bones.*'
Similarly, Hans-Joachin Klein, a member of an off-shoot of the West
German Baader-Meinhof Group identifies a series of critical points
that led to his active involvement in political violence. One was his
witnessing a policeman beating a young girl during a riot. He
describes himself as flying into an uncontrollable rage and attacking
the police officer, as a result of which he was beaten up. When he saw
the police beating the girl '. . . *two images collided, my image of women
and my image of cops . . . from that moment on, I began to think.*' A further
critical point for Klein was the death in prison of Holger Meins as a
result of hunger strike. Meins was a member of the Rote Armee
Faction, and was arrested with Andreas Baader. '*I put that first pistol of
mine into my pocket the night I heard Holger Meins had died in prison*'

As in the case of the German terrorists referred to above, the individual discussed at the beginning of this chapter had a gradual initial
engagement in terrorism. His particular degree of involvement with
the paramilitary organisation was limited and peripheral until the
death of a prominent paramilitary leader. This seemed to act as the
critical point which confirmed his membership, and facilitated the
transition to violence. '*This drew me in*' he said. '*I saw a way in which I
could contribute, and I am very proud of what I have been able to do . . .*'

Some care must be exercised here, however. The identification of
a precipitating event can also be a convenient *post hoc* rationalisation
for a much more mundane process of gradual involvement. A single

event can be more readily remembered than an array of influences, offering a spurious sense of order to what is in reality a much more complex and idiosyncratic process. Reference to a precipitating event can also serve as a justification, offering the individual the important psychological comfort of a moral position to justify involvement.

Organisations

We can accept the notion that individuals have goals, but it is much more difficult to see how individual goals relate to organisational goals or objectives. Yet in any organisation, we need to try to understand how it, as distinct from the individuals involved, makes decisions that are directive. To do this we need to conceptualise, at an organisational level, the processes and forces that are analogous to an individual's goals and aspirations.

Terrorist groups are, of course, organisations, and have many features in common with other organisations. As soon as individual terrorists join together to achieve some common objective, so is a form of organisation created. And like all organisations, the terrorist group will have multiple objectives, some of which are more important than others. Political or nationalist change may be the primary social goal, but this goal has to be achieved as a result of both dramatic and quite mundane activities. Whilst a terrorist organisation may wish to separate itself from the world (for security, for ideological purity) it has to live within the world. The organisation therefore has to acquire an income to obtain weapons and explosives, not to mention the sophisticated equipment needed to prosecute a successful terrorist campaign, to maintain safe houses in order to propagate its ideals through violence. As it develops further, so does the need to sustain an income grow, for terrorist organisations are expensive to maintain. For example, the families of imprisoned members have to be supported and media presences must be maintained.

In this sense, therefore, terrorist organisations are rather like businesses or commercial enterprises, whose main objective is to generate income and to maximise profit. In a paramilitary organisation, however, the beneficiaries of the profit are not shareholders, but the terrorist organisation where the profit is used to finance its other activities. Account books have to be kept, commercial decisions made, and structures put in place to manage the flow of funds. Indeed, this can in extreme situations lead to the terrorist organisation operating very effectively as a profit making concern.

Initially, terrorist organisations seem to achieve this income through robberies, contributions from supporters, and extortion.

But as an organisation matures and becomes better established, so other more sophisticated ways of generating income emerge, that are more secure from interference by the security forces, or the ebb and flow of operational successes.

Notable exponents of sophisticated ways of raising income are the Provisional IRA. They are, for example, thought to operate a chain of at least 25 pubs in the Dublin area, possibly with others in other parts of the Republic of Ireland. These pubs raise cash for the organisation through the profits they make, but they also serve as a base for money laundering, enabling the IRA to transfer the proceeds of robberies into the licensed trade. Cash which is passed through the pubs' accounts is then transferred into secret bank accounts, and then into the terrorist organisation. Hundreds of thousands of pounds are thought to have been used to buy the pubs, and care has been taken in using nominees, to ensure that there are no objections by the authorities to licensees. Professional and careful accounting practices have to be used to manage the cash flow generated by the pubs, and to ensure that the operation remains viable. The Provisional IRA, are also thought to have been heavily involved in the sale of illegal pirate copies of video films and audio tapes, including pornographic material. Members of the organisation were not themselves directly involved, but the business was directed by the organisation, and the proceeds of the business benefitted the IRA.

The management of these businesses requires considerable expertise, as with any successful commercial enterprise but with the added complication of the need to conceal the true disposal of the income thus generated. But a terrorist organisation has other functions than simply making a profit, and indeed profit is in one sense a secondary aspect of broader organisational objectives. People come together to form a terrorist group through a shared sense of ideological purpose. This ideological purpose provides the terrorist's organisational goals, and this serves to distinguish the terrorist organisation from a commercial enterprise.

But as an organisation becomes more sophisticated, and as intermediate objectives (such as raising funds) become more pressing, so distinctive organisational influences may begin to be apparent. The familiar, if complex, factors of group decision making then become influenced by further distinctive organisational influences. This is most apparent in the mature organisation, where objectives begin to shift from an ideological focus to organisational survival. Perhaps this occurs when members of the organisation begin to confuse and substitute organisational values for the attainment of ideological objectives. Keeping the movement together, fighting off rival claimants to leadership, simply managing a complex structure; after a time these become the dominant themes of the mature terrorist organisation. They offer immediacy and structure to the individual, in contrast to the much more diffuse ideological objectives. Maintaining impetus and direction is a common enough problem for any business organisation, and terrorist organisations are no different in this respect. A salient issue here is the sense in which success in fund raising not only facilitates a shift towards organisational priorities, but also confers independence from operational success or failure. It effectively reduces the links between the terrorist organisation and the 'constituency' from which it has developed.

In another context, the revolutionary theorist Régis Debray recognised the dangers of this process. He noted that when the conditions for achieving the ideological goal are not there, either through effective opposition by the State or because the terrorist group has failed to mobilise sufficient popular support, the terrorist organisation continues, but begins to substitute other goals from that of revolution. Debray does not make reference to organisational theory in his analysis, but the processes he identifies are similar to those described above. In the vacuum produced by the failure to attain ideological goals, the attainment of power or money begin to provide substitute goals. These are often the very things which the organisation is good at, giving members a sense of immediate achievement when ideological aims appear distant.

Whilst we can identify these factors at a relatively diffuse organisational level, they also have an effect on the individual. For the individual involved in the activities of a terrorist organisation, these processes create an important further boundary to be crossed. This is the boundary between the political act and the illegal act. Terrorism for it to be noticed is, of course, by definition illegal. But the justification for a bombing or kidnapping is generally expressed as a legitimate political act, which confers a sufficient sense of ambiguity to blur the issue. But terrorist action can be thought of as actually comprising two interrelated but different facets; there is the primary politically directed action, and there is the secondary support action. The former has an explicit ideological context, but the justification for the latter lies primarily in the organisational context of terrorism and only secondarily in the movement's ideological context.

As we have already seen, terrorists and their dependants are expensive people to maintain and substantial income must be generated to that end, even from the legitimate business enterprises described above. In Northern Ireland, for example, the Provisional IRA is estimated to need several million pounds a year. Thus, willy nilly, a terrorist organisation becomes not just a means of propagating political ends but a major business undertaking into the bargain. Hence it will often seek support from a wealthy third party (frequently a State) in addition to devoting a substantial proportion of its available effort to the perpetration of bank robberies, extortion and kidnapping. So, on the one hand, its members are involved in politically 'legitimate' acts against individuals or the forces of law and order and on the other in what amounts to violent illegality. Political purity often begins to blur as financial demands increase.

Most if not all terrorist groups in Western Europe and Northern Ireland have of necessity been involved in bank robberies to raise funds. The Basque organisation ETA, for example, raised several million dollars by this means during 1978 alone. But few organisations have developed the financial sophistication of the Provisional IRA. Of course, if an organisation subscribes to an ideology that seeks the overthrow of international capitalism, then attacking a bank may actually appear as part of the primary tasks. For less ideologically fortunate groups, the justification for such activity has to become more complex and pragmatic. There is clearly a pragmatic ideological virtue in standing against capitalism!

An extreme example of how the money raising priorities can come to distort a terrorist organisation can be seen in the Ulster Defence Association (UDA)[5]. During the period 1983–88, the UDA, a loyalist paramilitary group in Northern Ireland, increasingly became associated with extortion and what was termed gangsterism. It is impossible to guess the amounts of money raised through extortion, especially against building contractors. Although this was widely known, intimidation of the victims meant that it was almost impossible for the men responsible to be prosecuted successfully. For example, in 1985 a number of prominent loyalist leaders were charged at Belfast Magistrates Court with extortion from building sites. Witnesses identifying and accusing them were present in court, wearing masks and hooded jackets to protect their identity. They did not give their names, but identified themselves only as building company directors. Necessary as these precautions appeared, the defence successfully argued that it had not been given information about charges, locations, or accusers, and therefore could not properly make enquiries to conduct a defence. In all, 32 charges were made. The same men were also charged with possessing firearms to commit blackmail. For a time, the accused put on masks in court in mockery of the witnesses, but eventually the case collapsed as witnesses retracted their evidence.

Eventually, in 1990, some of those originally accused were sentenced to 10 years imprisonment for extortion. Many members of the

UDA during that period crossed the boundary between terrorist activity and straightforward acquisitive criminality. This example is an extreme case but, to a lesser extent, most terrorists cross that boundary at some time in their career. Strangely enough, at least in Northern Ireland, there is a sense of official recognition of the inevitability of paramilitary extortion. Business organisations subjected to extortion claim tax relief on extortion payments as a business expense! Up to 40 per cent of the money paid can be claimed back as tax allowance.

The relationship between terrorism and illegal and criminal activity can take other forms as well, as further examples from Northern Ireland illustrate. During 1992, the Irish People's Liberation Organisation (IPLO) became increasingly involved in drug dealing in Belfast. Suspicions that Irish paramilitary groups had been involved in the lucrative drugs trade have been high for some time, but towards the end of 1992, increasing evidence of drug dealing by the IPLO emerged. This resulted in a feud with the Provisional IRA, who despite their own involvement in extortion, have always taken a somewhat moralistic stand against drug dealing. After a number of deaths, and the eventual elimination of the active terrorist membership of the IPLO, it effectively ceased to exist as a paramilitary organisation. The IPLO illustrates how an organisation which started out with political aims can become distorted through over involvement with illegal activities to the point of these replacing the political aspirations. This can also happen at a personal level, where the individual terrorist begins to use his position to raise money for himself, rather than the organisation.

Individual Loyalist terrorists in Northern Ireland have also been attracted by the high rewards of drug dealing, but as in the case of the Provisional IRA, the major loyalist terrorist groupings have taken a stand against drug dealing as a means of raising money. As a result, the Ulster Freedom Fighters (UFF)[6] have killed some of its members suspected of involvement with the drugs trade. For example, in April 1992, a long standing member of the UDA, Ned McCreery, was shot dead as he was getting out of his car. McCreery was a publican, and was returning home after closing his bar. He had a long history of association with the UDA, and, in the early 1970's, was charged with being involved in a loyalist murder. At that time he was alleged to have been a member of a UFF assassination squad, although he was subsequently cleared of the murder charge. In a conversation with senior UDA leaders in mid-1992, it was confirmed that McCreery was shot for dealing in drugs '. . . *Ned was shot for drugs . . . we are not naive . . . if we wanted to make a lot of money that is the way to do it, but it's too dangerous. I have a family and I don't want them . . . it's anti-social . . .*'

The moral tone of condemnation may seem to sit oddly with the event, but it illustrates in that particular context the development of a more principled position on the part of the UDA leadership, distancing themselves from earlier corruption.

Unquestionably, the terrorist organisation plays an important role in the life of the terrorist. It supports the individual in both social and financial ways, and in the case of well developed terrorist groups, such as those operating in Northern Ireland, it can fulfil a wide range of social services for families as well as individual members. There is also undoubtedly a sense in which a terrorist organisation can lose its way when an emphasis on finance emerges and corruption develops. But for the active terrorist, no matter what happens, the organisation provides the base from which he develops and draws strength.

But the influence of the organisation on the terrorist member is not always benevolent. For example, where its ideology is expressed not simply in political terms, but extends to social relationships as well, the effects on the individual may be very stressful. Left wing terrorist organisations, in particular, may require of members ideologically appropriate social behaviour (ie. in terms of the relationships between members, especially sexual relationships). This, when allied to the strains of illegality, a clandestine lifestyle and the need to maintain security can severely diminish the quality of the individual's life, made worse by the sense in which once committed to a life of terrorism and wanted by the police, escape to the outside world is almost impossible. Alberto Franceschini, a leader of the Italian Red Brigades[7] describes his life within the organisation after he became an active terrorist as '. . . *depressing. Clandestinity reduced the quality of our lives. It was an ugly living, it wasn't a nice life . . . it was made with distant relationships . . . It was always a very solitary life. . . .*'

The terrorist organisation embraces most aspects of living. It provides structure and support, but that structure also implies discipline. When an individual member does something which is contrary to the needs of the organisation, then its response can be severe. It is in this area that we see the harshest aspect of organisational life for the terrorist. Perhaps the greatest crime a member can commit against an organisation is to compromise its activities by informing on it in some way, through giving information to the police or the security services. Retribution in such cases is usually swift and severe.

'*RE*[8] *was set up in prison. A . . . he went to the police in prison and told them where a shot gun would be and materials and stuff. Subsequently they raided the fella's house and found I think it was a sawn off shotgun. I don't know if there was any other hand guns found but I remember a sawn off shot* gun . . . and . . . I think there was ammunition. RE was the only person who knew it was there . . . he brought it to the house . . . RE turned around when questioned and said "yes, I couldn't do it, I couldn't do jail". His wife got a big claim and she was running around . . . he was sitting in jail and wanted to get out. A . . . he admitted it . . . and subsequently he was shot dead.'

'Informers have been acted on in various ways . . . if you know what I'm saying . . . other informers come along in our time and depending on the level of information they have . . . People in high class positions are different from others . . . you can't tar everyone with the same brush. . . . People who have responsible positions, who would be privy to high class information, that has been dealt with in a different manner. On a number of occasions we've put out amnesties and people have come forward . . . You can't be complacent about this, it's an ongoing thing. You have to be on your toes all the time, try to put in safeguards. . . .'

The role of the informant in the strategies of the security services in dealing with terrorism is very important. The opportunities for terrorist activity are very great in any society, and prevention in the absence of prior knowledge is almost impossible. Yet gaining knowledge about terrorist activities is very difficult. Contemporary terrorists are very sophisticated and knowledgeable about their own vulnerabilities. They are, for example, well aware of the potential for forensic identification and they take stringent precautions to avoid contamination by explosives, through disposing of clothes and gloves after handling explosives and scrubbing off residual skin contamination. The security services have had to rely more and more on informants in terrorist organisations to gain knowledge of their activities. But the risks for the individual concerned of being discovered as an informant are very high and probably lethal, as we have seen above.

This is an area where solid information is almost impossible to come by. It is clear that from time to time individuals emerge who have deliberately taken on the role of informant. Indeed, terrorist sources in Northern Ireland, for example, suggest that there are relatively frequent approaches to take on this role. Dangerous as it may be, there is clear advantage to a terrorist organisation to feed the security services wrong information, and the security services in turn are well aware of the potential for this in any agent. A number of these approaches would be from potential 'double agents' – agents who have access to terrorist information, (perhaps through membership of an organisation), who would enhance their own position in that organisation through information received from the security services. Double agents are inherently dangerous for both sides, because neither can be sure of the individual's loyalty; on the other hand, they offer opportunities for disinformation, and because they may have access to sensitive situations, they may produce highly useful information. The role of the double agent takes on a particular significance when the terrorist organisation is itself closely related to the state, or has objectives in common.

More often, however, informants are coerced by the security services to give information, either through blackmail, or through the offer of rewards. Criminal involvement of some kind increases the likelihood of blackmail. Such evidence that there is suggests that those who are coerced into acting as informants in this way lead sad and ultimately almost unendurable lives. Occasionally, informants of this kind do emerge in public, and offer tantalising glimpses into their world. The overwhelming impression is of a sordid and harsh environment, which leads to bitterness against the terrorist organisation as much as against the security services. Such informants are used, and then frequently abandoned to their fate should events go against them.

And that fate can be harsh. Betrayed terrorist organisations frequently resort to death as a punishment for betrayal, a fate of which the informer is well aware. In July 1990, Patrick Flood, for example, was found lying by the side of a road in South Armagh in Northern Ireland with his hands tied behind his back, and a plastic bag over his head. He had been shot in the head once from behind. The day after the body was found, the Provisional IRA announced that he had been executed as an informer. Subsequently, a tape recording of his interrogation and confession was made available to journalists. Flood does not appear to have been tortured, and apparently readily confessed to his interrogators. This cannot be said of many alleged informers, who have had to suffer appalling torture to extract 'confessions' of their guilt.

Whilst some informants act under duress, some may actively seek employment as agents; others however are inserted into terrorist organisations by the security services. Individuals involved in this way are almost always double agents of some kind. This is very murky water indeed, and reliable details rarely emerge. When they do, they are often sensationalised, and any information that emerges can generally be assumed to be released for a purpose. However one informant has emerged about whom there is some solid information. He is Brian Nelson, a long standing member of the Ulster Defence Association, who was acknowledged as a British Army informant during trials associated with allegations of security force collusion with the UDA[9].

The way in which Nelson's role emerged is probably unique, but his life illustrates the dangers of being a double informer. He undoubtedly gave information about UDA activities to his British Army handler. It seems likely, for example, that information from Nelson enabled the British Army to forestall a limpet mine attack on the car of the Sinn Fein President, Gerry Adams. '*He was quite specific – he knew where and when and the manner in which the attack would take place.*' However, it also appears that Nelson was himself involved in criminal acts, and there are suspicions as to the extent to which Nelson became over involved in the work of the UDA, in the sense that he became proactively involved in UDA activity. The loyalty of a double agent must always be a source for concern, and to counter this, the agent's handler will press him to demonstrate his loyalty through more and more dangerous acts. In Nelson's case, this probably resulted in pressure both from the British Army, and from the leadership of the UDA. The psychological pressures to which this gives rise are considerable, and it is difficult even to guess at the long term effects of such exposure on psychological wellbeing. Nelson's eventual imprisonment, however, illustrates the essentially no-win qualities of the life of an informant.

Threats to the organisation: arrest

Terrorism is a relatively risky business. The individual terrorist often presents himself as a member of an army 'fighting' another army, but of course the opponent to the terrorist usually is the array of services that a modern state can deploy against the terrorist. Detention and arrest are very real risks, therefore, with which the terrorist has to live. All terrorist organisations recognise the dangers to the organisation of an individual member being arrested. No matter what complex security structures are adopted by the terrorist organisation, it is inevitable that the individual will have some information of value to the security services which might be extracted under interrogation. Sensitisation to this is therefore an important element in the preparation of any terrorist.

As well as being a very real risk, however, the threat of apprehension by the security forces can serve paradoxically to bind the individual closer to the movement. It emphasises his specialness and separation from society, and the potential violence directed at him through interrogation can serve to reinforce his own righteousness in his cause.

Of all the European terrorist organisations, the Provisional IRA has probably one of the most effective programmes of anti-interrogation preparation. This is contained in a training manual, '*The Green Book*'[10], which provides the basis for a recruit training programme. It takes the individual through his or her likely feelings when arrested,

offers specific guidance on what to do on arrest, and on how to withstand interrogation techniques.

It notes that when arrested, the volunteer will '. . . feel that they
have failed, resulting in a deep sense of disappointment. The police
are aware of this disappointment and act upon this weakness by
insults. . . .'

1. The most important thing to bear in mind when arrested is that you
   are a Volunteer of a revolutionary Army, that you have been captured by an enemy force, that your cause is a just one, that you are
   right and that the enemy is wrong and that as a soldier you have
   taken the chance expected of a soldier and that there is nothing to
   be ashamed of in capture.
2. You must bear in mind that the treatment meted out to you is
   designed to break you and bleed you of all the information you may
   have with regard to the organisation to which you belong.
3. They will attempt to intimidate you by sheer force of numbers and
   by brutality. Volunteers who may feel disappointed are entering the
   first dangerous threshold because the police will act on this disappointment . . .

The process of interrogation is then described in detail, stressing
the brutal and violent acts that may occur. 'After the prisoner has
been placed in a cell, he may be left for some time alone . . .'
Interrogators may come and demand a confession from him, physically or verbally abusing him. He will then be taken for fingerprinting
and information about his name and background will be sought.
'Most probably "his associates" and general pattern of movement
will give a pretty good idea to the police if the person is involved in or
sympathetic to a political organisation . . . Armed with this information, the police will re-enter the cell and accuse the prisoner of all
sorts of activity. If the evidence does not indicate a degree of guilt on
a specific charge, he will be accused of all kinds of vague activity. The
purpose of these vague accusations is to implant a feeling of guilt in
the prisoner. . . .' Discussion of various kinds of interrogation techniques, such as hard followed by soft interrogation, then follows at
some length in the Green Book to orientate the recruit to the array
of techniques available to the police.

These accounts are given in some detail, for

    . . the best defence in anti-interrogation techniques is to understand
    the techniques as practised by police forces. The purpose of an inter-
    rogation is to get a confession; if the interrogators knew what they
    were searching for there would be no need for interrogation, therefore

interrogation is necessary only when the police are unaware of information which would lead to a conviction. The best anti-interrogation is to SAY NOTHING. All police forces work from a strong suspicion or a clue, therefore when a volunteer is arrested they strive to build that clue on that suspicion and the only way that can be done is to obtain information from their victim. They usually start by questioning their victim, writing down a recording of what he says, comparing this information with information already in their possession, looking for differences which contradict the information previously gained, going back to their victim, pointing out these differences, resulting in the victim changing his alibi in order to suit this difference. . . . This cannot be overstressed, when arrested SAY NOTHING. Ask to see your solicitor and doctor immediately and keep on doing so. DO NOT INDULGE IN CONVERSATION WITH THE POLICE.

The role of anxiety as a means of breaking people down is stressed at great length.

. . . an anxious or frightened man is easier to intimidate by interrogation than a cool, calculating person. . . . Most volunteers speak from a sense of fear thinking mistakenly that if they speak torture or ill treatment will not be used. It is a recorded fact that interrogators are guided by a simple rule of thumb – quote: "if a prisoner won't speak he may be innocent and interrogation may be a waste of time; if he speaks a little there is always more and so interrogation is necessary" therefore the prisoner who speaks a little is inviting more abuse from his interrogators . . . the best defence is to remain COOL, COLLECTED, CALM AND SAY NOTHING.

Various techniques are described to break down the prisoner – Top Secret File technique, the use of Pub Talk and Gossip, the fake confession.

Another dangerous technique employed is bringing the prisoner who made a statement into the same room as the volunteer who refuses to co-operate. Usually they are left on their own and the prisoner who made a statement may try to entice his comrade to do likewise. If this happens you have to bear in mind that you are not alone because the room is always bugged and any talk is recorded. . . . don't launch into a verbal attack upon him because this verbal attack on him would be an implication of your guilt, always speak friendly to him and suggest that he must be mistaken, that he is ill and advise him to seek medical attention. . . . DON'T GET INVOLVED IN A POLITICAL CONVERSATION.

Some interrogation techniques involve a friendly approach by the interrogator. These are thought to be particularly dangerous, and are strongly cautioned against.

> All volunteers must understand and understand in the clearest possible way that no interrogator is his friend, that they are the enemy, the instruments of coercion, the tools of suppression and a more dangerous enemy than the interrogators who will beat him up. These people act a part in a well rehearsed play, and are using subtle psychological techniques in order to undermine the morale of the volunteer. . . . The best anti-interrogation technique . . . is to look on the police interrogators as he would look on primitive people . . . All volunteers should look upon shouting, boasting policemen as they would look upon primitive people doing a war dance . . . While being tortured in a brutal, physical manner it is important that the volunteer should consolidate his position, he should realise that it's seven days if he keeps silent, perhaps seventeen years if he speaks.

The volunteer is also given some advice on how to withstand brutal interrogation. A technique recommended is forming

> . . images in their minds or on the surrounding walls . . . people who were brutalised found that by directing their powers of concentration away from their interrogators and diverting it onto images formed in their own mind, they could in effect overcome the physical pain . . . In conclusion, if and when arrested: SAY NOTHING, SIGN NOTHING, SEE NOTHING, HEAR NOTHING.

The Provisional IRA take these matters very seriously, which is presumably an indication of the threat of interrogation to the organisation, and the volunteer is instructed that

> Volunteers who are arrested and interrogated must upon release report IN DETAIL all things which happened from the time of arrest to their release to their IO.[11] This report is extremely important because it helps and assists the Intelligence Department of the Army to build up a detailed picture of events throughout the whole occupied area on interrogation methods and techniques as they evolve . . . Volunteers who are sent to prison must also do likewise to the IO on the Prison Staff.

The anti-interrogation techniques described above are developed further through practice mock interrogations.

Some final reflections on being a terrorist

The psychological forces that result in the development of the terrorist are complex and obscure. But that there are psychological forces, and that these may well be more important than political or social forces is a case that can be argued. Quite clearly, however, in something so complex as terrorism there is no simple single dimensional answer to give to explain an individual's involvement.

Perhaps the most useful way of trying to understand the issue is to think of becoming a terrorist as a process – one that certainly involves choices on the part of the individual, but a process which also has elements of chance within it. A process can be understood, but yet still have elements of uncertainty in it when it comes to the individual. The circumstances that result in engagement with political violence when experienced by the individual can be very powerful, and given a facilitating context, can result in psychological forces of enormous pressure.

Once engaged, the terrorist seems to cross a number of boundaries. Political purity becomes compromised in the reality of terrorist life, with its mistakes, bad fortune, or simple inefficiency which results in the wrong victim. But the negative elements of the lifestyle have their compensations. Such things as excitement or social approval carry the individual along, confirming and sustaining his or her involvement. The organisation he or she belongs to provides the framework and rewards of life. It sets the agenda and structures activity. It also exerts its toll in terms of loyalty and obedience, as transgressors find to their cost.

The active terrorists whose words appear in this chapter were drawn from a variety of backgrounds, but many seem to be aware of the moral context of their acts. Perhaps the most revealing feature of this chapter is the way in which we can see that they develop psychological strategies to accommodate their behaviour. Once an individual, by chance or intention, becomes engaged in terrorism, it is extremely difficult to move away from it. It is an absorbing and inclusive lifestyle that to a large extent sustains itself.

3

Terrorist Organisations in Ireland: a case study of change.

'Terrorism as I know it here is like a trade or an occupation, you know. Certainly the volunteers who are on the payroll [in the case of the Provisional IRA] – paid weekly did you know – have acquired an expertise in some form or forms of activity. You know, shootings, explosions, things like that there, and these become a full-time activity even though efforts may come to fruition only occasionally.' '. . . Yes, I suppose there are parallels with other aspects of criminality, like you'd say especially in terms of planning or improvisation and execution. . . .' 'Altogether, they are few in number, but activists regard themselves as professionals and adopt what you'd call a professional profile for recruits, if you see what I mean.'

'PIRA has been in business for so long that it has now become quite structured, even to the extent for example of having its own security teams who specialise in internal investigation. They're quite good . . . I suppose like most hierarchies, it sometimes works to our disadvantage and sometimes to our advantage. Depends how you look at it I suppose. . . .'

'. . . The longer the structures last, the more rigid they become you know . . . that can be a problem.'

Contemporary terrorism, as we saw in Chapter 2, is an expensive and often complex activity, and to be effective, a terrorist group must have some measure of organisation to structure and control its activities. Supplies, funding, personnel all need to be obtained, and complex decisions need to be made about such matters as the choice of targets or maintaining logistics. At the political level, the terrorist organisation also has to relate its activities to broader objectives around which its violence is focused. In this chapter we will explore some of these issues focussing on the organisational context of terrorism. It will supplement and extend our earlier discussion of the experience of terrorism from a psychological perspective, developing here a more organisational rather than individual focus. To do this, we will focus primarily on Irish terrorism; Irish Terrorism has the unenviable reputation of being well-organised, sophisticated and brutal. But looked at dispassionately, perhaps its most distinctive feature is its structure and organisation, and the sense in which terrorist organisations (both republican and loyalist) and their aspirations and ways of seeing the world have become a part of most people's lives in Northern Ireland, whether or not they are directly involved.

Nationalist Terrorism

The largest and certainly the best known nationalist terrorist group in Northern Ireland is the Provisional IRA. This organisation is actively engaged in a conflict which aims to eliminate what it regards as British occupation of Northern Ireland and to thereby achieve a united Ireland. All republican paramilitaries would describe their principal target for terrorist attack at the moment as 'the British war machine' and the British State. Although bystander and more obviously sectarian killings are often committed, the security services, and those associated with them, have born the brunt of its attacks in Northern Ireland. Republican paramilitaries were responsible for the death of some 850 members of the security forces from 1969–89. In that same period, however, they killed some 574 civilians, of whom 66 per cent were Protestant. The amount of property damage, and general disruption to the economic life of Northern Ireland is beyond estimate, exceeding billions of pounds.

Nationalist groups draw their support almost exclusively from the Roman Catholic community. The Provisional IRA has been engaged in the current campaign for some twenty years, with limited political and military success, but with considerable success in terms of its own development. It draws upon a complex and emotive historical background, and presents itself as the contemporary inheritor of the rich Irish radical and anti-authoritarian tradition.

The complexity and confusions that tradition and history can bring to the present, and the importance of the labels linking present events to the past can be seen in the contemporary use of the term Irish Republican Army. The IRA was the term that began to be used to describe the volunteers who fought against British rule in the period from 1916 until the founding of the modern Irish State in 1922. Both the people and government of the modern Irish Republic show little support for the activities of the contemporary Provisional IRA, and indeed the Irish State would probably be at great, and probably unmanageable risk from them should the Provisional IRA emerge victorious from the conflict in Northern Ireland. Yet the visitor to Dublin may well see invitations in newspapers to attend meetings of old IRA members, which often command official support. Indeed, the portrait of the commander of the IRA, Michael Collins, hangs in the Irish Parliament. This IRA, however, belongs to a different era from the present organisation with which it shares a name. But it can be seen that the term IRA strikes a popular resonance amongst nationalists in Ireland claiming legitimacy and continuity for a contemporary organisation which has in fact very little in common with its precursor. That resonance seems all the stronger when Irish people leave Ireland, when the folk memories of emigration, the famine, the war of independence and the civil war merge and are tapped by emotive terms and associations. There may well be as many, if not more, ardent republicans and Provisional IRA supporters in New York and Boston than in the whole of Ireland. The reality of terrorist bloodshed can be conveniently obscured at a distance.

The Provisional IRA is a sophisticated and complex organisation, with the capacity, (both financial and military) to undertake carefully planned and effective operations largely at will, in either Northern Ireland, the United Kingdom, or against British targets in Europe. Some measure of this can be seen in the fact that since the Provisional IRA launched its present bombing campaign in the United Kingdom with the Mill Hill barracks bombing in north London in 1988, from 1988 to 1992 no-one was convicted for any of the main crimes. In 1992–3, it was thought that up to five terrorist active service units were operating in the United Kingdom, and probably all the individuals involved in these units remained free and were able to operate largely unhindered by the actions of the security services. Such arrests as did occur were confined to less important support elements.

In Chapter 2 we considered the ways in which terrorist organisations will seek to finance and equip their operations by methods ranging from sheer banditry to the maintenance of bona fide commercial undertakings, such as the ownership of public houses. An important element of the provisional IRA's capacity to sustain its operations is the availability of hard cash. Some of this is derived from donations from a variety of support groups – not just from within Ireland but especially from the United States. Much of their local funding stems from such illegal activities as protection rackets, blackmail, extortion and bank robberies. Over the years, they have had access to large stocks of weapons and explosives – to the extent that the organisation is now virtually self-sufficient for the foreseeable future, so having no immediate need to become involved in further forays into the dangerous fields of arms purchase and importation.

The extent of the supplies available became apparent after a ship, the *Eksund*, was seized off the French coast in 1987 with a large cargo of weapons and explosives from Libya. Three other equally substantial cargoes are thought to have entered Ireland before that, of which the Irish and British security services were wholly unaware. These munitions have fuelled the campaign and still remain largely available and undetected. On arrival in Ireland, the cargoes were broken up and distributed to safe stores. Substantial elements of these cargoes appear to have been hidden in the South West of Ireland, mainly in the counties of North Cork, Kerry and Limerick, where they are usually hidden underground, sometimes in well prepared bunkers. Six substantial stores of arms and explosives were found in these areas by the Irish police between February and May 1992, but large quantities still remain undetected. Unknown, but probably large amounts of these cargoes were also sent to the United Kingdom, where they were hidden for later use in the bombing campaign there.

Although more ideologically sophisticated terrorist groups may find the Provisional IRA's political programmes unappealing because of its lack of a clearly articulated political and social philosophy, the organisation nevertheless commands very high status and interest amongst those committed to political violence world wide for its sophisticated activities and its evident success in evading the security services. Its media presence is considerable, but it has generally not found common cause with the various European terrorist groups; a prominent European terrorist leader recently said that he had no contacts with the Provisional IRA because '. . . *to me the IRA could very well have been a fascist movement . . . but I always followed with great attention the stories of their activities.*'

One feature of the Provisional IRA which is in part responsible for its success is its capacity to penetrate prestige or high profile targets using innovative methods. These serve as important propaganda and morale boosts for the organisation, and are seen as having a role in enhancing their public image. For example, on the 1st of May, 1992, the Provisional IRA bombed a permanent border checkpoint manned by the British Army. This checkpoint, on the main Belfast to Dublin road, had been subjected to attack before and considerable steps had been taken to protect it. However, those preventative measures had not extended to an adjacent railway line. The terrorists recognised this, and after successfully testing out the extent of protection on the line, improvised a railway bogey, loaded it with a massive 2000 lbs of explosives, and pushed it down the track. When opposite the checkpoint, it was detonated, killing one soldier and injuring others, including a motorist stopped at the checkpoint. This audacious attack was a considerable propaganda coup for the Provisional IRA, causing extensive and highly visible damage at a sensitive point on one of the busiest roads in Northern Ireland. The Provisional IRA have consistently shown the capacity for what can only be described as 'lateral thinking' in their planning of attacks, and frequently seem to leave the security forces nonplussed by their capacity to organise and execute complex operations.

To describe the Provisional IRA as a political movement would, in one sense, be wrong. The Provisional IRA itself claims that it does not overtly engage in political activity. This is left to its political wing, Sinn Fein, which whilst it denies its explicit links with the Provisional IRA, nevertheless is clearly recognisable as its political front. In so far as it is possible to judge, the Provisional IRA, through its political wing, Sinn Fein, commands the unwavering support of 30–35 per cent of the nationalist electorate (about 10 per cent of the total electorate of Northern Ireland), and has an emotional and historic appeal to the Roman Catholic community that, in particular circumstances, can transcend the violence of its terrorist activities. The number of Provisional IRA members *actively* involved in terrorist actions probably does not exceed 200 at any one time.

The Provisional IRA is characterised by a very efficient and differentiated organisational structure. It is organised on a cell system, in which members on 'active service' only know a very small group of others immediately involved. Only the leader of the cell has access to the organisation's hierarchy. This makes penetration by the security services very difficult. Within the organisational framework are highly differentiated regional and support services, also using a cell structure, such as logistic and intelligence units. Recently, it has been making increased use of members who lack criminal records (and who therefore have had no previous contact with the security services) in active roles. This implies a considerable capacity effectively to train people prior to exposure to terrorist action. Reports have suggested that this training sometimes takes place in the Middle East amongst Palestinian groups, but evidence also suggests that locations in the Irish Republic are used.

The Provisional IRA is often presented as a monolithic organisation. This is a convenient point to make for propaganda purposes, enhancing its image as 'an army of liberation', analogous to a state army. But the reality may be somewhat different. The cell structure on which the organisation is premised can act as a pressure towards local rather than national control. There is undoubtedly a tension at times between the independence of operation of local units, and the continuity and control of action within a broader organisational framework.

The Provisional IRA has the capacity to undertake sophisticated political analyses of its actions, and to plan its activities to meet long term goals. In doing this, it can draw on a network of well positioned supporters (many with access to sophisticated information) who whilst not directly contributing to violence (and not committing any offences), nevertheless contribute materially to the analysis, planning, targeting, and effectiveness of its actions. This capacity for long term thinking gives the Provisional IRA an enormous advantage over the security services who seem to be constantly disadvantaged by the shifting patterns of terrorist action, especially within the United Kingdom. Indeed, long term and sophisticated planning can be seen particularly in its activities there, where members have been settled into local communities, only to be activated as need arises. It has also repeatedly demonstrated a capacity to make effective use of its sympathisers in sensitive positions. The extent of this capacity is unclear, but some of its more audacious operations suggest, if not complicity, then a very well developed capacity to gather information. Complicity may extend to official organs of the Irish State, for in 1992, for example, a member of the Irish Police force (*An Garda Siochana*) was convicted of passing sensitive information to the Provisional IRA.

The potential for sophisticated analysis of their own activities which the Provisional IRA undoubtedly have, has not diminished the barbarity and bloodiness of its members' actions. From time to time, it has ruthlessly oppressed and victimised the nationalist community from which it emerged, as well as its own recalcitrant or deviant members. Knee-capping (shooting through the knee joint, or drilling holes in the knee with an electric power drill), beatings and executions have all been routinely used as punishments for people who transgress its rules. For example, three men were killed in South Armagh in July, 1992 in a dispute over racketeering and embezzlement. All three bodies showed evidence of brutal beating, and at least one was scalded, either by boiling water or hot oil. Whilst it has repeatedly demonstrated the capacity to undertake highly effective targeting in attacks (such as the mortar bomb attack on the residence of the British Prime Minister in 1991), it has also been responsible for deliberate bombing of targets which inevitably killed civilians.

Much less numerous, but probably rather more aggressively vicious, are the various minor republican organisations, who are generally politically to the left, and adopt more radical and extreme ideologies. The INLA (Irish National Liberation Army) and its political front the

IRSP (Irish Republican Socialist Party)) and IPLO (Irish Peoples
Liberation Organisation) are the major groupings. These groupings
have generally split from the larger organisation over some point of
principle, and have from time to time engaged in bitter feuds between
themselves, and with the Provisional IRA. These groups have been
responsible for a number of civilian murders, some of which were
clearly sectarian. Recent events related to drug dealing may have
effectively removed the IPLO from active terrorist involvement (see
Chapter 2).

Loyalist Terrorism

Protestant or loyalist paramilitary groupings have as long and complex a history as their republican equivalents. The historical origins
of the contemporary loyalist groups can be traced to the irregular
and part time forces recruited by the British authorities to contain
the periodic violence in Ireland during the nineteenth and twentieth
centuries. Part time police units, such as the 'B' Specials, have a justified position in the demonology of Republicanism, but they were
also an expression of the loyalist community's attempts to defend
what it saw as its interests. More recently, loyalist groupings have
become more distant from the official security forces, and from mainstream loyalist politics and, at the moment, it seems that early
collusion between the security forces and loyalist paramilitary groups
has now largely disappeared.

Until recently, loyalists groups have been poorly organised and
generally brutal in their activities. When attempting to influence the
political process they have tended to rely on mass action such as
large scale protests, or strikes, to produce political pressure, rather
than targeted attacks. This, however was to a large extent a reflection of their genuine popular support. When they have been
engaged in violent attacks, the targets have usually (and necessarily)
been republican activists or sympathisers, for there are, of course,
no state structures in Northern Ireland associated with Nationalism.
This inevitably lends itself to accusations of sectarianism, as the victims, even if they are paramilitary supporters or activists, are also
almost necessarily Roman Catholics and civilians. Republican violence directed against the security forces serves as an almost direct
mirror image of this, as members of the security services are largely
(but not necessarily) Protestant. On the other hand, there have
been a number of well documented frank sectarian killings by loyalist paramilitaries. The reality of collusion from time to time with
the largely Protestant security forces further adds to accusations of
sectarian influence.

The pre-eminence of particular groupings tends to relate (at least in the past) to shifting alliances and the availability of weapons. Numerically the largest grouping is the UDA (Ulster Defence Association), which has used the name UFF (Ulster Freedom Fighters) when involved in attacks. This organisation was founded in the early 1970s, and was responsible for the mass mobilisation of the loyalist community on a number of occasions during the 1970's. These mobilisations of popular support effectively exercised a veto on political change until the period of the Republican hunger strikes in the early 1980's. During the 1970's, the UDA also took on a vigilante role, patrolling loyalist areas. The organisation was proscribed by the British Government in 1992.

During the period 1987–1990, the UDA went through a process of change in which its activist 'roots' were re-asserted. The factors that contributed to this change remain unclear, but nevertheless, the events that took place within the UDA have now become clearer. The latter part of this chapter describes these events as an illustration of how a terrorist organisation can change and regenerate itself. This revitalisation of the UDA has served to stem its political and paramilitary decline from its heights in the 1970's. Indeed. that decline now seems to have been reversed, and an upsurge of violence since 1990 appears to herald a much better organised and more effective political as well as paramilitary organisation. As we will see below, a clearer command structure has been put in place. For the moment it has a collective leadership made up of relatively young activists. There is an undoubted sense of buoyancy in that leadership, and they are rediscovering the emphases on politics and paramilitary violence originally developed by the murdered UFF leader, John McMichael. It is presumably in part in recognition of this that the UDA was made a proscribed organisation in 1992.

The active paramilitary membership of the UDA has recently been estimated by the security forces in Ulster to number about seventy. However, as this chapter shows, there are good grounds for the belief that this is a substantial underestimate. Like the Provisional IRA, the UDA had recently received large shipments of weapons from the Middle East although, as we shall see, there is every likelihood that they originated through South African contacts. Only about a third of these shipments are believed to have been seized by the security forces, leaving the UDA as a very well armed force with the capacity to continue its acts of violence. It is noticeable that there have been comparatively few intelligence successes against the UDA paramilitaries since the upheavals of the late 1980's. They now have a sophisticated organisation and are probably more deadly than they have ever been. They are sensitive to the forensic and logistical

problems of evading capture and are now reorganised into a geo-
graphically based cell structure. They continue to be grouped in
'Brigades' with their leaders, who collectively constitute the leadership of the UDA, using the title 'Brigadier'. The Association now has
a growing capacity to continue and to escalate acts of violence – a violence that has, so far, tended to take the form of shooting rather than
bombing.

A numerically smaller group is the UVF (Ulster Volunteer Force).
Although founded in 1966, the term UVF has considerable emotional connotations for the Ulster Protestant community, and takes its
name from a force founded in 1916 to fight home rule in Ireland.
This original organisation was absorbed into the British Army during
the First World War, after which it suffered enormous casualties. To
the confusion of the outsider, there still exists a quite legitimate UVF
Hospital in Belfast which dates from that time. In the same way that
the Provisional IRA can command broad emotional support amongst
its community through emotive use of names suggesting links with
past events, so can the UVF and UDA for similar reasons command
considerable latent emotional support from the loyalist community
from time to time.

Change in a terrorist organisation – a view from the inside.

Even after more than 20 years of attempting to bring the conflict in
Northern Ireland under control, using what are probably the best
equipped, informed and financed administrative and security
resources available in Europe, the violence in the Province shows no
sign of diminishing. Indeed, there has been a marked increase in the
late 1980's and 1990's. To a large extent, this recent growth in violence is the result of increased activity by the loyalist paramilitary
organisations, and in particular by the Ulster Defence Association
(UDA). In the remainder of this chapter, we will attempt to throw
some light on the reasons for this. We will examine how the UDA
endured and revitalised itself in spite of internal conflict, corruption
on a large scale and a lassitude on security which allowed British
Military Intelligence to penetrate an agent into the UDA leadership
at a level never previously achieved in field intelligence in Northern
Ireland.

This account will also give some idea of the complexity of the situation in the province. For example, it may no doubt surprise many
readers that there have been periods of contact and a measure of co-
operation between apparently opposing loyalist and republican
terrorist organisations. Whilst these contacts have diminished greatly
during the 1990's, they certainly existed at a variety of levels during

the 1980's, where all sides found common cause primarily in better organising and co-ordinating their capacity to raise money through extortion. Thus rhetorical and actual attacks on each other were paralleled by discrete and covert communication and agreement over specific issues.

In 1989 the security forces in Northern Ireland came as near as is probably possible to undermining the UDA. The organisation was in disarray, its leadership discredited, dead or imprisoned. Yet since 1989, the organisation has re-emerged as a highly dangerous force capable of influencing political events and challenging the security forces. Although rarely acknowledged in official circles until recently, an active and effective UDA (with other loyalist paramilitaries) probably represents as great a threat to the security of Northern Ireland as republican violence. As the momentum for political dialogue between the British Government and Republican paramilitaries grows, so will the counterbalance of this threat increase. As noted earlier, it is presumably in recognition of this that the UDA was made a proscribed organisation in July, 1992 by the Government of the United Kingdom.

The popular image of the terrorist in Northern Ireland is that of a member of a Republican terrorist organisation, most notably from the Provisional Irish Republican Army (IRA). The loyalist terrorist, if recognised at all, is seen as being synonymous with a gangster, and is rarely given the political 'legitimacy' and 'status' that his republican counterpart attracts: there is no doubt that, until recently, they merited no more. Given these stereotypes, it is perhaps not surprising that the extensive literature on political violence in Northern Ireland has largely ignored loyalist terrorism. Indeed, such analyses that there are suggest that loyalist terrorism, and in particular the UDA, was effectively in terminal decline.

In its early days, the UDA had considerable political success in terms of mass mobilisation and through the loyalist workers' strikes which it organised and led. But in the decade from 1977 to 1987, it is generally viewed as lacking the psychological and organisational base of a strong ideological commitment, and was thoroughly penetrated by the security forces. Debray, an influential writer on terrorism, has drawn our attention to the problems faced by revolutionaries when the revolution loses its momentum. It may well be that the experiences of the UDA reflected a loss of momentum, and are illustrative of Debray's analysis.

In numerical terms, the UDA is the largest paramilitary organisation in Northern Ireland and, since the renewal of the current conflict, it is generally agreed that they have been responsible overall for more civilian deaths and violence in the Province than the

Provisional IRA. Loyalist paramilitaries were responsible for some 41 per cent of civilian deaths during the period 1969–89 compared with 37 per cent for Republican paramilitaries. On the other hand, if security force personnel are included in the calculation along with civilians, loyalist paramilitaries have been responsible for some 25 per cent of deaths, compared with 57 per cent for republican paramilitaries.

There has been a marked rise in loyalist killings since 1986, the year of the signing of the Anglo-Irish Agreement. Furthermore, from a plateau at 16–19 deaths per year from 1986 to 1990, itself a rise over previous years, there has been a striking rise in deaths since 1991. Whilst a number of these deaths are undoubtedly vicious sectarian attacks, loyalist paramilitaries have also shown themselves capable of sophisticated targeting and planning from time to time. Many of these deaths were those of members, or associates, of militant republican organisations.

In 1992, both the Alliance Party and former loyalist figures have warned of yet worse violence to come from both major loyalist paramilitary organisations, the UDA and the Ulster Volunteer Force. For the first time in almost two decades, the catchphrase of a 'loyalist backlash' has reappeared in the media and amongst political circles. Indeed, in an interview in the *Belfast News Letter* on February 18, 1992, the Church of Ireland Primate said the threat from 'so called loyalist sources is one of the most sinister, ruthless and best-organised ingredients of our tragic situation'. The Democratic Unionist Party Deputy leader, Mr Peter Robinson; the Alliance party leader, Dr John Alderdice; and the former UDA leader when it was a legal organisation, Glen Barr, have expressed similar sentiments.

At the heart of this new loyalist militancy is a group of largely unknown paramilitary figures who have salvaged the near dormant remains of the monolithic Ulster Defence Association of the early 1970's and turned it into a highly effective terrorist group. The new UDA, which was proscribed in July 1992 after 20 years of legal existence, can be seen as the product not only of renewed militancy and better organisation among the loyalist paramilitaries, but of a series of chance events and of internal conflict and upheaval within the organisation's leadership. Of especial significance, the security forces' high level penetration of the UDA leadership has been lost since the late 1980's. The organisation simultaneously rid itself of its older, less militant leadership.

Tensions within the loyalist community had been mounting since the 1986 Anglo-Irish Agreement, which set up the inter-governmental process and the establishment of an Irish government secretariat at Maryfield in Belfast. Until the Anglo-Irish Agreement was signed,

the early 1980's was a relatively quiet period within the loyalist community, and the UDA, in particular, moved away from political protest
to concentrate increasingly on illegal money raising activities. The
protests against the Anglo-Irish Agreement were the first major concentration of loyalist anger since the Carson Trail protests in the
winter of 1981. It is of some significance that the decline of the UDA
in this period was associated both with increasing racketeering and
extensive penetration of the UDA by a security force double agent,
and other agents. Indeed, it is tempting to speculate on the extent to
which these are related. By the mid-1980's, the UDA's senior intelligence officer, Brian Nelson, and, possibly, one of the UDA's six Inner
Council members were working as agents for either British Army
Intelligence or the Royal Ulster Constabulary (RUC) Special Branch.
The current UDA leadership also admits that other UDA members
were involved in criminal activities that involved them with republican paramilitaries and which may have led to collaboration in the
assassination of other loyalists.

An extensive series of demonstrations, known as the Carson Trail
protest of 1981, were prompted by loyalist concerns that the British
Government was failing to respond to the IRA threat in general and
particularly to the murder by the IRA of the Official Unionist MP for
Belfast South, the Rev Robert Bradford. During the Carson Trail
protest the Democratic Unionist Party (DUP), led by Dr Ian Paisley,
helped form the Third Force. This organisation appeared to gain its
greatest response from rural loyalists, but after a series of publicity-
driven late night demonstrations, the Third Force petered out.
During later protests in 1985–86 against the Anglo-Irish Agreement
the DUP formed Ulster Resistance. The name of this organisation,
unlike the Third Force, appears to have survived after the Rev. Paisley
and his fellow DUP members tired of a series of night time rallies and
the name of the organisation disappeared from media reports in
1987. The name Ulster Resistance was to play a highly significant
role in the subsequent development of loyalist paramilitary violence.

The significance of Ulster Resistance is still unclear, but it has certainly played a role in the development of loyalist protest. In 1989
three Ulster Resistance members were arrested in Paris during an
attempt to trade secrets about the Shorts-manufactured Starstreak
missile to the South African Government, in return for weapons and
explosives. These men were under surveillance by the British security
services, and their arrest in Paris was prompted by a request from
Britain, rather than any particular concern on the part of the French
security services. There are continuing rumours that it was a connection between South African agents and Ulster loyalists that
rearmed the loyalist paramilitaries.

Indeed, in 1989 loyalist paramilitary groups received a major arms shipment. Whilst the origins of the weapons still remain somewhat obscure, the shipment, which was paid for with £150,000 raised in a loyalist bank robbery in Co. Armagh in July 1987, was reported to have consisted of 200 Czech-manufactured assault rifles, 90 Browning pistols, 10 RPG7 rocket systems and 150 warheads, 450 fragmentation grenades and ammunition for the rifles and handguns. The weapons have been used consistently by the UDA and Ulster Volunteer Force (UVF) since. Ulster Resistance does not appear to have further developed as an active paramilitary group, but appears to remain a shadowy organisation in the background.

This arsenal may have been augmented recently by a further arms shipment. It has provided the loyalist paramilitaries with sufficient resources to pose a major security threat within Northern Ireland. The resultant increase in violence, as well as striking fear into the Catholic community, is stretching security force resources and diverting attention away from the IRA. Indeed, there must be fears that the drain on police and army resources could allow the IRA to reorganise in areas where it had been brought under control.

The Cook Report, the murder of John McMichael and the loss of weapons

A series of seemingly unconnected events between 1987 and 1990 contributed to the re-emergence of the UDA as an effective terrorist organisation. These events began to be noticed at the time of a British television investigation into UDA racketeering.

The UDA's western brigadier, Eddie Sayers, was filmed attempting to extort money from a reporter posing as a businessman. This served as a catalyst, prompting internal upheavals in the UDA leadership, which had until then been largely unchanged since the early 1970s.

In March 1987, Central Television's Cook Report programme set up a meeting with Sayers. Sayers fell for the trick in spite, other UDA figures say, of being warned that an investigation by TV journalists was going on into extortion. The present UDA leadership suspects the television programme received help from the security forces.

The programme appeared in the late Summer of 1988, and caused immense embarrassment to the leadership, especially to the senior loyalist leader, John McMichael. McMichael had attempted to develop a public image as a more thoughtful loyalist paramilitary, who supported power sharing with Catholics. He was appalled by the effect the programme had on the organisation's public image. Others in the UDA Inner Council were simply appalled that Sayers should fall for so obvious a trick and appear on the film. At one stage in the secretly-filmed meeting with Roger Cook, Sayers struggled over simple arithmetic as he worked out the cost of his extortion demand.

The programme also exposed the activities of Jimmy Craig, the Shankill Road, Belfast, UDA figure who had at one stage been a senior 'military commander' in the UDA, but who had moved into controlling rackets in Belfast. Craig was an archetypal gangster figure, fond of expensive clothes and jewellery and holidaying in the Costa del Sol and Florida. He was a familiar figure in Belfast, where his extortion activities were an open secret. Craig had a long history of involvement in crime and loyalist politics. His criminal career extends beyond 1971, when he was sentenced to 7 years for armed robbery of Mr Simon Seith, a warehouse manager. Craig and 2 other men burst into Mr Seith's house and viciously assaulted him, beating him about the head, and stealing £50. After sentencing, Craig also pleaded guilty to assault with intent to rob, and received a concurrent 3 year sentence. In passing sentence, the Judge made reference to Craig's criminal record going back over the years which included previous cases of assault.

The first public acknowledgement of Craig's senior role in the UDA occurred in September 1974, when Craig was described as UDA commander in the Maze prison and was involved in protests over prison conditions following disturbances at the jail. He subsequently acted as liaison between prisoners and authorities. In 1981, he first appeared in court on charges directly related to loyalist terrorism, jointly accused with Arthur Bettice of having guns under suspicious circumstances and membership of the UFF. These charges arose out of a press conference, allegedly addressed by Craig, where seven hooded men displayed weapons. Craig was eventually acquitted of these charges, as he was on several further occasions between 1981 and 1986 when he appeared in court on charges related to paramilitary activities and extortion.

The Central Television programme featured Craig prominently and by the late 1980's Craig's gangster activities had begun to overwhelm McMichael's attempts to improve the UDA's image. In spite of this, there seems to have been little antipathy to Craig amongst the UDA's Inner Council. Craig had been an important organising figure in the highly successful campaign of assassination of leading republican H Block and hunger strike activists during 1979-1981. Even as he had slid into deep involvement in racketeering, much of which was clearly for personal gain and which involved his collaboration

with republican paramilitaries, he had managed to remain in favour
with the Inner Council of the UDA.

Craig was responsible for extortion on a previously unexperienced
scale in loyalist paramilitary circles. During a period of massive public sector development in Belfast, involving huge public housing and
civil engineering projects, he was raking in large amounts of money
from building contractors pressing to win and complete public contracts.

The extent of extortion at the time was well known to the public
authorities in Northern Ireland. In fact, the view was held by some in
public authority that without Craig's 'protection', many large housing and other contracts would not have been completed in
Protestant areas. Craig's profits ensured that any reservations
amongst the UDA leadership about his free spending activities were
tempered by his ability effectively to bankroll the entire organisation.
His free spending included taking a party of more than 20 friends
and relatives on holiday in Spain. It has even been reported that his
corrupting influence extended to making a 'loan' of several thousand pounds to McMichael, whose sole income was from a rented
public house in Lisburn, Co. Antrim and who had recently divorced
and remarried.

During this period, however, an important development occurred
which ultimately played a significant role in the struggle for power
within the UDA leadership. Since the early 1980's the UDA had
almost incidentally developed a co-ordinated second tier of management. At the start of the 1980's the UDA Chairman, Andy Tyrie, and
John McMichael, who was the South Belfast Brigadier and overall military commander, had set up a recruitment and training programme
to which younger, more enthusiastic, loyalists were attracted. This
element was given a separate title, the Ulster Defence Force (UDF).
Its members underwent a training programme, which included some
ideological instruction, as well as survival and combat training in isolated rural areas in Ulster. As well as providing a well trained element
and directing and sustaining the motivation of younger members, the
UDF initiative was also the first time that the previously separate
members of the UDA's six Brigades met regularly. These opportunities for meetings may well be the most significant aspect of the UDF
which contributed eventually to the resurgence of the UDA.

There is some dispute about the significance of the UDF. The current UDA Inner Council say that it was membership of the UDF
which allowed those members committed to the organisation and its
aims to exchange views and express concerns about the activities of
the then UDA leadership. This provided one of the foundations
upon which the subsequent regeneration of the UDA was based.

'I thought . . . that one big plus was that it brought all the various geographical areas together. I'm talking about north, south, east, west Belfast, south east Antrim, north Antrim and Londonderry and so on. . . . Whereas lads had social contact with each other in Belfast, it drew the country people in . . . it set up the network where views were exchanged that maybe didn't reflect the views of the leadership.' *'It gave the organisation a broader pool to draw from while they were doing the training in various camps. To me that was the one big plus.'*

'It was the first time we ever crossed the [Brigade] borders. They used to call it Andy's Army. Certain Brigades told men in it, from their own areas, they weren't to join us because if they failed obviously they couldn't hold rank . . . if they failed the tests. But people joined it anyway'.

Some of the existing Brigadiers of the time were unhappy with the development, and actively took steps to discourage membership. *'. . . them Brigadiers were frightened of it because, as I say, it was the first time that people knew what was going on in different areas'.* *'I think what scared the higher ones at that time was seeing the quality of the leadership, the quality of personnel that was coming through. They were showing very distinct leadership skills and a good leader should always ensure there is someone to replace him no matter what comes or goes. If he fails to do that, there are two things wrong – either he hasn't the ability to be a leader himself or he's shit scared of the lad taking over'.*

'I think that he [Tyrie] said it must go on, it must continue. And I think his council round him were starting to get a bit afraid of it – is that fair comment?'

'Because Andy [Tyrie] had no Brigade behind him at that time, he was sort of isolated and then, all of sudden, there was this crowd coming up that he took a personal interest in'. This continuing interest seems to have been shared by John McMichael.

The concerns of this broad group included the apparently ostentatious lifestyle being led by Craig and his coterie, and suspicions that a pact had been agreed between the UDA leaders and some leaders of republican paramilitaries, the IRA, INLA and the Official IRA to protect each other from assassination. By 1987, the dissent within the ranks was growing, reaching levels of near mutiny in the North Belfast area. This brigade area in particular was additionally annoyed at the imposition of David Payne as its Brigadier by the Inner Council. Payne had previously been the subject of an attempted assassination allegedly by some members of the UDA in north Belfast and appears to have been seen as a highly unsuitable local leader by the membership. The North Belfast Brigade had been put in charge of robbing a Co. Armagh bank in the summer of 1986 to raise funds for buying arms. When money from the proceeds of the robbery went missing, and Payne went on holiday to

Florida, the local members acted and sent a delegate to the Inner Council to complain.

The disquiet over Payne, the developing relationship amongst the second tier leadership and the public disclosures of the Cook Report precipitated a leadership crisis in the UDA. In response, the Inner Council announced that an investigation into the racketeering allegations would be carried out by John McMichael. In part this investigation was undoubtedly as much a public relations exercise as a serious attempt to explore the allegations, and was designed to address both internal as well as external pressures. A significant internal pressure was concern that the UDA was moving away from a paramilitary role. However, as it progressed, the investigation does seem to have gained a momentum of its own.

The most significant pressure for some form of inquiry came from the second-tier leadership. This group is officially referred to as the UDA's 'Outer Council'. It has around 30 members, about five from each of the UDA's six Brigade areas. Four of these Brigade areas coincide roughly with Westminster parliamentary constituencies in Belfast. The fifth is South East Antrim, which contains the predominantly loyalist towns and suburbs from Newtownabbey to Larne and inland to Ballymena. The sixth is referred to as either the Londonderry or Western Brigade. As noted above, the current leadership say that many members of the 'Outer Council' came together through participation in the activities of the UDF. As a result of sharing experiences outside of their own Brigade, members at this level began to feel they had little knowledge of why decisions were being made, and increasingly began to distrust the leadership. '. . . *we were kept like mushrooms . . .*'

Whilst the public view was that McMichael's investigation was directed at the Cook Report allegations, a further immediate interest within the UDA itself appears to have been centred on the move against Payne in north Belfast. Payne is one of the most notorious of the UDA figures. In the early 1970's, he was closely associated with torture killings of Catholics, and whilst previously Brigadier of North Belfast he was also said to have practised torture on his own Brigade members. The popular myth in Northern Ireland that loyalists use electric drills on victims' knees stems from Payne who is alleged to have threatened this against other UDA members. It was, however, never carried out.

Payne had been thrown out of the UDA in the mid 1970's and was later the subject of the assassination attempt already described. However, by the mid 1980's, after suffering heart trouble, he was again associating with the UDA Inner Council who re-selected him as North Belfast Brigadier when the incumbent fell ill.

By the closing months of 1987, McMichael was indicating that he had prepared a report on allegations of racketeering and misappropriation of funds. However, before he could announce his findings, he was killed on December 22, 1987 by a bomb attached to the underside of his car. The bomb was of a type made only by the IRA and the IRA subsequently claimed responsibility for the killing. A later hint by the RUC that McMichael's death may have been a result of collaboration between certain members of the UDA and republican paramilitaries fuelled the mounting suspicions amongst those in the UDA who suspected treachery. There still seems to be some ambiguities about the events which resulted in McMichael's death, which may revolve around the nature and extent of the links between some of the then loyalist leadership and republican paramilitaries. '. . . *we have not closed the file on John's death . . . we have not closed it. . . .*' The report prepared by McMichael appears to have disappeared, and its findings have never been made public.

McMichael's killing coincided with the arrival in Northern Ireland of the arms shipment organised through Ulster Resistance. The weapons are believed to have been supplied by an arms dealer, and there are continuing unverified speculations about the involvement of the South African security services in this. These arms were brought to a location in North Armagh, where they were to be split between the UDA, the UVF and Ulster Resistance in January 1988. Payne, as leader of the UDA Brigade which had played a principal role in organising the raid which raised the money for the weapons, apparently saw this as his chance to counter his detractors within the organisation by being the man who collected the weapons and brought them to Belfast. He hired two Ford Granada cars which were driven by James McCullough and Thomas Aitkin. These two men, and Payne who drove a further car, a Metro, went to Armagh to collect the weapons. All three men were arrested near Portadown as they drove away from collecting the UDA's portion of the shipment, which consisted of 61 rifles, 124 magazines, 11,500 rounds of ammunition, 30 pistols, 150 fuses and 150 grenades. Payne had moved the weapons against advice from other UDA leaders, and was almost certainly informed on – '. . . *he was told not to physically go because it was high profile . . . you do what you like, organise it but under no circumstances would you go yourself because of the high profile that you have*'.

The present Inner Council believe that Payne precipitated this disaster for the UDA because he was aware of the declining standards in the organisation, and the opportunities this presented for him to rehabilitate himself within the UDA. To have been associated with the successful movement of the arms would have bolstered, or even secured his position – '. . . *if Payne hada pulled that off he would have been in some position. Look at the allegations what were made against Payne. If he hada done that those allegations would have been swept under the table. . . .'* As it was, he was arrested by the RUC, and subsequently sentenced to 19 years' imprisonment in October 1988.

These events had shaken the UDA dramatically. In less than a year, the UDA, once the largest private army in Western Europe, that had provided the power behind the Ulster Workers' Council strike to bring down the 1974 power sharing initiatives, had been exposed on television as a criminal conspiracy. Its most articulate leader John McMichael was assassinated in circumstances which gave rise to suspicions about conspiracies and collusion, and it had lost its share of the arms shipment.

Brian Nelson and the Stevens Inquiry

Yet in a way, the worst was still to come as far as the UDA as a paramilitary organisation was concerned. It now appears that the information which led to the capture of the arms, probably came from Brian Nelson, the UDA's senior intelligence officer who was also a double agent working for British Army Intelligence. Nelson, it is now known, was one of the most effective informants ever operated by the security forces in Northern Ireland. It was later stated in court by his British Army 'handler', a Scottish Colonel, that Nelson had passed a total of 730 reports to his Army handlers including information on plots to kill 217 republicans.

Unusually, Nelson's role as a double agent was acknowledged at his trial. An officer from British Army Military Intelligence, identified in court only as Colonel J, admitted that '. . . *We wished to infiltrate him into the loyalist paramilitaries . . . to gain inside knowledge of their workings and to prevent or at the very least limit their murderous activity. . . . Our aim was to get inside knowledge, but we didn't want him to get involved with murder gangs. We had to decide where he should be infiltrated where he could get information for us which we would pass on to the RUC.'* In later evidence, it was explicitly admitted that Nelson was a British Army agent '. . . *We would run the agent – he was always our agent, and we would be responsible for passing on the information to the RUC, which we did in all cases.'* There was even acknowledgement of payment to Nelson. Referring to his return to Northern Ireland in 1987, the officer stated that Nelson was given a salary of £200 per week to recompense for the disruption of his family life.

Brian Nelson was arrested in Belfast on the 12 January, 1990 and charged with aiding and abetting the murder of 2 men in 1988, conspiracy to murder 4 further men, and 26 counts of possessing information. All the people referred to in the accusations against

Nelson had links either with the Provisional IRA, or the republican movement in Northern Ireland. In February 1992, Nelson was eventually convicted and sentenced to 10 years imprisonment on 5 charges of conspiracy to murder, receiving also a 6 year concurrent sentence for possession of a machine gun, a 4 years concurrent sentence on 3 charges of collecting information useful to terrorists, and a further concurrent 3 years on 11 counts of possessing documents useful to terrorists.

Nelson's career as an informant offers some insights into a shadowy area of the state's response to terrorism. He was born in Northern Ireland in 1948, and after what appears to be an uneventful childhood, like many Northern Ireland youths he eventually joined the British Army. Around 1971, he received a medical discharge from the Black Watch, and in 1972 seems to have become a member of the UDA. He was a relatively minor figure in the early days of the organisation and his precise activities then remain obscure, but in 1974 he received a 7 year prison sentence for the kidnapping of a Roman Catholic man. In 1977 he was released from prison, and seems to have immediately rejoined the UDA.

There are some suggestions that it was around this time that Nelson was recruited by the British Army as an informant, but there is clearer acknowledgement that he was recruited by 1983 when he became the UDA intelligence officer. In 1985, for reasons which are unclear, but may relate to doubts about his role, he left Northern Ireland for Germany. He appears to have settled well in Germany, but also retained his contacts with the British Army. Early in 1987, the British Army appears to have felt that there was an intelligence gap in the UDA, and Nelson was invited to return to Northern Ireland and resume his role as an informant. In April 1987, he returned to Northern Ireland and became the head of the UDA Intelligence Section in West Belfast, a role he occupied until his arrest in 1990. Nelson appears to have become one of the few British Army agents operating in Northern Ireland, and probably the only one operating within the UDA.

It appears that Nelson was known by the UDA to be a double informer. He supplied the UDA with information much in the same way that he supplied the British Army, and the UDA as much as the British Army recognised the risks involved.

'*I knew Brian Nelson very very well . . . he was a friend of mine and . . . was . . . I believe now . . . have gone over things with a couple of people in his immediate family and all, and some of the ordinary men on the ground . . . Brian Nelson had never really left the Army if you know what I mean. He, he always did work for them . . . When something falls into your hands as good as that you have to grab it and that's the way it was. In hindsight it was def-*

initely an own goal. Well he started going around and getting things going, and his intelligence was becoming more and more . . . very very good . . .' 'You might think we was a bit naive like . . . but we knew he was getting good information, and that carried risks'.

It seems likely that there were suspicions about Nelson quite early in his career with the UDA.

'An incident occurred in 1985 when four men were arrested for shooting a Sinn Fein councillor . . . Brian Nelson did the whole intelligence that day. Now the four men arrested should never have been arrested if you know what I'm saying to ye . . . I mean questioned sorry, they were brought in for questioning and no charges were preferred against them. . . . After 7 days the four men got out of Castlereagh. The UDA had an enquiry into it . . . [the findings came back] . . . a week later and said it was down to good police work . . . just shortly after that Brian Nelson went down the road to Germany.'

'He was getting information and people were saying how can he get this type of great information and all these photographs . . . people were saying this is great and not thinking what was behind it . . . but things started to go wrong . . . people were saying there is only so many people knew this . . . a lot of things came out about him. . . . People would not act even when things were going down. . . .' It seems likely that Nelson was himself protected by someone within the UDA. *'Nelson was a shrewd man, but I would have to say to you here that I believe . . . You know what I mean . . . more like a Lord Nelson.'*

As we have already stated, Nelson returned to the UDA in 1987, after being approached by the British Army in Germany. The information he now provided to the UDA appears to have been of a significantly higher quality than when he was previously involved. *'He was a very meticulous wee man . . . if you had something on, he would tell you the colour of his eyes . . . he was good, good, right down to the last point.' 'Yea, oh he was great. He used to have a computer in the background . . . he used to have everything logged. He was very meticulous . . . very very good at the job he done . . . his intelligence was becoming very very good so he was took back, and '85, that was sort of like swept under the rug you know . . . two years had elapsed . . . we had seen it working'.*

The UDA became suspicious of Nelson again in 1988, and he was apparently roughly interrogated. This may have related to Nelson's release by the RUC whilst he was known by the UDA to be in possession of certain documents hidden in a false spirit level which might normally have been found in a police search, and resulted in arrest. It seems that there was continuing suspicion about him during this period, to the extent that one UDA unit refused to carry out operations in which he was involved. *'West Belfast took Nelson to Lyttle, but he did nothing. . . .'* and Nelson survived, largely under the protection of

Tommy Lyttle, UDA Brigadier of West Belfast. He remained in his post as Intelligence Officer until his arrest by the Stevens Inquiry in 1990. '*Brian Nelson was a terrible nervous fella . . . I mean he was always shaking . . . always had a suspicious air about him. That was the type he was, terrible nervous.*'

It seems now that the British Army may at times have had almost complete access to information about the inner workings of the military wing of the UDA from Nelson's weekly reports. The security services must have been able to use this intelligence to reduce the UDA's military activity. His eventual exposure arose from a set of circumstances apparently involving the UDA's attempts to justify the killing of a Co. Down Catholic man and the establishment of an investigation into collaboration between members of the security forces and loyalist paramilitaries.

After shooting dead a Catholic, Loughlin Maginn, at this home in Rathfriland in August 1989, a member of the UDA Inner Council, identified by the current leaders as Tommy Lyttle, sought to justify the act by revealing to journalists that Maginn appeared on a security force intelligence file in the UDA's possession. Lyttle was then West Belfast Brigadier, and for many years had been the UDA's spokesman and principal source of contact with the media. The story caused a controversy about collaboration between the security forces and loyalist paramilitaries, and resulted in a chorus of calls from the Republic's government and nationalist politicians in Northern Ireland for an inquiry. The later revelation of other security force documents in the possession of the UDA fuelled the demands for an inquiry. However, damaging as the Stevens Inquiry might have appeared to be to the UDA, recent evidence suggests that sources within the UDA may have either deliberately engineered Lyttle's justification to precipitate a crisis, or at the least deliberately fuelled the resultant controversy after the public revelation of security force files.

Within a month, the RUC had appointed the Chief Constable of Cambridgeshire, Mr John Stevens to investigate allegations of collusion. Mr Stevens and his team of English detectives carried out an exceptionally thorough and robust investigation and quickly began arresting members of the loyalist paramilitary organisations and members of the Ulster Defence Regiment (UDR), since re-titled the Royal Irish Regiment. The arrest of UDR members caused particular disquiet among the unionist community and the Stevens Inquiry sparked off a series of disputes at operational level between the RUC and the UDR.

The 28th person arrested by the Stevens' team in January 1990 was Brian Nelson. The day Nelson appeared before Belfast Magistrate's

Court, his wife, children and all their family possessions were moved from their home in North Belfast under police protection. This is a well recognised sign in Northern Ireland that a paramilitary member has turned informer and has opted to escape retribution with his family to the 'protective custody' of the security forces.

It now seems that the arrest of Nelson may in fact have been an error resulting from poor co-ordination between the various arms of the British security services in Northern Ireland. Some support for this view can be seen in the fact that in the summer of 1992, a respectable length of time after the publication of the Steven's Report and the hearing of most of the cases arising from his investigation, it was announced that a new co-ordinating committee had been set up to oversee improved liaison between the Army, the RUC and the Intelligence Services in Northern Ireland.

There is no doubt that the Stevens Inquiry proved to be a watershed in the subsequent development of the UDA. That watershed marked not decline, however, but change and regeneration; it is from Nelson's arrest that the revival of the UDA can be dated. Paradoxically, the Stevens Inquiry, while achieving the object of assuaging Irish Government concerns about security force collusion, had the far more serious and far reaching consequence of removing the mechanism which had allowed the security forces to subvert the UDA and reduce, and in some measure, to control its violence.

In tandem with the Stevens/Nelson affair, the shift of power to a group of figures who had risen from the ranks of the UDA and who constitute the present leadership, was almost complete. Andy Tyrie, the chairman of the Inner Council of the UDA from 1973, had been forced to leave his position and resign in March 1988. Tyrie was held responsible for the organisation's problems and particularly for the appointment of Payne as North Belfast Brigadier against the wishes of local members, and of then refusing to acknowledge complaints that Payne was stealing UDA funds.

Tyrie was also regarded as Craig's 'protector' in the organisation against elements in the West Belfast UDA who wished to see Craig '... *put off the [Shankill] road*'. Stories began to circulate that Craig was collaborating with republicans and had passed information leading to the assassination of loyalist politician George Seawright; the Shankill Road UDA member William McCullough; and UVF members Hugh Murphy and John Bingham. There are also whispered allegations that Tyrie had an agreement with the Northern Ireland Office to restrain UDA violence and that he was aware that UDA members were acting as informants to the security services and allowed it to continue. A senior UDA figure perhaps alluded to this when he said '. . . *I would say there were ones above Nelson* . . .' In March 1988, Tyrie resigned a few days after a crude booby-trap bomb was left under his car at his home in East Belfast.

With his protector gone, Craig's time was quickly running out and he was assassinated in an east Belfast public house in October 1989. Two gunmen shot Craig repeatedly in an almost frenzied attack which also left a 68-year-old customer dead and 4 other men injured, one seriously. The UFF, in a statement admitting the killing later said that Craig was 'executed for treason and other activities which resulted in death of innocent people, including John McMichael.' Craig was said to have been lured to the pub, reputedly by a call from another UDA member about handling stolen goods.

Tommy Little, the West Belfast Brigadier and a member of the UDA Inner Council, who had been Nelson's protector, was arrested with him by the Stevens team and was eventually sentenced to seven years' imprisonment in July 1991 for possession of documents likely to be of use to terrorists. The judge at Lyttle's trial referred to Lyttle's 'evil'plotting to kill witnesses in the trial of UDA men charged with racketeering.

Consolidation and developments

By the early 1990's changes had taken place in all four Belfast brigades of the UDA. In South Belfast, John McMichael had been assassinated. The appointment of John McDonald as McMichael's successor had much the same effect as Payne's appointment had in North Belfast. McDonald lasted less than a year before being deposed, having been arrested, and subsequently imprisoned for 10 years on extortion charges in January 1990. In East Belfast William Elliott, Brigadier since the 1970's resigned along with Andy Tyrie. Elliott appears to have been held in very low regard by the present leadership who have made it clear that the decision not to assassinate him had been a narrow one. The present leadership say that he has bought his safety from the RUC by revealing to the RUC the whereabouts of RPG7 rocket launchers from the arms shipment of 1988.

In West Belfast, Lyttle was replaced by a much younger man, typical of a number of members of the second generation of UDA membership. Many of these men have links with the UDF, are in their late twenties and early thirties, and had fathers or uncles involved with the UDA in the early days. Members of that same group now command East, West and South Belfast, as well as Londonderry. The North Belfast and South East Antrim Brigadiers are all that remain of the first generation UDA members in the present Inner Council.

The strongest supporters of the internal power struggle that deposed the Tyrie leadership were the North, West and South Belfast 'Outer Councils'. These groups are based in the urban cockpits of sectarian conflict. The North Belfast UDA in particular has consistently been at the centre of the bloodiest sectarian violence in Northern Ireland. The inner Northern suburbs of Belfast are a jigsaw of already segregated or segregating areas. One in every five deaths in the conflict takes place in North Belfast, which in its 40–60 per cent Catholic to Protestant mix is like Northern Ireland in microcosm. There are similar growing tensions in South Belfast, and the West Belfast area contains the long unbroken 'peace line' division between the Catholic Falls Road and the Protestant Shankill Road heartland. In fuelling the pressure for change within the UDA, it seems possible that these front line UDA Brigades were more concerned that the old Inner Council was leading the UDA towards becoming a political pressure group rather than a paramilitary army, than they were about the alleged pilfering and colluding of some of the then leadership.

One of the first acts of the new Inner Council after Tyrie was deposed was to remove the large oval table where the old Inner Council had met in the chairman's office at the old UDA headquarters on the Newtownards Road. A smaller, round table was bought at a local furniture shop and installed in its place. This symbolic change in arrangements recognises a more substantial change in the structure of the leadership – there is now no longer an official chairman of the UDA. Interviews with the media are no longer conducted on an individual basis, emphasising the collective nature of the new leadership, and perhaps also suggesting a certain nervousness that may stem from their predecessors' tendency to float stories about each other in the press. Interviews with the press, which are the principal form of outside communication used by the UDA leadership, are now held by the full Inner Council; journalists who were thought to have associations with the old UDA leadership appear no longer to be given interviews.

The leadership now appears united and firm in its resolve to pursue its own ends. They show a growing sophistication in tactics, and a more explicit development of the political and 'military' roles. There is also a recognition that the days of mass mobilisation of loyalist working classes are over, and that new tactics to exert political pressure need to be developed.

Some purging of figures associated with the old leadership has continued into 1992–93, and a number of assassinations and attempted assassinations have taken place. For example, the long standing East Belfast UDA figure, Edward 'Ned' McGreary, who was implicated in the 1973 'romper room' killings trial, was shot dead in a public house he ran on the Beersbridge Road. He was described in a UFF statement later as 'an enemy of Ulster' and was implicated in drug dealing. There have also been active efforts to identify informers within the organisation. Some have emerged as a result of an 'amnesty', others have been assassinated or fled.

The old leadership had a number of individuals, particularly Tyrie, McMichael and Lyttle, who were open to interview, and would comment on both political and military matters. Indeed, in many ways, McMichael had been both the political and military leader of the organisation. The new leadership continue to comment as a group on both political and military matters, but say that any involvement in negotiations or participation in elections, meetings or other political affairs should be undertaken by the political party which most closely shares its views, the Ulster Democratic Party. This Party has yet to make any significant impact on the Ulster political scene.

The UDA has had earlier political groups associated with it, although these too have never been particularly strong, nor successful in electoral terms. In the 1970's, the Ulster Political Research Group was formed, and in the early 1980's the Ulster Loyalist Democratic Party (ULDP) was established as the official electoral vehicle to be headed by John McMichael. In early 1974, the UDA's political spokesman, Glen Barr, was elected to the Northern Ireland Assembly, but such modest early electoral appeal there was seems to have quickly disappeared. McMichael stood for the Assembly elections in South Belfast in 1982 as the ULDP candidate, but received a very small vote.

A small number of UDA members have been elected to and successfully held council seats in some of the 26 local government constituencies from time to time, but few of these have made any significant political impact. Some councillors associated with the UDA have also stood as independent loyalists, and have been elected largely on personal votes. It is notable that within a short period of the UDA providing the power behind the 1974 Ulster Workers Council strike, its political standing and ambitions were dashed quite rapidly. Mainstream Unionist political parties were quick to disassociate themselves from the UDA when it became too openly involved in acts of terrorism. McMichael expressed some disillusionment in private at his rejection by the electorate, but maintained that the unionist community would again turn to the UDA when the Union was under threat. Recent events may well support this view at an emotional if not electoral level.

Aside from electoral politics and its military campaign, the UDA has produced two policy documents which have been taken seriously by political commentators and politicians outside Northern Ireland. These are '*Beyond the Religious Divide*' published in 1979, and '*Common Sense*' published in 1987.

'*Beyond the Religious Divide*' was the Ulster Political Research Group's largest and most important report. It proposed negotiated independence for Northern Ireland with a new constitution and Bill of Rights. The UDA members involved in its production, mainly Barr, Tyrie and Chicken, had assistance from a Californian lawyer and local academics. The report coincided with a period when the UDA was in some dispute with the constitutional Unionist parties. Some reflection of this can be seen in the following quotation:

> Without the evolution of proper politics the people of Northern Ireland will continue to be manipulated by sectarian politicians who make no contribution to the social and economic well being of the people or the country, but only continue to fan the flames of religious bigotry for self gain and preservation.

The present UDA leadership, and the Ulster Democratic Party, express their adherence to the '*Common Sense*' document as a way forward for political change in Northern Ireland, and as a means of reducing violence. Subtitled '*Northern Ireland – an agreed process*', it proposes a written constitution as '. . . a foundation on which to build a new pluralist society.' This includes a provision that the status of Northern Ireland could not be altered without the acceptance of a two-thirds majority in a referendum. The Foreword to the document by John McMichael said it proposed a '. . . modern democratic political structure based on consensus government, proportional representation and shared responsibility'. An important element of '*Common Sense*' is a proposal for independence for Ulster, both as a response to the continuing violence, and emphasising a sense of Ulster identity. Related to this, the new leaders also continue to support the cultural and historical ideas of Adamson[1] who has emphasised the social and cultural integrity of Ulster, and indeed suggested that a separate Ulster race existed in pre-christian times from which the population of North-East Ireland is derived.

Bombs and weapons – an indicator of terrorist development

Until March 1993 the rise in UDA violence had been largely restricted to assassinations of targeted individuals, random assassinations of people in Catholic areas and indiscriminate shooting attacks, such as the gun attacks on bookmakers' shops in Belfast in March and October 1992. No significant use was made of explosives or rockets in attacks. This necessarily limits the extent and nature of targets available to the terrorist, and confines them to relatively high risk shooting attacks. It might be argued that a measure of the development of the UDA's lethal capacity, and in a sense its strength as a terrorist organisation, lies in its capacity to extend its violence beyond shootings to safer and more flexible methods. A visible indicator of this is its capacity to make and place bombs.

Available evidence suggests that loyalist bomb-making, once more advanced than the IRA's, has reverted to a primitive stage. Attacks in Donegal, Dublin and Dundalk in 1992 indicated that the loyalists have not yet developed a strategy for incendiary attacks in Northern Ireland or in the Republic of Ireland, although these attacks caused considerable financial damage to the shops involved. This weakness in the array of tactics available to the UDA is recognised by the present Inner Council, and in 1992 the UDA attempted to detonate two van bombs using Butane gas as the explosive. These devices were placed in Catholic housing areas in West Belfast and in Downpatrick, Co Down. However, both devices were incapable of detonating, and revealed the lack of loyalists' bomb-making skills. In these incidents, the would-be bombers had sealed the doors and other openings of the vans and before abandoning them had opened the gas cylinders. Small incendiary devices similar to the type which were being left in shops in the Republic of Ireland were expected to detonate the escaped gas, but failed.

These bombs were to have been the UDA's response to the huge IRA bombs, up to four tonnes in weight, which have caused damage to some 1,800 houses, mainly in Protestant areas, in 1992. This republican campaign, largely unreported outside Northern Ireland, has been a cause of extreme aggravation to the Protestant population and undoubtedly is one of the contributory causes of the retributive loyalist assassination campaign against Catholics.

However in March 1993, a number of attacks occurred in which a development in loyalist bomb-making skills can be seen. In that month, a British Army bomb disposal officer and a Roman Catholic construction worker both suffered severe hand and arm injuries whilst handling a new type of anti-personnel device. A customer at a Catholic owned public house in West Belfast also suffered severe injuries to the hand and face when another UDA bomb exploded in the entrance to the bar. Home-made grenades have also been thrown into the homes of two Sinn Fein members in North Belfast. In August 1993, a co-ordinated attack of five '. . . *token bombs*' were placed at the homes of SDLP public representatives. These bombs all detonated at around the same time, and herald a significant shift in bomb-making capabilities. Furthermore a '. . . *sabotage attack* . . .' was made in Dublin in August 1993 by the UDA. Three underground telephone cables and a data link cable were cut in Central Dublin, with an anti-handling device being left in one location. '. . . *one day we will get it right* . . . *it is coming* . . .' The UDA is clearly actively developing its bomb-making skills, and it seems that only the lack of a safe base in the Republic of Ireland is for the moment restricting their actions across the border. Evidence in mid-1993 suggests that this is changing.

The last serious loyalist bombing campaign aimed at civilian targets in both Northern Ireland and the Republic ended in early 1977. At around this time loyalists entered a state of much reduced activity. This was probably related to the commitment by the then Secretary of State for Northern Ireland, Mr Roy Mason, of the Special Air Service troops in numbers, mainly aimed at increased activity against the IRA.

Loyalist bomb makers were also being imprisoned at about this time, and their less experienced successors were having difficulties. Indeed, in early 1977, four loyalist bomb makers, killed themselves while making bombs. Additionally, the loyalists' (both UFF and UVF) main source of bomb-making materials also disappeared in the late 1970's. Scottish Police Special Branch, in co-operation with the RUC, British Army and security services, uncovered and disrupted the loyalists' main supply of explosives and bomb-making equipment. Scottish miners, sympathetic to the loyalist cause had been supplying commercial explosive and detonators, but were stopped when Scottish Special Branch detectives thoroughly infiltrated the loyalist support organisations in Scottish communities.

In contrast to the weaknesses in its bomb-making capacity, the UDA has considerable strength in its other munitions capabilities. Aside from the increased supply of weapons available to the UDA from the arms shipments, it has shown that it has the capacity to manufacture its own weapons, as distinct from explosives. During the 1970's, using locally available machine tools and patterns 'borrowed' from the British arms industry, loyalists were able to make a working replica of the Sterling sub-machine gun. Hundreds were manufactured and used, and the discovery of these guns in or around loyalist premises was a regular occurrence.

In September, 1988, the RUC raided a small engineering facility in a farm at Ballynahinch, Co. Down. They found there the largest illicit weapons factory ever uncovered in Northern Ireland, and possibly in western Europe. In this factory, the loyalists were close to completing almost 800 sub-machine guns, based on the Israeli Uzi. Thirty machine-guns were completed, and when tested were shown to be highly serviceable weapons. Little attention has been paid to this surprisingly large arms making capacity, and what it implies in terms of the UDA technical skills and resources, but the RUC described the find as 'very significant'.

Returning to the basic principles

The following observations in many ways summarise the events which have led to the present resurgence of loyalist terrorism, and their effects on the UDA.

'If Ballynahinch had come off we would not have been looking anywhere else. . . . The things that hurt us most was the Cook Report, John's death, the arms find in Portadown and the weapons factory in Ballynahinch . . .'

'. . . some of the old leadership was corrupt, sitting back, not rocking the boat. In this way the Government was able to introduce the Anglo-Irish Agreement without fear of any . . . a . . . real retribution because they had informers. . . .'

'. . . . overt corruption has been wiped out and there is a policy now of cleaning up the act and making the organisation acceptable to the people. A phrase I often hear . . . mentioned . . . is "returning to the basic principles of the organisation" and for what my opinion's worth, I believe, I believe these guys mean it . . .'

'. . . the UDA was always the last line of defence between us and an enforced United Ireland . . . we can't trust the British Government and we can't trust anyone else. . . . Without us being here, it would be so much easier for our country, and our way of life to be taken from us.'

'. . . Stevens was a blessing in disguise, you know. . . .'

These comments capture the spirit of the reinvigorated UDA, and undoubtedly herald a new phase in the balance of paramilitary activity in Northern Ireland. Amongst the current UDA leadership, the event that might have been thought to be the final nail in the coffin of the UDA after a catalogue of disasters, the Stevens Inquiry, is now frequently referred to as '. . . *a blessing in disguise . . .'*

It is quite clear that leadership is a central quality of the factors that shape organisational behaviour. In the case of the UDA, the importance of the leadership in shaping organisational development cannot be overemphasised. During the period 1980–89 the old 'Inner Council' leadership appears to have been very suspect in terms of political motivation, and some of the individuals in power during the late 1970's and early 1980's significantly directed the organisation away from its original ideological and political objectives. Either by accident or design, a situation emerged where the non-political activities continued, were condoned by the leadership and assumed exaggerated importance and influence. In this context gangsterism and corruption flourished under the guidance and direction of UDA leaders such as Craig, Payne and their allies.

The series of events described here, set in motion by the Central Television programme and ending with the Stevens Inquiry seems to have created the conditions that eventually either removed or discredited the old leadership and allowed a more politically directed and ideologically committed group to emerge. In a sense, this provided the necessary stimulus to the organisation to allow the changed external environment to impinge on it. As a result, politics and ideology exerted an increasing influence.

It is of some significance to note that in areas where corruption penetrated less (the 'Outer Council' and many rank and file members), the ideological and political objectives of the UDA survived. Corruption in this context is of course quite a complex notion. At one level, it clearly relates to gangsterism, but it can also be seen as a form of 'revolutionary taxation'. Indeed, current UDA leaders have offered the view that they don't mind some corruption where it helps to keep the member engaged in the organisation. However, that the political aims of the UDA did survive in spite of the corruption, may in the long run prove to be the most important factor to emerge from this period. The high levels of corruption for personal gain amongst the old leadership has perhaps distracted analysts and commentators from this strength of commitment to what in present terms are politically incorrect views. The increase in alienation and disaffection with British Government policy within the Loyalist community will undoubtedly augment the ideological appeal of loyalist paramilitaries. Recruitment and membership of the UDA is undoubtedly growing, and a cynical view from an authoritative UDA source suggests that proscription of the organisation has given it an added glamour!

It is often asserted that democratic states that are subject to terrorism must maintain the rule of law when dealing with terrorists to preserve fundamental freedoms and human rights. Thus due process, and the disposition of offenders as a result of due process, is seen as a critical element in the state's response to terrorism. Frequently, however, accusations of failure to maintain the rule of law and of abuses of human rights are made as propaganda against a state by terrorist organisations. The Stevens Inquiry was established in the spirit of maintaining respect for the rule of law, and in response to criticism by the Republican organisations and the Irish Government. The suspicion that there was security force co-operation with loyalist paramilitaries made necessary the Inquiry to maintain the credibility of assertions about fairness and the rule of law in Northern Ireland. It is ironic that this inquiry, which in one sense was virtuous and appropriate, through its actions seems to have tipped the balance in favour of the regeneration of the UDA. It can now be seen as a watershed, heralding a revival of loyalist extremism in a way not seen for 15 years. Despite the high level of penetration by the security services, hindsight suggests at the very least a lack of adequate analysis and understanding of the organisation and membership of the UDA on the part of the British Security Services and the British political establishment.

There may be political merit in reducing the problems of Northern Ireland to a single republican-British dimension. This may have indeed effectively been the political reality of the situation up to 1989, but the current realities appear to be that loyalist political violence is as pressing an issue as republican violence in Northern Ireland. Loyalist terrorism does not command the media attention of republican terrorism, nor can it draw upon the extensive tacit support available for republican political violence; the views and aspirations of the loyalist terrorists are definitely not in current terms 'politically correct'. For many political commentators and policy makers, loyalist concern expressed through loyalist terrorism is an inconvenience, a distraction, from what appears to be the main agenda. The events described above suggest this view is flawed.

4

Two Crazed Peoples: Northern Ireland and 'the troubles'

January 1981 in Northern Ireland was seasonably wet and cold. In contrast, the political environment was intensely hot and turbulent even in Northern Ireland terms. Superlatives are often used to describe events in Northern Ireland, as one atrocity bids to outrival the next. But at that time, something new and totally unknown emerged into the political arena in the Province – the dirty protest and the hunger strikes. A force was unleashed that almost destroyed the fabric of Northern Ireland, and which still has resonances today.

The dirty protests arose when Republican prisoners convicted of paramilitary offenses engaged in an attempt to seek political status by deliberately fouling their cells, smearing the walls with faeces and refusing to wear prison clothes. They created for themselves perhaps the most degrading conditions imaginable, and in doing so either by accident or design created a political and propaganda weapon of enormous power. The hunger strike followed, as initially a group, and later a staggered sequence of prisoners, embarked on a process of starvation. Ten prisoners eventually died.

The dirty protests and the subsequent hunger strikes touched many of the most fundamental myths around which much of the nationalist Irish sense of identity is built, drawing on a rich tradition of folk history of victimisation and affront by the British authorities. Through a strange reversal of relationships, the prisoners on the dirty protest created a potent form of self-victimisation. Through a process that seems to be best described in terms of wish fulfilment, it created its own impetus and came to be seen as a form of victimisation. This same process later metamorphosed voluntary starvation (and what seems in rational terms suicide) to a state of martyrdom.

The protests were nurtured by an explosive mix of folk history, Irish Nationalism and Irish Roman Catholicism. This general process of protest became known as the H Block campaign, so named after the H Blocks in which prisoners were housed in the Maze Prison.

The political consequences of the H Block campaign were enormous. The dirty protests and hunger strikes were associated with a highly co-ordinated and structured campaign to politicise the Nationalist population within Northern Ireland and in the Irish Republic, and to mobilise support in Northern Ireland, the Republic of Ireland and indeed in the world at large. At the very outset, the need to translate the prisoners' protest into a broader political weapon was recognised by all concerned, and the development of a co-ordinating body was seen to be a critical element by the prisoners themselves. '*We asked the people on the outside for formal consideration, and what they said was that while there were protests and protest movements on the outside, that they weren't pulled together, there wasn't any common band that linked them together. In the case of a hunger strike you needed that sort of unified movement on the outside before you could move into hunger strike. So we were persuaded to postpone the hunger strike for a period until they would found what became known as the National H Blocks Armagh Committee . . . so throughout late 79 and early 80's . . . we literally sat back . . .*' These comments are from a prisoner who was involved in the hunger strikes. The logic is compelling; but the discussion of a lengthy and painful death in such an unconcerned fashion is chilling and horrific.

The National H Block Committee became the critical agency co-ordinating and developing the protests associated with the hunger strikes. Through the publicity and the various actions achieved, the farthest corners of the world became aware of the events in Northern Ireland. Within Northern Ireland itself, the H Block campaign created a highly potent and dangerous situation, and it is no exaggeration to say that the riots and civil disturbances associated with it almost resulted in overt civil war, involving not just paramilitary groups, but the civilian population as well. Indeed, there were many periods when government control was barely maintained, and the security services were strained almost to breaking point. Feelings ran extraordinarily high not only amongst the politically committed, but also amongst the general population at all levels of society. No-one was untouched by those events.

The H Block campaign proved to be a very effective weapon of the various Republican groupings in Northern Ireland in their attempts to create a united Ireland. But the majority Loyalist community in Northern Ireland has never accepted this aspiration, and inevitably, so effective and strident a weapon provoked a response. This took the form of a series of murders and attempted murders directed against the leadership of the H Block protests, and in particular against the more prominent members of the National H Block Committee. These murders were part of an organised and deliberate campaign to undermine the protest through the elimination of activists. It was organised and undertaken by loyalist paramilitaries, the historical enemy of the republican movement. Some appreciation of the loyalist response to this very effective protest can be seen in the following account of an involved loyalist paramilitary: '*I worked in and around West Belfast on a daily basis, Catholic West Belfast in those days, and I could see the hype, you know, real hype, there was real tension. They were trying for a civil war. We felt that perhaps by taking out the leaders we could sap the morale you know . . . You don't want your leadership knocked off . . . at that particular time there was a campaign against the INLA, IPLO, IRSP whatever they called themselves at that particular time. It was a very successful campaign.*'

Unlike many of the loyalist terrorist incidents of that time, or indeed since then, these attacks were noteworthy because they were well organised and highly specific. The reputation of incompetence which at that time loyalist terrorists had acquired was largely merited, as evidenced by a series of bungled and poorly planned attacks on inappropriate targets causing death to entirely innocent people. But these new attacks betrayed a much more sophisticated approach than before. All the people murdered were actively involved in the H Block protest, and belonged mainly to the republican political fringe, rather than the mainstream. This accurately reflected a shift in the relative political momentum of the time, where much of the impetus came from more radical and left wing elements within the republican movement rather than the larger and more traditional conservative republican organisations.

What particularly attracted loyalist attention to the hunger strike was the bringing together within one campaign of paramilitary violence and effective political protest. Prime movers in this, and the main focus for the loyalist attacks, was the leadership of the small Irish Republican Socialist Party (IRSP). In the labyrinthine politics of Northern Ireland, the IRSP is a recognisably Marxist grouping which acts as a political front for the Irish National Liberation Army (INLA), a paramilitary organisation responsible for a number of murders, and sometimes frankly sectarian deaths. The IRSP emerged from a split within the major republican grouping (the Official IRA) in 1974, and since then has adopted an extreme radical republican position. Its members were actively and publicly involved in the H Block political process.

In 1980 and 1981, loyalist terrorists murdered three prominent

IRSP members – Mrs Miriam Daly, Mr Ronnie Bunting and Mr Noel Little. They also murdered Mr John Turnly, a leading political figure in the SDLP who was subsequently a founder member of the Irish Independence Party. All these murders showed evidence of organisation, good intelligence and planning, as did a number of other murders of less prominent republican figures. The murders all followed a similar pattern. The house where the victim lived was broken into early in the morning, and the victim was shot either whilst still in bed, or whilst still half asleep and confused by the break in.

Of all the people at that time who were evident in fringe republican activity around the H Block protest, one prominent figure stood out – Bernadette McAliskey. Bernadette McAliskey, born Bernadette Devlin, was a central and prominent figure in the politicising movement in the H Block protest on the nationalist side. Although only 33, she was already a major controversial figure in republican politics in 1981, and indeed remains one today. She first came to prominence in 1968 at the start of a period of civil rights agitation when, as Bernadette Devlin, she was a student at Queen's University, Belfast. A student civil rights group, the People's Democracy, was founded as a result of a civil rights protest march being broken up by a police baton charge. Bernadette Devlin was a prominent figure amongst the student leaders of the People's Democracy, taking part in a number of well publicised protests. She was elected to the British Parliament in April 1969 as the Independent Unity candidate for the Mid-Ulster constituency, beating the widow of the former Unionist MP by 4,200 votes.

On her 22nd birthday later that month, she took her seat in the House of Commons, the youngest woman MP ever elected, and the youngest MP to be elected in 200 years. She broke all traditions by making her maiden speech within hours of taking her seat, when with eloquence and passion she denounced the Government of Northern Ireland, and called for its abolition. Regardless of her views, she attracted at that time admiration from members of parliament from all sides of the House for her sincerity and honesty.

Whilst remaining a member of parliament, she continued to be actively engaged in the civil rights movement in Northern Ireland, and in December, 1969, was sentenced to imprisonment for 6 months for incitement to riot against the Royal Ulster Constabulary. She was imprisoned in June, 1970, shortly after she had increased her parliamentary majority to 6,000. The aura of controversy surrounding her increased in June, 1971, when she announced that she was expecting a baby. She gave birth to a girl, Roisín in July and, despite criticism of her private life, she announced that she intended to remain in politics. Her most controversial parliamentary act occurred in January, 1972, when she physically attacked the then British Home Secretary, Mr Reginald Maudling, punching and scratching him and accusing him of having lied about the events surrounding 'Bloody Sunday', when earlier that month, 14 people were shot dead in controversial circumstances by members of the Parachute Regiment.

After almost 5 years in the British Parliament, in February, 1974, she lost her seat to the Unionist candidate after the intervention of the Social Democratic and Labour Party (SDLP), a moderate nationalist political party, split the nationalist vote. In the meantime, she had quietly married a schoolteacher and former member of the Official Republican Clubs, Michael McAliskey, in April 1973. Her parliamentary defeat resulted in a less prominent public political role for her, although her political involvement continued. In 1974, she emerged as one of the co-founders of the IRSP, which seems to have marked an increased tendency for her to embrace more consistently left wing ideals and values. But it was not until the dirty protest and H Block campaign of 1979 that she again emerged as a prominent public figure.

Her background as a well known IRSP activist made her a highly attractive target for loyalist attention. She lived, with her husband and three children, in an isolated and remote small cottage near to the shores of Lough Neagh in County Tyrone. It is difficult to imagine a more inaccessible and isolated house. Vehicles could only reach it along a muddy, potholed road that led only to the house. Other access was by foot through a marsh.

At about 7 o'clock on the morning of Friday, the 16th of January, 1981, three men met on the outskirts of a town near to Belfast. One man, a firearms officer and member of the loyalist Ulster Defence Association (UDA), had with him a 9mm high-powered Browning pistol, a .38 revolver and a .22 pistol with a silencer. He kept the Browning, and gave each of the others a weapon. These weapons were acquired from a very senior UDA figure. The weather was cold and wet as they set off towards Derrylaughan, the home of Michael and Bernadette McAliskey and their three children. The intention of those three men was simply to kill the McAliskeys.

'I don't like the idea of being involved in taking anybody's life, but . . . the facts as I saw them were that this individual . . . was . . . her purpose . . . certainly her activities were such that, in my view she brought about a great deal of loss of life and rather than take out all the wee gunmen that she created, her and them all created in my view, I thought take out the source of the problem.'
' . . . you don't want your leadership knocked off . . . it was a very successful campaign which many journalists gave us credit for' . . . ' . . . when I was

involved, it wasn't reactive it was . . . the particular campaign was . . . the opposite, proactive'. These are the words of one of the men who was later convicted of the attack against Bernadette McAliskey. They reveal something of the thinking which lay behind the event itself, and the way in which it was part of a co-ordinated campaign against H Block activists.

This attack was planned and organised by the South Belfast UDA. Prior to the attack, the three men involved were identified and briefed by senior UDA officials. In the briefing, they were shown detailed maps of the McAliskeys house and its surrounds. These same UDA officials were behind the other attacks at that time against H Block activists, and knowledge and planning of the attacks extended to the very highest reaches of the UDA leadership. *'Well . . . a . . . . I came into contact, I met this individual who was responsible for that type of thing in the course of the day, and he said to me a . . . he said there's a job on if you want it, and that's how it was put . . . it was accepted it was a dangerous operation. A high risk operation maybe and that's why I was offered it, because it was known I was totally committed, you know . . . now I didn't go away elated or anything (laugh) it was new ground right.'*

About half an hour after setting out in their orange Avenger car, the three men, now hooded, drove slowly down the lane, and arrived at the McAliskeys home. One man caught a glimpse of Michael McAliskey through a window, and immediately fired at him. Michael McAliskey also saw the hooded men, and alerted to the attack, threw himself to the ground behind the front door in an attempt to stop them entering. The attackers, however, were able to force the door open with a sledgehammer, and shoot at him. Although wounded, McAliskey then fled to the kitchen, where he collapsed feigning death after being shot again. Once inside the cottage, one man went straight to the bedroom, where he saw Bernadette McAliskey trying to hide her infant son, Fintan, under the bedclothes. The attacker pushed the child away, and fired at Bernadette McAliskey at close range, hitting her 9 times with high velocity bullets, and seriously wounding her. Six bullets passed right through her body, and left strike marks on the concrete floor. One shot hit the back of her head, and passed through her body to exit from her left leg. She was also shot by one of the other attackers, and two low velocity bullets were subsequently removed from her under surgery. Michael McAliskey was seriously wounded, receiving a total of 6 shots. One shot severed a main artery, and he bled profusely.

Unlike other UDA targets at this time, the McAliskeys survived this attack. Although seriously injured, they were able to reach hospital quickly, through the actions of British soldiers, who arrived after the attack. A medical orderly helped to stop Michael McAliskey's bleeding and gave immediate first aid to Mrs McAliskey. The attackers were arrested at the scene and detained by the British Army. The attackers were subsequently tried, convicted and sentenced to life, 15 years and 20 years imprisonment. After being sentenced, the three raised their fists in clenched salute.

'*She was one of the foremost exponents of the hunger strike . . . I had a determination to do something you know . . . atrocities like the Kingsmill and so on had an effect. Ah . . . equally, equally the effects of the British Government, the treacherous . . . the treacherous activities of the British Government as I saw them . . . for me I've got to say it was the isolation of the loyalists, protestants . . . All this was happening, and that's why my target wasn't an accident. I don't like politicians, you know. Ah . . . I believe that the, the nationalist politicians in particular, but certainly the Unionist too have a lot to answer for because they created the situation*'

'*. . . I remember her photograph on the Roseville flats in Londonderry, I don't know whether you remember it . . . her words when the army moved in, I haven't got them word for word, . . . not "now we're safe, we've got the army in" but in essence what she said was "that's the end of Northern Ireland, the constitution is in shreds, keep fighting" . . . she was a founder member of the IRSP which spawned the INLA, a vicious sectarian gang . . . I knew what was going on . . . I put it down to leadership that creates this situation, and that's who you crack at, you know . . . I think it should be directed exactly where the problem is and that's what I was doing. I was directing it at what I perceived to be the problem*'

'*. . . I just did what I felt was right . . . the dangers may have been there or whatever, I let my . . . my . . . if I felt something had to be done I went ahead and did it regardless of . . . of . . . of what the cost might be . . . I always tried to keep things right. I can't think of anything in particular that I was, that I was ashamed of . . . individually that I was involved in . . .*'

The arrival of the British Army on the scene undoubtedly saved the lives of the McAliskeys. But it also raises issues about why the Army was present in the vicinity and able to respond so quickly, *but* did nothing to hinder the attack. Doubts of this kind are so typical of the Ulster situation, and can often be dismissed as being either evidence of paranoia, or attempts at generating propaganda. In this case, however, there *is* a suspicion of issues which make the circumstances of the army presence, and the implication that the Army therefore had foreknowledge of the attack, possible and therefore worrying. These issues also relate to the sense in which double standards, from the perspective of the terrorist, sometimes appear to operate in the response of the security services to terrorism.

Unlike the Provisional IRA, it is known that the activities of the

UDA have been penetrated for a long time by British security forces[1]. However, there have been, and continue to be, suspicions that such penetration has been used not only for gaining information, but also to manipulate the paramilitary leadership through the use of double agents. This can be achieved by selectively feeding into the organisation information to focus activity, or by not acting on information received from an informant allowing something illegal to take place. At best, this might result in the creation of traps to apprehend activists – but at worst it can result in the paramilitary organisation becoming either an explicit or unwitting agent of the security forces themselves, enabling illegal activity to be undertaken without in any way compromising the State services. Allegations of this type are commonplace in Northern Ireland, and are virtually impossible to check. The propaganda value of the allegation alone makes it worthwhile, regardless of the truth of the situation. Allegations of this kind lie at the heart of criticism of the role of the UDA informer, Brian Nelson, who is discussed in Chapter 3.

Units of the British Army arrived in the vicinity of the McAliskeys' home *the night before* the attack. Mrs McAliskey arrived home that night between 1 to 1.30 am after attending an H Block meeting. She recalls seeing 4 soldiers lying on the ground directly opposite the backdoor of the house. She spoke to them, asking *'have you no home to go to on a cold night like this?'* The soldiers, she says, grunted at her, and she went indoors. Given the context, the presence of the Army is not in itself particularly surprising. It did not give rise to much concern on the part of the McAliskeys, who were quite frequently subject to surveillance by the security forces. But it does give rise to the suspicion that something, perhaps the threat of an attack, at least merited attention by the security forces. Other independent evidence suggests that in fact there was prior knowledge of the planning of an attack although that knowledge may not have extended to precise details of date or time. The McAliskeys were obvious targets, given the murders that had gone before, and therefore placing them under observation might be thought to have been a prudent step. If this was so, then the presence of the Army seems appropriate.

Immediately after the attack by the gunmen, soldiers arrived and arrested the attackers who had no opportunity to escape, a sequence of events which at first sight seems to justify both the Army's presence and actions. But given the evidence of army surveillance, the terrain around the house and the visibility of the road, the question has to be asked as to why the soldiers did not intervene *before* the shooting. The British Army response to questions at the time was that it was simply a routine patrol in the area.

Mrs McAliskey remembers the shooting, although she lost consciousness from time to time. She remembers the initial commotions, as her husband saw the hooded men outside and tried to warn her, but she recalls that she did not take any immediate action to hide. She also remembers the shooting beginning, but did not see the man who shot her – she was turned round facing the bed trying to hide her son, and he shot her in the back. Her initial reaction was that it was the soldiers whom she had seen outside the night before who had broken in and shot them. It was only when the shooting had died down, that she heard an English voice saying something like 'get your hands up' to the gunmen, and a Northern Ireland voice replying 'fuck this for a double cross'. Hearing this comment, Mrs McAliskey began for the first time to doubt the involvement of the security forces in the attack. Although Michael McAliskey was seriously injured, he also heard outside the cottage an English voice say (of a soldier presumably to the attackers) 'if you move you're dead', whilst attempting to drag himself to the phone.

After this, Mrs McAliskey clearly recalls a soldier coming to the door of the house and shouting several times 'Is there anybody alive in there?'. The two older McAliskey children were in another bedroom, and were unhurt in the attack, but they remained silent – they also thought that the Army had carried out the attack. Mrs McAliskey then made a noise and a young member of the Parachute Regiment came in, looking very shaken.

She remembers four soldiers from the Parachute Regiment being initially at the scene, one of whom she says stood guard over her. They appear not to have had a functioning radio, and summoned assistance by putting up a flare. One of the gunmen had disabled the McAliskey telephone, so another one of the four soldiers ran down the lane and commandeered a car, asking the driver to get him to the nearest telephone. This was at a local councillor's home, and when he got there the soldier asked the occupants to dial Army Headquarters in Lisburn. What he actually said on the telephone is not known. By this time, soldiers from the Argyll and Sutherland Highlanders had arrived by road, presumably in response to the flare. Shortly after, a military helicopter arrived. It must be inferred that whilst this was happening, the remaining two soldiers guarded the gunmen. A medical orderly from the Argylls gave the two McAliskeys medical attention, until they were evacuated to Musgrave Park Hospital, Belfast, by Army helicopter.

Were either the McAliskeys, or the attackers, or both, 'set up' as a result of an informant within the loyalist terrorist organisation? The reported comment of one of the gunmen at the scene suggests this was their immediate reaction. On the other hand, one of the attackers thinks this is unlikely, but possible – '*I don't think the person that gave me the job to do set me up . . . it's possible, anything's possible . . . There's only four people to my knowledge who know exactly what happened there on the ground that day, and that's the three soldiers and me because I wasn't in the house, I was outside the house. And the reaction of those three soldiers . . . was not the reaction of people who were expecting something to happen . . . these soldiers came into a sort of yard, if you want, an open garden, shoulder to shoulder carrying their rifles they had and I say to you and if you know there's three gunmen cornered and you're aware of that happening, you will have worked something out a wee bit better than running shoulder to shoulder presenting an unmissable target.*' '*There was a big winding lane . . . full of potholes, you had to drive very slowly. At any point soldiers could a let us come in, do our business and at any point stepped out without any danger to themselves. But they come in here three of them shoulder to shoulder presenting a target for cornered people. There was no need for it, those soldiers were caught unawares.*' '*Now loyalists don't traditionally shoot at soldiers, but cornered gunmen do strange things . . . so my view is, and always has been that . . . it's possible, perhaps even probable, I don't know. It's possible, perhaps probable, that the people who sent the soldiers and put them in there knew that we were coming, but I don't believe they told the soldiers . . . those soldiers were caught unawares . . . the boys on the ground didn't know*'.

Despite minor discrepancies, Bernadette McAliskey's view of the event broadly agrees with this. She does not feel that the soldiers on the ground were aware of the attack, and that they were shocked and surprised by its occurrence and by its ferocity.

The sense of conspiracy deepens, however, when the memory of the oldest McAliskey daughter is noted. During the period of the attack, neither of the older McAliskey children were hurt. They hid in their bedroom. The oldest daughter, a 9-year-old, clearly remembers seeing the three gunmen, but also very firmly believes she saw a fourth masked man, dressed in blue overalls and holding a sawn off shotgun. This fourth man stood at the door of the children's room looking in, and then he walked away. The child is quite certain she saw him walk past her bedroom window away from the house in the opposite direction to where the soldiers came from. The suggestion must be that this fourth man, if he exists, was a local who knew the terrain. The fact that the UDA had considerable knowledge of the building and surrounds of the McAliskeys' house lends at least some credence to this suggestion.

Was there a fourth man? Did the security forces know of his presence and allow him to escape? Those involved deny it, the official version made no reference to it and it was not raised at the trial; even the McAliskey family initially discounted the child's evidence.

There is yet a further layer of complexity to the attacks on prominent H Block activists. John Turnly, another H Block activist, was murdered in June 1980, some 6 months before the attack on Bernadette McAliskey. In March, 1982, a UDA activist from Larne, Co. Antrim, Robert McConnell, was convicted of Turnly's murder. In a statement read to the court after being sentenced, McConnell alleged that he had received material assistance from the SAS in murdering Turnly. His allegation was that a member of the SAS provided him with information and advice specifically about Turnly and weapons, but he also alleged that Bernadette McAliskey was included in his discussions with the SAS man. This was denied by the Army. It is important to note that there is no suggestion that the SAS participated in the murder of Turnly or anyone else.

Complex sequences of events, suspicions of complicity and tantalising evidence of things happening beneath the surface, propaganda accusation and counter-accusation: these are all part of the reality of terrorism in Northern Ireland. Unspecific knowledge of, or suspicions about an event do not amount to conspiracy, and assurances that there was no official condonement of this attempted murder seem to be accurate. We know rather more about the events in this case because unusually, the intended victims survived and they were notable enough to command media attention in the aftermath.

One of the tragedies of Northern Ireland is the routinisation of violence. Our knowledge of events are filtered by media attention, and all too often, the media prominence given to events relates to its 'newsworthiness', rather than the personal tragedy involved. The attack on Bernadette McAliskey was newsworthy; this cannot be said of another murder which occurred on the same day. The Provisional IRA shot dead a part-time major in the Ulster Defence Regiment, Mr Ivan Toombs, a 42-year-old married man with five children. Mr Toombs was working in his office in Warrenpoint, County Down, when two youths on a motor cycle drove up to the office. One of the youths held up the office staff, whilst the other went into Mr Toombs's office and shot him several times with a handgun. The youths then drove away. This murder was later claimed by the Provisional IRA in South Down. Mr Toombs death attracted relatively little attention, other than a minor headline and a brief paragraph of detail. It failed to attract the attention of the national media on such a busy day, and the tragedy for the Toombs family was relegated to little more than the statistics of violence.

Also on the same day, a well known restaurant in Belfast, *The Gables*, was badly damaged by a fire bomb attack, and in the city of Armagh, an RUC Landrover patrol narrowly escaped death when a 200lb milk churn bomb failed to detonate near to them. The

Provisional IRA claimed responsibility for both attacks. A suspect device was also defused in the centre of Belfast. The 16th of January 1981 was quite a busy day for the terrorists.

The Irish Terrorist

It is not difficult to meet people engaged in terrorism in Northern Ireland. Both republican and loyalist organisations will facilitate meetings at various levels. There are also other less sanctioned ways of meeting people actively involved, and of course there are a number of ex-terrorists who have either repented, or are no longer engaged in direct political action. There are always potential uncertainties in any meeting, especially where the meeting is in some way clandestine – are the individuals you meet telling the truth, are they who they say they are and have they done what they claim, or do they have the knowledge they claim. If a meeting is arranged by a paramilitary organisation, it is a reasonable assumption that they expect to gain something from it, and it is also a reasonable assumption that the interviewee will have clear limits to what he will say, and a purpose in saying it. As we noted in Chapter 1, in this world, all involved are alert to the dangers of exposure and entrapment, but also to the benefits of gaining or influencing publicity.

Descriptions of events can be checked, of course, and after time, an experienced ear begins to distinguish factual and psychological elaborations, rationalisations and justifications from the substance of an account. Because organisations such as the Provisional IRA, the INLA, the UVF and the UFF are proscribed, an individual will rarely admit to membership of them in any public way. Similarly, individuals involved in particular crimes are unlikely to admit to that involvement, especially if access to them has been arranged through a paramilitary organisation; people met through more informal means, however, may be less circumspect.

It is possible to build up through interviews and discussions a picture of the active terrorist in Northern Ireland, and in what follows we will attempt to do this. The material on which this picture is based is drawn from interviews and meetings with republican and loyalist activists engaged in political violence, and other sources. Some were accessed through paramilitary organisations (especially recent interviews with loyalist sources), others through less formal contacts and other sources. The material was collected at irregular intervals in the course of research during the 1980's and 90's. Some very lengthy psychological interviews were conducted which followed a quite formal structure, and were analogous to clinical interviews. Others were of necessity much less formal, and should probably be characterised as discussions, rather than interviews. In reporting the interviews, individuals are not identified and in some circumstances, where appropriate, efforts have been made to obscure identification of the people concerned. Direct quotations are indicated in the text, but modified comments directly based on interview material are not. At least three of the people interviewed have died through or in terrorist action.

We can create a composite picture of those Irish terrorists, loyalist and republican, which will serve to make our discussion more concrete. The person involved in violent action, is likely to be up to 30 years old, or perhaps a little older and usually male. Early loyalists tended to be older, but now seem to be approaching the age-range of the Provisional IRA. The leadership of both republican and loyalist groups tend to be somewhat older. The terrorist is almost certainly from a working class background either still living in the area in which he was born, or has relatively recently left it for operational reasons. He has probably not received much by way of education, having left school at 15 or 16 without formal qualifications, although more recent recruits are becoming better educated. It is quite likely that he has always been unemployed, or has experienced a period of unemployment. Consistent with the discussion in Chapter 2, he probably had a period of increasing involvement with the organisation of which he is a member for more than a year before becoming involved in direct violence, probably as a member of a junior wing. As a member, he will have received training in weapons and perhaps explosives, but is unlikely to be technically proficient in specialised areas – this is someone else's job. Women are less numerous than men, (even more so amongst loyalist groups), but follow broadly similar patterns. A republican activist operates in a much more structured and controlled world than the loyalist, although this situation is changing in the 1990's as the loyalist groups have become more sophisticated and structured, as we saw in Chapter 3.

Northern Ireland terrorists are frequently articulate and give the impression of being worldly. Republican terrorists would have stood out in his respect compared to loyalist terrorists some years ago, but this difference is no longer apparent. Individual terrorists do not live in a world of intense political pressure, and remain in touch with the day-to-day fabric of life. Often well dressed, or at least appropriately dressed in the fashion of the time, they blend into the community which they claim to defend with ease. And so they should – they are of that community, and in a very real sense the inheritors and expression of the folk memory and traditions of their particular view of Irish identity.

At the psychological level, the picture is more complex, but nevertheless generalisations emerge. As we noted in Chapter 1, a popular image of the terrorist is that he or she is abnormal in some way, and that the violence associated with terrorism can only be understood by reference to madness, psychopathology, or deviance of some form. Yet perhaps the most striking feature of those discussed here is the lack of signs of psychopathology, at least in any overt clinical sense. With rare exceptions, and contrary to popular misconceptions, the Irish terrorists are neither madmen nor blind bigots. They have considerable insight into their own actions, and often show a striking awareness of how others view them. In the main, they have come to terms with the violence they commit, and are able to justify it in terms of their own perception of the world, and their role in its maintenance.

For example, few object to the use of the term terrorist to describe themselves, although euphemisms such as volunteers or members are generally preferred descriptions. Relatively few individuals offer sophisticated political justifications of the violence they may admit to or imply being involved in, yet all show a strength of what can only be described as belief in the rightness of their actions. What strongly emerges from them is a sense of understanding and order in what they do, a claim to rationality and intention which lies behind their acts when seen from their perspective. It seems to take a period of imprisonment for relatively sophisticated political rationales to emerge, a reflection of the active programmes for the development of political awareness amongst both republican and loyalist prisoners. Probing beneath the surface of discussion, however, often reveals little more than cliché and ritualised assertion.

Sectarian violence is an issue which is frequently referred to in conversation, either as a cause or justification for some act, and some further discussion of this will help to illustrate some of the points made above. This is an emotive issue in Northern Ireland striking at the core of religious and national identity, and the allegation of sectarian murder is used for propaganda purposes from time to time by both loyalist and republican paramilitaries.

From a psychological perspective, sectarianism as an aspect of the broader issue of prejudice seems to lie inescapably at the heart of much of the violence in Northern Ireland. There is no doubt that deliberate sectarian killings occur on both sides. From the loyalist perspective, the selective targeting of the security forces (who are largely protestant), random attacks against civilian targets (frequently killing protestants), and the murder of prominent loyalist political and paramilitary figures by republican groups are acts of sectarian violence. Similarly, loyalist attacks on Sinn Fein activists and

supporters are often presented by republican organisations as unpro-
voked sectarian attacks on Roman Catholics. As paramilitary
organisations are tightly structured and generally secretive about
their membership, checking allegations can be very difficult. The
propaganda value of accusations of sectarianism is recognised by all
sides. Vociferous denials of the connection of a victim with a paramilitary grouping, for example, may later be followed after perhaps
several years, by an acknowledgement of membership. Even in death,
members have a value!

In a sense, republican opportunities for sectarian killing are both
greater and more readily disguised than loyalist attack, but in the
truly awful balance of justification for murder, loyalist groups have
been involved in more frankly sectarian attacks than republican
groups. Many individuals murdered by loyalist paramilitaries can
only be described as representing Roman Catholics, rather than individuals with specific political involvement. *'Pride isn't a word I could use
in relation to my involvement [in a sectarian attack] . . . the word pride just
doesn't ring right. But what I would feel best about is I did what I felt was
necessary . . . I felt something had to be done, I went ahead and did it
regardless of . . . of . . . of what the cost might be . . . mistakes are regrettable . . .'* But there is need for a note of caution here. During the
1980's, much loyalist paramilitary attention was directed towards
raising money through intimidation of the business community.
Given this, what might sometimes appear to be a sectarian attack has
more to do with the process of extorting money rather than the religion of the victim.

The reality of terrorism in Ireland is horrific. A young Roman
Catholic woman was killed in April 1992 by the UFF. She worked in a
chemist's shop, and was described by the Royal Ulster Constabulary
as 'a paradigm within her community'. She travelled around the area
of West Belfast without any apparent contact with the security forces
or paramilitaries. She seems to have been an ordinary respectable
person, whose only quality which made her a target was that she was
Roman Catholic.

How do those involved make sense of this? How do they come to
terms with the victimisation of someone who is quite clearly innocent? When faced with potential psychological conflicts, we all resort
to a number of strategies to protect ourselves. One of the most common of these is to reinterpret a situation in such a way that the
conduct of the victim or his or her qualities created a justification for
what happened. Echoes of this can be seen in the ways in which justifications for sectarian murders can emerge in discussion. *'Striking
fear into them'* '*. . . it's retribution . . .*' and forms of victim denigration
'*. . . he deserved it, and was probably a supporter anyway*' reflect important

processes of rationalisation for sectarian attacks given by members of both republican and loyalist terrorist groups.

Another related strategy is to place the blame on an outside agency, especially the security forces, rather than on yourself. This was discussed at some length in Chapters 1 and 2. In psychological terms, the processes involved are referred to as attribution, and it is a common feature of terrorist justifications for violence. '. . . *the blame lies with the British Government, not in our actions. They created the situation . . .' '. . . a clear warning was given, but they didn't act on it . . . yea we understand they do this to discredit us . . . we understand this*'.

Joe Doherty, a self-confessed Provisional IRA member, who admits to the killing of a British Army captain, illustrated both these processes. Whilst in prison in the USA, fighting extradition proceedings to the United Kingdom, he gave a number of interviews in which he talked about and justified his activities: '*You don't think you're going to murder someone. It's not this 23-year-old Captain Westmacott [his victim]. It's what he's representing. I don't know if he was married or if he had kids. I didn't know what he thought about. I didn't know and I didn't care. People have asked me if I felt remorse for Westmacott. No, I was not responsible for his death. British intransigence was responsible for his death.*' Words like these can be heard from activists on both sides of the sectarian divide in Northern Ireland, drawing on the same depressingly familiar justification. But the almost clichéd quality of the accounts should not lead us to underestimate their power as a psychological support for violence and murder.

A more sophisticated response can sometimes emerge in terms of conspiracies 'hiding' real issues [again discussed in general terms in Chapter 2]. Recognising that sectarian attacks had happened, and that loyalists are often accused of random sectarian attacks against Roman Catholics, a loyalist terrorist nevertheless made the following point '*Yes, sometimes there's a sectarian attack, you know, but there's no need for it . . . if you follow the situation and ignore what the police say, there is evidence to show that people are targeting what they, what their information suggests. – even if they don't admit it . . .' '. . . we don't need to . . . our information is accurate*'. The problem for the listener is that there may sometimes be some truth in all these explanations.

It seems likely that current changes in the loyalist terrorist organisations will reduce their lack of control over sectarian violence, which has certainly seemed to be the case in the past. This does not mean that sectarian killings will necessarily diminish, (and indeed evidence suggests that they are on the increase), but perhaps that when they do occur as a result of loyalist action, they will be more likely to be part of a plan or campaign. Nevertheless, the underlying psychological justification for this behaviour in terms of the broader conflict, republican and loyalist, remains . . . '*I can defend to my con-science . . . and the right of the IRA to wage an armed struggle*' . . . A rampant protestant voice says '*I want to see a fair society for Catholic and Protestant . . . a free society. But if they try to impose their will on us, we will crush them*'. . . but it is matched by an equalling chilling republican view . . . '*It's our historical right . . . it's what we have died for.*'

The vigorous rejection of sectarianism, but the pervasive recognition of religion as a factor in events and upbringing, even when later denied, flavours many terrorists' accounts of their lives. The rather stereotyped political rhetoric of '. . . *freedom*' '. . . *liberation from British colonialism*' '. . . *response to the brutality of British oppression*' that especially emerges in discussions with some Republicans seems less vibrant and more superficial. The meaning of freedom and oppression as the words emerge in discussion of reasons for action seem to have an automatic cliché quality to them, which contrast with accounts of everyday living which often relate to deeper historical and perhaps uglier notions. Indeed, in a paradoxical way, the more vigorous the denial, the greater the listener is left with a sense of unease at underlying sectarian influences. '. . . *as a matter of fact my mother was a Roman Catholic and my father a Protestant and as it would happen we were brought up as Presbyterians . . . the idea of politics and religion was absent in my life . . .*'

But the recognition of religious affiliation is an inescapable reality in Northern Ireland . . . '. . . *it was just something you were aware of . . . you didn't take it any further than that.*' '. . . *I remember symbols sort of are a great thing in this country . . . I do remember my father never put his [Union Flag] until the twelfth of July and then he put it up again on the twelfth of August.*' A Protestant view describes the influence of religion in terms of '. . . *a set of moral values based on religion rather than religion . . . and a kind of badge for your own people*'. A Roman Catholic terrorist described '. . . *Church and Mass was a social gathering, we all went . . . Yes, it meant a lot to me at the time, and it still does. I go to Mass . . sometimes anyway.*' As for many people in Northern Ireland, childhood memories tie early experiences to religion '. . . *the original school is still the old church building, you know still part of the church, very much you know, typical of these old schools.*' Family relationships also are often structured in religious and essentially sectarian terms. '*I have one, two, two sisters married to Roman Catholics. One lives as a Roman Catholic in Londonderry one lives as a Protestant this side of the country . . . so there's no sectarianism*'.

Awareness of sectarian difference is an underlying fact of life amongst Northern Ireland terrorists. It is of course impossible to know the extent to which this is also a characteristic of many non-terrorists in Northern Ireland. It is impossible therefore to know whether its expression in the politically violent is in some sense an expression of a fundamental and largely shared view, even if unacknowledged. This does not make it acceptable, of course.

Whilst we might want to assert that sectarianism is undesirable, inappropriate and inexcusable, it is not in itself evidence of any form of psychological abnormality in any recognised sense. Sectarian murders from both sides of the Northern Ireland community may at times be random, but the bombings or shootings that produce the deaths are generally deliberate, and often well planned and executed. Such acts lack the qualities of uncontrolled, irrational violence that would characterise a psychopathic state, for example. Indeed, terrorists themselves are well aware of and alert to the expression of violence outside the appropriate ideological context. A republican terrorist emphatically made the following point '. . . *there are very very few obvious what do you call them . . . psychopaths . . . they'd stand out like sore thumbs, and everyone would know them.*' There is considerable truth in this. The planners and strategists in charge of Northern Ireland's controlled violence would not welcome the unpredictable, inherently unsafe security risk of a psychopathic killer. It is a convenient way of denigrating the image of the terrorist by claiming he is mad – the reality is much more uncomfortable.

Involvement in terrorism seems to be for much more familiar reasons. '*Most volunteers – ours and theirs – are in the game for something, be it status and this certainly applies to the hierarchy, excitement, power, or even that at the end of the struggle they will find a place in the sun. This last thing was extremely important in the early years, but not so much now.*' This revealing comment captures the reality of terrorist involvement not just in Ireland but elsewhere.

'*People join for various reasons, and some even 'drift' into membership but once involved the struggle always becomes a way of life, even to the extent that the main reason for the movement is overlooked in the excitement and action of day-to-day events. This can be a problem. Once in, most people progress eventually in one of two directions. Either the acceptable – becoming involved with the political and propaganda, or educational and cultural side – or the physical force side. Seldom both, but when someone is heavily involved in both, the result is an extremely effective animal indeed.*' Terrorists may from time to time be selfless and altruistic or they may be frankly sectarian, but in the main they also do what they do for something. They attain goals, gain satisfaction and seem to experience excitement and an enormous sense of fulfilment in contributing to the success of their movement. '*. . . I wanted to make a contribution*' . . . '*. . . I think I am achieving something . . .*' '*. . . it's not just the excitement, although that does give you a buzz . . . it's afterwards, you do feel you have made a contribution.*' Being violent can serve to empower people, and to give a sense of personal agency within the broader and rather impersonal conflict. We should not underestimate the strength of commitment, nor the desire many terrorists have to contribute to their community; nor does this diminish the horror of random violence and murder. But if we look on them with the same sense of rational analysis that we might bring to describing non-terrorist political activists, or indeed ordinary people engaged in any occupation, we will probably better understand their motivations.

One thing is quite clear; neither republican nor loyalist terrorists are mercenaries at the beginning of their career in terrorism. As one Republican volunteer said '. . . *one factor which is not of consuming importance is the economic, because most active and dedicated members exist on minimal monetary rewards.*' Except for some loyalists leaders of the 1980's and '. . . *very very few republicans, we make little in the way of riches . . .*' However, some developments in Northern Ireland may lead to this ideologically pure beginning becoming somewhat corrupted. As we will note later in this Chapter and discussed at some length in Chapter 3, protestant paramilitaries have had a long involvement in corruption and extortion to raise money for personal rather than political ends. Similarly, some of the lesser nationalist groupings (especially the Irish Peoples Liberation Organisation – IPLO) have been extensively involved in extortion, and drug dealing.

The Latin American revolutionary, Regis Debray, observed that when the conditions for success for a terrorist organisation were absent, then the 'armed struggle' will continue, but lead to the corruption and debasement of the original ideals of the terrorist movement. Similarly, a noted American academic author on terrorism, Martha Crenshaw, has noted that after a time, terrorist groups tend to begin to pay more attention to organisational pressures in the development of violence, rather than ideological. Both these pressures tend to lead to increased engagement with money raising activities, and shift political aspirations to stereotyped sectarianism.

Terrorists generally have to resort to illegal means to raise money, and they are often very successful at this. The mechanisms for illegally raising money therefore exist and are well developed. When the pressures of ideology diminish, violence and illegality acquires a life of their own, and the organisation subtly shifts its priorities to sustaining itself rather than its ideology. In this shift, the acquisition of funds becomes the principal objective of the organisation, and this, in turn, leads the way to personal acquisitiveness asserting itself. This does not exclude ideological justification for acts, but the justification acquires a ritual quality far removed from the vibrancy and moral authority of a terrorist group in its early stages of development. All of the Northern Ireland terrorist organisations have gone down this road in some measure.

Chapter 2 describes the process that seems to characterise the initiation of the terrorist into his life style, and uses an Irish example to illustrate the process. What then sustains his involvement? Why, once committed, do Irish Terrorists continue in a very dangerous occupation? Familiar, even mundane, factors seem to be important. A republican comment illustrates one set of critical issues . . . '*Excitement and interest are always there. The only time volunteers become disgruntled is when the calendar is blank. Or when the leadership is questioned or when success is lacking*'. This is clearly mirrored by a loyalist comment . . . '*I was involved like, heavily involved, and everybody knew. It was exciting, and great. Moving around, a bit like a deadly game. But sometimes it became more real . . . you gotta trust people like.*'

Excitement, success, involvement, trust and belonging: these are features that emerge time and time again in discussions. Paradoxically, being a terrorist, at least in Northern Ireland, can at times be a rather mundane occupation. These comments by Republican terrorists illustrate something of the normality of the reality of terrorist involvement '*You gossip about and criticise each other and the topics tend to be normal – who's doing a line with who, who's in the family way and by who, who can't hold his or her drink, who got duffed in a fight, who is past it. The one thing you don't do is live in a world where the cause is the sole topic . . . where you are continually looking over your shoulder to see who is following or watching. The only time extra caution is exercised is when you are on a job . . . or in a strange place.*' But that normality has a decidedly cutting edge to it . . . '*Days are full like, because when there's no action ordinary demands have to be met just like anybody else – you know the family, the house. When detailed for a job though the job takes precedence and no matter what hour of the day or night you're at the place you're told . . . only when you're practically on your way will you be told what the job is.*'

Sometimes, a less formal commitment to terrorism is apparent, especially amongst early loyalist activists . . . '*My days and nights were taken up with work . . . my work at night enabled me to . . . to carry on whatever associations I had.*' There can therefore be a part-time quality to involvement. But for those currently involved in violence, as distinct from support operations, most are effectively full-time terrorists, engaged in and supported by their movement.

If you are known, or wanted for a particular incident, then you may have to change your life style quickly, move to safe houses and lead a clandestine life to evade capture. Normal social contact becomes more difficult, but even then, the routine of living remains, and the circle you mix with perhaps diminishes but does not disappear. Life may become less pleasant in one sense, but the excitement, and the support and sense of community which being clandestine

helps to produce, can offer attractions. A Republican comments that
'*I have contacts and friends all over who can help me . . . it takes some getting
used to, but I know there is always somewhere safe to go. Our people help each
other . . . it's a sense of community and commitment*'.

An important factor which underpins much of the sense of
engagement and support within the community, and probably the
sense of commitment to the organisation, is the idea of trust. This
recurs over and over again in different contexts as a critical sustaining element. Living a life on the margins of the law, perhaps having
to live a clandestine existence, forces active terrorists into a state of
dependence on both the community and their organisation. '*. . . you
have to trust people*' . . . '*I know I can rely on our people . . they take risks
for us*' . . . '*Sometimes it makes you feel very proud to be a part of it . . . they
trust us to defend their interest, but we have to trust them too . . . it seems right,
doesn't it*' These are quotations from both loyalist and republican
sources and they illustrate an almost brittle sense of vulnerability in
the dependence they imply.

The sense of trust permeates terrorist life in other ways. A Loyalist
commenting about relationships within his group notes '*. . . how shall
I say, if you were the man in charge for me to become active I've got to trust you
and respect you, right. So having given the trust and respect in your leadership
and your ability then if you tell me to . . . be involved with . . . [name] . . . in
any particular way then I will respect. Because of my trust and respect for you
I will automatically take him . . . that relationship would then build right. I
don't know who else out there might want to do something. It's not my job as
a volunteer to know that. It's somebody else's job to monitor the situation and
see who's coming in.*' . . . '*I progressed through . . . and so on and so on you
know, to where I ended up would be people within the organisation, people . . .
the senior ranks would listen and watch and they would know who is keen to
do things, they would know who would keep their mouth shut and so on and
so on. And then they would . . . you would be . . . shall we say tested . . . you
know in minor ways, you'd work your way let's say. It's down to trust in the
end isn't it*'.

Trust also seems to be related to the individual's sense of belonging
to the terrorist organisation. '*You started to take on a sort of a . . . a different feeling about it. You belonged to an organisation.*' '*I was impressed you
know*' '*I was proud.*' The peculiar circumstances of leading a clandestine life, of being totally absorbed within an organisation which is
organised on a cell system to limit the individual's knowledge of others involved creates a strange intense world. Conspiracy, camaraderie,
complicity in a shared secret, the excitement of action, a sense of historical appropriateness and communion with the past; all of these
create intense forces to bind the individual to the organisation, and to
make him dependent on it. These give rise to powerful psychological

forces which above all else, sustain the terrorist, and enable him to tolerate the ambiguities and cruelties of his life.

Paradoxically, trust and dependence, and the vulnerability they can imply when trust is misplaced, are the Achilles heel of terrorism in Ireland, and elsewhere. The extensive active and passive support enjoyed by terrorists in both loyalist and republican communities is on the one hand a great source of strength but on the other it offers a potential weakness. The strength of community support which sustains the terrorist, and the sense of belonging to an organisation which is strong and successful are recurrent underlying motifs in the terrorist's view of his world. The need to minimise damage when trust is broken (through capture and confession, or through informants) creates the organisational structure into which the active terrorist fits, and which, in turn, sustains his commitment. This also shapes the supportive political structures. Breaking this self-sustaining cycle seems to offer the only psychologically coherent way in which terrorism can be modified in the mature Irish terrorist organisations.

The context

Should we expect the terrorist to be in some sense different from the rest of society? Are there qualities that distinguish him in some way, that would enable us to recognise him? The people whose voices are recorded above are not distinguishable in any way from most people – in a very real sense they are ordinary people. Sometimes meeting them can be frightening, but it is often the context, and the knowledge of what they have been involved in that strikes fear, rather than the people themselves. The surrounding of secrecy, the preliminary negotiations necessary to arrange a meeting, sometimes the deliberate obscuration of location; all these things contribute to a sense of apprehension. The overwhelming impression left is of meetings taking place in tacky surroundings, places of formica and cheap plastic furnishings. Sometimes the people have been met in clubs or pubs (especially the early interviews), sometimes they have been conducted in private safe houses or other places. The circumstances can be intimidating, but the people are rarely so.

The extensive media coverage of events in Northern Ireland mean that the broad outlines of the conflict are probably familiar to most readers, even if the details are not. What may be somewhat surprising in the above, however, is the intermixing of loyalist and republican terrorist voices. The popular image of the terrorist in Northern Ireland is the republican terrorist most probably from the Provisional Irish Republican Army (IRA). As noted in Chapter 3, the loyalist terrorist, if recognised at all, is frequently seen as being synonymous with a gangster, and is rarely given the political 'legitimacy' and 'status' that his republican counterpart attracts.

Analysis of the complexities of the conflict in Northern Ireland are beyond the scope of this chapter. But we cannot complete our psychological exploration of terrorism in Northern Ireland without some further reference to social context and the terrorist. Terrorism does not exist in isolation, and the psychological reality of involvement for the individual rests upon a collective foundation of both organisational membership and tradition and history. This has been in some measure already explored in Chapters 2 and 3, but it cannot be ignored in this discussion

The broad historical and social pressures that provide the context to the conflict impinge on the individual, and provide the setting in which the individual lives. However ill defined these pressures may be, they are tangible enough to provide the psychological structures from which the individual tries to understand and organise the world as he experiences it. In this sense they are factors in the process of engagement with political violence and condition the psychological reality of engagement.

The Social Context to Terrorists and Terrorist Groups in Northern Ireland

We must note at the outset that terrorism in Northern Ireland is different from other forms of terrorist activity in Europe. One simple quality that distinguishes Northern Ireland from other places is that in its relatively small geographical area, terrorists are probably more numerous than anywhere else in the Western World. There are thought to be in the region of 500 active terrorists, loyalist and republican, operating at any one time in the Province. The number appears to remain largely constant, with losses through death and imprisonment, or other causes being quickly replaced. There is a large pool of potential terrorists ready to move into active roles when the need arises.

Many ordinary people, of course, have contact with paramilitary organisations through family, friends or acquaintances. Terrorist organisations are the ubiquitous background presence in many communities. The other side to this is that there exists in Northern Ireland a very large sector of the economy which is dependent on terrorism. The damage caused by explosions requires builders and other service providers, the security situation creates a demand for a wide array of State and non-State security services. Very many people are employed either directly or indirectly in a job related to the security situation. Because of these factors, the influence attained by terrorism over the lives of ordinary people is more extensive and pervasive than in most other countries with active terrorist conflicts.

Another factor which distinguishes Nationalist Irish from European terrorism is the availability of readily identifiable sub-goals for the Irish situation. Whilst the ultimate aspiration may be the attainment of Irish unity, sub-goals such as the withdrawal of the United Kingdom from Northern Ireland, give the terrorist groups more readily attainable aspirations that contribute to the ultimate ideological goal. The more monolithic aspirations of the European terrorist organisation, fighting international capitalism or the establishment of a socialist Utopia, are less amenable to expression in terms of such sub-goals. Similarly, the focus of loyalist activity in terms of sustaining the union with Britain finds little expression at the level of sub-goals.

The origins of the conflict in Northern Ireland have complex and unique historical roots. It is these historical roots that give the impetus to the violence of Northern Ireland, for the political ideologies of the various factions involved are generally rather naive, and lack links with the concerns of contemporary European political life. For many people, the conflict is as much about the past as the present, and historical legitimacy and claims to moral authority are powerful factors sustaining and feeding the present conflict. Indeed, it sometimes seems that a cycle of retribution and revenge has been established between the different communities which is now to a large extent self-sustaining because it is based on an unchanging and inaccessible past.

The Northern Irish community broadly divides along sectarian lines, with the predominantly Roman Catholic community (which accounts for some 40 per cent of the total population) having a general sympathy with an aspiration to a united Ireland (with the Irish Republic), whilst the predominantly Protestant majority community seeks to maintain its constitutional links with the United Kingdom. Thus, nation and identity are at the heart of the Northern Irish situation.

Whilst the reality of peoples' attitudes in Northern Ireland are far more complex than this gross simplification would suggest, it does nevertheless broadly capture the core of the essentially nationalist and confessional political aspirations of the *terrorist groups* associated with each community. Social class and economic well-being are factors that are relevant in Northern Ireland, but in a much more complex fashion than in similar, economically deprived, areas in Europe. Both communities in Northern Ireland are relatively economically disadvantaged when compared to the United Kingdom. Generally speaking, the nationalist community is more economically disadvantaged than the loyalist community, having higher rates of unemployment. There has been and probably remains today, discrimination against the nationalist community, in employment and civil affairs.

Comparisons are sometimes made between the situation in Northern Ireland and the Basque regions of Spain, where there has also been a continuing terrorist conflict focused on demands for Basque independence. Certainly, the principal Irish nationalist terrorist group, the Provisional IRA, have had contact with the Basque separatist group, ETA in a way that contacts with other European groups have not developed. There is an obvious sense of common ground between them at a number of levels in terms of their essentially nationalist aspirations. But unlike the situation in the Basque region, in Northern Ireland the loyalist paramilitaries constitute a third element in the conflict of an organised popular resistance to separatism *as well* as the conventional apparatus of the State which resists the separatist demands. The complexity of the problem in Northern Ireland is enhanced by the varying agendas of the three principal elements involved in the conflict – the nationalist republican movement, the loyalist movements and the largely Protestant security forces.

Terrorist organisations in Northern Ireland draw their recruits chiefly from working class areas. But social class, in any obvious Marxist sense, is not a major driving force in Northern Ireland terrorism from either loyalist or republican perspectives. Identifiable loyalist and republican areas of Northern Ireland are primarily working class, and indeed the Northern Irish terrorist from both communities is distinguished by his working class background from the more typical middle class European terrorist. The class basis of the geography of terrorism in Belfast, for example, can be seen vividly in the maps privately published by the security forces which indicate affiliation by colour – green for republican, orange for loyalist. The green and orange coloured areas cluster in low cost or local authority housing areas in the inner city, or in large public authority housing estates on the periphery, all of which are widely recognised as being socially deprived. Given the scale of violence in Belfast, the coloured areas occupy a surprisingly small part of the total area of the city. The much larger uncoloured areas, which largely lack terrorist affiliation, cover the higher cost areas where occupants generally have a higher standard of living, and live in more religiously mixed communities.

But social class does not characterise adequately the conflicting aspirations of the two communities. Although there may be almost ritual references to 'class struggle' in the political rhetoric of the various organisations, the sophisticated class based analyses of European terrorist groups, for example, have little currency in the Irish context. Tradition (in both a political and religious sense) and the past are far more potent factors in driving the continuing conflict. Civil Rights, and the resistance to very real discrimination against Roman Catholics in employment and in civil affairs was the precipitating factor in initiating this current phase of conflict. But this seems to have been a trigger, rather than a cause. The present conflict is one of a series of conflicts in and about Northern Ireland, and it is not unreasonable to suppose that they largely defy political analysis in conventional terms.

Preparation and Training

In Chapter 2, some of the general psychological processes involved in becoming a terrorist were discussed. There is, however, a more explicit and directive sense in which an individual 'becomes' a terrorist – through training and induction. In Northern Ireland, once someone has become involved with a terrorist organisation, and once that person has been recognised as having qualities which make them attractive to the organisation, both loyalist and republican terrorist groups have programmes of training. Training extends from use of weapons, to planning and preparation of attacks, to dealing with interrogation if arrested, to more ideologically orientated preparation allowing the volunteer to place his actions within the broader historical perspective of the organisation as that organisation would see it.

Of the terrorist groups in Northern Ireland, the Provisional IRA has the most sophisticated training capacity. This capacity extends to a relatively formal training structure, including the production of a training manual, known as 'The Green Book' (already referred to in Chapter 2). The ideas presented in the Green Book are worth examining in some detail, because they reveal a great deal about the organisation as experienced by the individual terrorist, as well as its approach to the problems of Northern Ireland.

The material in the Green Book is presented in the form of a series of lectures, with notes for discussion and further reading, as you would expect to find in any training manual. The topics dealt with include Recruiting, History, The Republican Alternative addressing topics such as long and short term objectives, an analysis of the IRA volunteer compared with members of the security forces, and anti-interrogation techniques.

The seeds of the sense of isolation of the terrorist are sown and developed in the early lectures in The Green Book, along with the sense in which he or she is encouraged to feel different, superior, and in a sense disassociated from the normal constraints of living. The first lecture, on 'Recruiting', begins with a warning of the need for security:

> The most important aspect of any organisation, party, group or army is security. Security binds all people within that organisation together in confidence . . . Any weakening in the individual means a weakening in his organisation as a whole . . . volunteers very often see the Army as a distant thing and feel that they play only a minor role in its affairs and objects. This assumption is a truly false, misleading and dangerous assumption . . .
>
> So the most important thing is security, that means you:- DON'T TALK IN PUBLIC OR PRIVATE PLACES.: YOU DON'T TELL YOUR FAMILY, FRIENDS, GIRLFRIENDS OR WORKMATES THAT YOU ARE A MEMBER OF THE IRA: DON'T EXPRESS VIEWS ABOUT MILITARY MATTERS, IN OTHER WORDS YOU SAY NOTHING to any person. Don't be seen in public marches, demonstrations or protests. Don't be seen in the company of known Republicans, don't frequent known Republican houses. Your prime duty is to remain unknown to the enemy forces and the public at large . . . Quite a body of information has been gathered in the past by enemy forces and their touts from volunteers who drank and who under the influence of alcohol spoke of their exploits and the exploits of others: this is the MOST POTENTIAL DANGER facing any organisation . . . It does and can lead people into prison, it does and can kill volunteers . . . the best security is total security, and total security means in effect not speaking in public, and treating all those you don't know as informers, and all those you do know outside the army as potential touts.

This lecture then goes on to emphasise the importance of commitment and confidence in Victory, Loyalty to the Movement and the Moral Superiority of the Volunteer:

> Commitment to the Army is total belief in the Army, in its aims and objects, in its style of war, in its method of struggle, and in its political foundations. Commitment means standing steadfast to principles when all others condemn those principles and vilify the Army . . . Commitment to the Republican Movement is the firm belief that its struggle is morally justified and that the Army is the direct representative of the 1918 Dail Eireann parliament, and that as such [it is] the legal and lawful government of the Irish Republic . . .'

The issue of legitimacy is important for any terrorist organisation. In the context of Ireland, this is particularly so for the Republican Movement, given the bitter civil war fought after independence, and this topic receives further emphasis. It is also important, however, for the individual volunteer, for it is probably the sense of legitimacy which provides an important element in both the moral and the psychological justification for involvement in killing and injuring people:

> This belief, this ethical fact, should and must give moral strength to all volunteers, and all members of the Republican Movement. The Irish Republican Army, its leadership, is the lawful government of the Irish Republic, all other parliaments or assemblies claiming the right to speak for and to pass laws on behalf of the Irish people are illegal assemblies, puppet governments of a foreign power, and willing tools of an occupying force. Volunteers must firmly believe without doubt and without reservation that as members of the Irish Republican Army, all orders issued by the Army Authority, and all actions directed by the Army Authority are the legal orders and the lawful actions of the Government of the Irish Republic.

This is one of the most important mainstays of the Republican Movement, the firm belief that all operations and actions directed by the Army are in effect lawful and legal actions of the Government of all Irish people. The logic of this is to question all the political structures of modern Ireland, North and South, and in particular to condemn as illegitimate all the agents of law enforcement and security. In doing this, of course, the Provisional IRA presents itself as filling this vacuum

> '. . . All volunteers are and must feel morally justified in carrying out the dictates of the legal government, they as the Army are the legal and lawful Army of the Irish Republic which has been forced underground by overwhelming forces. All volunteers must look on the British Army as an occupying force, must look upon the RUC, the Gardai, the UDR and the Free State Army as illegal armies and illegal forces whose main tasks are treasonable and as such morally wrong, politically unacceptable and ethically inexcusable . . . Churches too have attempted to and are attempting to find some form of theological justification for those corrupted and illegal assemblies. They have twisted and bent their theology, warped their logic and disregarded their ethics in a vain attempt to justify the unjustifiable illegal set ups.

The lecture ends with an account of what it means to be a volunteer. It emphasises the seriousness of the oath taken by members

> . . . to obey all orders issued to them by their superior officers and by the Army Authorities. This means what it is supposed to mean literally, that you obey all orders, whether you like them or not. Orders and instructions sometimes may be distasteful to the Volunteer, but this is what is involved in being a Volunteer, and this is the meaning of being a Volunteer – the ability to take orders and to carry them out . . .

This approach is common to all terrorist groups, although rarely so clearly and unambiguously expressed. In it we can see the origins of what has been termed the 'conforming anti-authoritarian' terrorist – the paradoxical juxtaposition of the rebel kicking against society, who conforms absolutely to the commands of his leaders.

The Provisional IRA also alerts its volunteers to both the military and political aspects of being a volunteer. It is probably this emphasis on the combination of political activism and military activity that characterises one of the main strengths of the movement:

> In THE MILITARY ASPECT after an initial training, volunteers are expected to wage military war against a numerically superior force. This involves the use of Arms and explosives . . . volunteers are trained to kill people. It is not an easy thing to take up a gun and go out to kill some person without strong conviction of justification. The Army, its motivating force is based upon strong convictions, convictions of justification . . . before any potential volunteer decides to join the Army he must have these strong convictions. Convictions which are strong enough to give him confidence to kill someone without hesitation and without regret The same can be said about a bombing campaign . . . If you go out to shoot soldiers or police you must fully realise that they can shoot you too. It is a dangerous thing to join the Army . . . The Army as an organisation claims and expects your total allegiance without reservation. It enters into every aspect of your life. It invades the privacy of your home life, it fragments your family and friends, in other words claims your total allegiance

The primacy of the political over the military is clearly emphasised.

> Military action is an extension of political action, therefore the military campaign being waged by the Irish Republican Army is in effect a political campaign. People with no political concepts have no place in the Army, because the actions of the Army are directed towards a political objective that is the real meaning of the present military

campaign. The Army as a political force are intent on creating a socialist Republic in this country, therefore all potential volunteers must be socialist in outlook . . . he should examine his political motives bearing in mind that the Army are intent on creating a Socialist Republic.

The rousing, if total, condemnation of the social and political structures of modern Ireland referred to above is justified further in the lectures on History and Ideology, both in terms of an analysis of the recent past, and in terms of a far reaching overview of Irish history since the Norman Conquest. A central assertion is the continuity of an Irish entity, initially in the form of a kingship, from the earliest of times, and the sense of recovery from defeat and of the successful overthrow of invaders. 'In 1169 the Norman invasion of Ireland began and with it commenced more than 8 centuries of RELENTLESS AND UNREMITTING WARFARE that has lasted down to this very day.' The analysis continues, emphasising not only the military struggle, but its associated economic and political struggles. The issues raised, such as emigration and poverty, touch a profound collective memory, but of course also have resonance today.

The long term Republican Alternative described in 'The Green Book' is rather amorphous and ill defined, but very clearly radical socialist in character. To the typical republican supporter, at least in the Republic of Ireland and the USA, this is probably rather a surprising emphasis, at variance with the more traditional conservative and sectarian qualities of republicanism. Recognition of this difficulty probably accounts for its lack of emphasis amongst the uninitiated. In the future state, reference is made to terms like 'freedom' and 'democracy' but these are placed in a clear radical framework:

> . . . our task will be to tackle the inherent injustices of the present system by replacing it with another, both Democratic and Socialist.

This new state will emphasise the decentralisation of political power, returning:

> . . . the ownership of the wealth of Ireland through a system of cooperativism, of worker ownership and control of industry, Agriculture and Fisheries . . . Internationally our alignments would hopefully be with the Progressive Governments or former colonies like ourselves with the dual purpose of mutual advantage and curbing the endeavours of imperialistic military and economic power blocks throughout the world.

Whilst the long term is expressed in very general terms, the short term process of achieving this is much more clearly articulated. It is, of course, on this process that our interests focus. The principal focus of the short term is 'Brits out'. '. . . the Brits out campaign is . . . our 'National' short term objective. . . .' Within the context of potential discussions with the Provisional IRA in the hope of achieving peace, this forthright statement of objectives should raise the suspicions of anyone who seeks compromise.

> . . . But priority dictates that, of equal if not greater importance if we are to achieve that national objective is the need for the individual member, unit or branch of the movement to clearly analyse their own particular obstacles or short term objectives which hinders the achievement of that national objective and how best to remove it. In simple terms: a new recruit's immediate obstacle is the removal of his (her) ignorance about how to handle weapons, military tactics, security interrogations, etc. An O.C.'s[2] might be how to put a unit on a military footing: An I.O.'s[3] how to create an effective intelligence network: A Cumann[4] Chairman's how best to mount a campaign on a given issue . . .'

Two kinds of supporters are identified – active and passive. Active supporters are those members of the movement who are involved with the Provisional IRA in its activities – 'people who billet us, hold our dumps, provide transport, contribute to our collections, etc.' Passive supporters:

> . . . are those who condone our activities by not informing when they see an IRA operation being set up, know of IRA Billets, Call Houses, etc., who attend Republican funerals even if only in an observer capacity.' Both passive and active '. . . support at least our short term objective of Brits out while an indeterminate percentage also support our long term objective . . . All support lost by us from either category is potential support for our Irish Reformist and Brit imperialist enemies.

The lecture material on Tactics is more revealing of the nature of Republican terrorist activity. It expresses two rules which dictate the choice of tactics: 'get your defensive before your offensive', and 'Tactics are dictated by existing conditions'. The first rule emphasises '. . . that before we go on the offensive politically or militarily we take the greatest defensive precautions possible to ensure success'. The second emphasises flexibility of response appropriate to the political conditions of the time:

In September of 1969 the existing conditions dictated that Brits were not to be shot, but after the Falls curfew all Brits were to the people acceptable targets. The existing conditions had changed.

A further example relates to the tolerance extended to the SDLP[5] whilst it proves useful, despite the ability of the IRA to make '. . . them the subject of ridicule by tarring and feathering them . . .'

The lecture then goes on to emphasise a further rather more sophisticated tactical element – THE ENEMY – CATEGORISE – CURE:

> The enemy generally speaking are all those opposed to our short term or long term objectives. But having said that we must realise that all our enemies are not the same and therefore there is no common cure for their enmity. The conclusion then is that we must categorise and then suggest cures for each category.

There are '. . . enemies through ignorance, enemies through our own fault or default, and of course the main enemy which is the establishment.' The means of education are:

> . . . marches, demonstrations, wall slogans, press statements, Republican press and publications and of course person to person communication. But . . . we must first educate ourselves, we must organise the protests and demonstrations efficiently, we must prepare to paint the wall slogans and to sell and contribute to Republican press, Publications and Press statements.
>
> The enemy through our own fault or default is the one we create ourselves through our personal conduct and through our collective conduct of the struggle: the wee woman whose gate or back door gets pulled off its hinges by a Volunteer evading arrest and who doesn't get an apology as soon as possible afterwards or more preferably has the damage repaired by one of our supporters: the family friends and neighbours of a criminal or informer who has been punished without their being informed why.

The category of the establishment is very broadly defined in 'The Green Book'. It includes what is referred to as 'the British War Machine' (the British Army, the RUC, etc), but it notes that the 'overtly unarmed' branches of the establishment:

> . . . are not so clearly identifiable to the people as say the armed Brits or RUC. It is our task therefore to clearly identify them to the people as such and again depending on the existing conditions and

our ability to get our defensive before offensive, effect a cure. Execution . . . is not the only way of making this category of establishment enemy ineffective: we can variously expose them as liars, hypocrites, collaborators, make them subjects of ridicule, etc.

There then follows a discussion of the IRA's long term Guerrilla Strategy. This discussion is of some significance, for we can see from it the essential guiding principles that have characterised the Provisional IRA's campaign for the past 20 years. The strategy is likened to the war of the flea:

> . . . a Guerrilla Army such as the IRA . . . employs hit and run tactics against the Brits while at the same time striking at the soft economic underbelly of the enemy, not with the hope of physically driving them into the sea but nevertheless expecting to effect their withdrawal by an effective campaign of continuing harassment contained in a fivefold guerrilla strategy.
> That strategy is:
> 1. A war of attrition against enemy personnel which is aimed at causing as many casualties and deaths as possible so as to create a demand for their withdrawal.
> 2. A bombing campaign aimed at making the enemy's financial interests in our country unprofitable, whilst at the same time curbing long term financial investment in our country.
> 3. To make the six counties[6] as at present and for the past several years ungovernable except by colonial military rule.
> 4. To sustain the war and gain support for its ends by National and International propaganda and publicity campaigns.
> 5. By defending the war of liberation by punishing criminals, collaborators and informers.

To a large extent a critical element underpinning that strategy is to:

> . . . EXPLOIT A GIVEN SITUATION OR CREATE A SITUATION AND THEN EXPLOIT IT. Exploiting a given situation simply means taking advantage of our enemies' political or military mistakes. If the Brits pass the same point at the same time every day we exploit their mistake by mounting an operation against them. Similarly when they make the mistake of wrecking homes, assaulting our people, etc. We exploit these mistakes by propagating the facts . . . Likewise we can create a situation ourselves and then exploit it to our advantage eg. if the Brits don't make themselves available to be shot when and where it suits us we attempt to get them to an area where we can operate against them at a time when we can operate against them on some

bogus pretext or other; bomb scare, body found, reported robbery, etc. Likewise we exploit their political mistakes . . . they make the mistake, we exploit their mistake by propagating it, which in turn creates a new situation where we could at least embarrass them.

. . . the factors analysed above must be considered as a whole and FOR THE MOST PART' they govern our actions. That means we do not exclude taking an action which does not completely fill the criteria of this analysis on how to conduct the struggle. Many instances have arisen and will arise again when we have had to step outside these general terms of reference to our immediate detriment propaganda wise and support wise. However, even in such an eventuality, if we rationalise our actions, get our defensive before our offensive, try to ensure that we have an alternative, relatively unaffected area of support from which to operate if the support in the area in which the detrimental but unavoidable action takes place we are adhering as best as possible under the circumstances to a proper conduct of the war.'

This discussion of IRA tactics is complemented by a discussion of the long and short term objectives of the enemy. The long term objective of the British involvement in Northern Ireland is identified as preserving the *status quo* '. . . regardless of whether that *status quo* is maintained in a partitioned Ireland, a Unitary Ireland or in any form of federal or confederated Ireland.' This analysis is of considerable interest within the context of the Anglo-Irish Agreement, because it suggests that no solution outside the '. . . establishment of a Democratic Socialist Republic' would be acceptable in the long term to the Provisional IRA. The enemy's short term objective is identified as the political and military defeat of the Republican movement, as the biggest stumbling block to maintaining the *status quo*.

This analysis is conducted using a similar format to the earlier analysis of the Provisional IRA's objectives. It identifies the British Government's passive and active supporters emphasising in the active supporters, of course, the relationship between the Northern Ireland establishment and the broader British State. The greatest passive supporter is identified as the Catholic Hierarchy. The Hierarchy ' . . . by its silence condoned the activities of the establishment while regularly attacking the IRA'.

The British Government is acknowledged as having broadly similar tactical considerations as the IRA, but at a different level and with different motivations. A contrast in particular is drawn between a major consideration of the IRA, which '. . . in deciding tactics is the concern for our friends, relatives, neighbours, our people in the midst of whom we operate' in contrast to the British who are

'. . . simply dealing with an impersonal, inferior foreigner, a "Paddy", "Muck-Savage" or "Bog-Wog".'

The British are also seen as exploiting and creating situations – using the mistakes of the IRA to its own advantage. The major over-all strategy of the British is seen as isolation – isolation '. . . from our support from those who supply the dumps, billets, etc., who passively condone our activities by their silence.' Were this to be successful:

> . . . it would in effect achieve for him his short term objective of defeat-ing the republican Movement, albeit temporary as history has proved if partition were to continue. But it would give him sufficient breath-ing space to attempt the long term objective of preserving the status quo by creating some form of all Ireland institutions which would maintain the political, social and economic situations he desires. Our task is to conduct ourselves and the struggle in such a fashion that the enemy's attempted isolation does not come to fruition.

At a later point, the motivations of 'The Brit and the IRA Volunteer' are contrasted. This element of the Green Book is probably amongst the most valuable parts as far as the new volunteer is concerned, for it deliberately contrasts his or her own state with that of the enemy, adding to their understanding of what they are embarking on, and helping them to place their activities within a broader context. By emphasising negative qualities, and the use of terms like freedom and free will, to characterise IRA motivations, through denigration it enhances the volunteer's own role. The British, for example, are described as gaining support purely from the organs and finances of the state, in contrast with the IRA volunteer '. . . who receives all his support voluntarily from his people'.

> The Brit has . . . no motivation for being here . . . A member of the IRA is such by his own choice . . . his objectives the political freedom and social and economic justice for his people . . . apart from the few min-utes in the career of the average Brit that he comes under attack, the Brit has no freedom or personal initiative. He is told when to sleep, where to sleep, when to get up, where to spend his free time.

The conclusion of this section summarises in a very clear way the quite complex and sophisticated objectives of the Provisional IRA:

> By now it is clear that our task is not only to kill as many enemy per-sonnel as possible or to cause as much economic damage as possible but of equal importance to create support which will carry us not only through a war of liberation which could last another decade but which

will support us past the 'Brits Out' stage to the ultimate aim of a Democratic Socialist Republic . . . Our analysis of the overall Irish society is that it is unjust: unjust that a small minority of Irish Nationals and Foreign investors own or control most of the wealth of our country, and, that conditions in which that unjust situation can be successfully resisted and overturned will exist only in a United Ireland . . . Our aim therefore must be . . . we force by compulsion of their own convictions as many of the disenchanted . . . to bring them as far along the road to a Democratic Socialist Republic as possible.

In practical terms that means that in the war zone we must channel all the resentment felt by the nationalist population . . . Then resistance thus created must in turn be channelled into active and passive support with an ongoing process through our actions, our education programmes, our policies, of attempting to turn the passive supporter into a dump holder, a member of the movement, a paper seller, etc. with the purpose of building protective support barriers between the enemy and ourselves, thus curbing the enemy's attempted isolation policy. And, of course, the more barriers there are, the harder it is for the enemy to get at us while at the same time we increase the potential for active support in its various forms.

The immediate protective barriers are, of course, our own security, the other branches of the movement, our billets, etc. But we must build up other barriers by championing the various causes in our support areas through involvement in the various peoples committees in those areas. More important still is the need for us as a movement to replace the various enemy structures which have been brought down as a result of the war: Policing, Transport, Bin Collection, Advice Centres, etc.

From the above, a picture emerges of a complex sophisticated organisation, that has a clear view of its objectives, and the role of the volunteer in achieving those objectives. Above all, it is clear that the Provisional IRA has a broad social, as well as political agenda. The organisation has, of course, had a long time to develop its social perspectives. But its sophistication is revealed in the sense in which its concerns have broadened from the purely violent to a recognition of the significance of local politics as the support for the broader political agenda. The organisation is generally very secretive, and not prone to public explanation of its actions. The material presented above, however, throws an unusual light on the thinking that guides the organisation. In particular, its sophistication in recognising the need to temper political objectives with the social realities of the situation, and to take a step by step approach to achieving its long term objectives, both indicates its strength and the extent to which it has integrated political violence with its political agenda.

The above lengthy discussion also serves two other purposes. It introduces and develops in a very clear way the ideological and practical considerations of the Provisional IRA. The material presented on strategy and tactics in particular helps to place into context many of the actions of the IRA over the past 20 years, and reveals it to be a sophisticated, well controlled and creative organisation. But the material also illustrates some of the factors that go towards moulding the volunteer into an effective terrorist. Its emphasis on the moral and ideological bases to terrorist behaviour are important elements in the individual's own justification for the acts he commits. There may be a sense in which the experienced terrorist does not need these supports – perhaps he has been desensitised to the death and injury he might cause. But the new recruit needs the sense of moral and ideological superiority to embark on his acts. We can see in this training scheme, how that sense of righteousness is developed within its broader ideological framework.

Irish terrorism

Whilst loyalist and republican terrorists strive for opposite and irreconcilable ends, the individuals involved show surprising similarities at a psychological level. If the particular nationalistic aspirations are set to one side, a number of common qualities emerge. For example, when pressed, most make use of sophisticated sounding rhetoric to describe their cause. Words like 'freedom', 'defence', 'justice', 'values' litter the conversation. Both loyalists and republicans look back to the past more clearly than they look to the future, to a sense of historical necessity, to the need to defend fundamental qualities in the face of aggression and potential assimilation into the opposing camp. Underneath the rhetoric, however, there is often an inarticulate, but nevertheless real, uglier and less acceptable sectarianism and nationalism. This is at its most apparent in images and examples used to illustrate points, or to provoke amusement. National and confessional stereotypes are frequently referred to, poking fun at putative collective qualities, but distancing the individual from direct acknowledgement of their bases. These are the familiar qualities of prejudice; these processes serve to categorise and dehumanise the targets of their ire.

Perhaps this is the only way in which people involved in murder can rationalise and legitimise their activities. Recognition and acceptance of blame, allowing feelings of guilt, showing some sympathy or understanding of the plight of the victim; all these present a fundamentally insurmountable conflict for the active terrorist which can only be resolved by some form of cognitive reconstruction of the world into a framework more accepting of their behaviour.

Both loyalists and nationalists embrace a frankly militant ideology. Its simplicity, and its transparent links with the past (real or imagined) adds to its appeal. It is often said that the past is ever present in Ireland, and no more so is this the case with Irish nationalism (loyalist or republican). The past is merged with the present by family stories, a facilitating cultural ambience, and particularly at a popular level by song. The confessional attributes of a working class club or pub can be identified immediately by the songs which patrons sing. Current events are drawn into song, and relayed to people in a particularly powerful, emotive and effective way. Songs in all cultures serve to reinterpret the complexities of the world into acceptable structures, but this is particularly the case in Ireland. Because of the sectarian divisions within the community, social life, especially pub or club related, tends to be largely inward looking. Communal gatherings tend to be from the same religious affiliation for very practical reasons; in a society where sectarian violence occurs, it is safer to mix with your own kind. In this world, song is the repository at a popular level of the cultural fundamentals and aspirations in both loyalist and nationalist communities.

Because of the illegal nature of their actions, terrorists by definition need to lead cautious and circumspect lives if they are to evade capture. However, awareness of the potential of forensic science of crime testing, and the development of a capacity to safeguard against leaving forensic evidence tempers and limits the extent to which the legal system can acquire sufficient evidence for a conviction for a terrorist offence, unless the perpetrator is caught in the act. This means that the active terrorist can still interact within his culture, socialising amongst a safe group without particular regard to the attentions of the security forces. A safe group, of course, is one which does not question values, and which accords some status to the commitment of the terrorist to violence. The terrorist drinks and socialises with others of his group. He is sustained by his culture, he sings the songs in which he may himself be playing a distant part. A very powerful force is thereby created which sustains its members, offers considerable attractions for membership, and dispenses status and rewards. The importance of this level of day-to-day support for the terrorist cannot be underestimated.

Furthermore, because of their very nature, terrorist organisations exercise tight control over their members, creating a social context where doubt, questioning and reflection on what is occurring is difficult and discouraged. The net result of this is the creation of a self contained social system that propagates, values and rewards commitment to particular kinds of communal values. The tragedy of Northern Ireland, and perhaps Ireland as a whole, is that the pinnacle of these values has become associated with violence in the service of 'the cause'.

The strength of community support, the exclusivity of social relationships and settings, the illegality of their actions, the militancy of their ideology, and the very real sense of personal agency contributing to the attainment of their goals creates, therefore, a potent force for sustaining and developing terrorist behaviour. These processes are given direction and focus by an underlying ideology. We will see in the next chapter how in different social contexts these general features affect members of terrorist groups more explicitly linked to radical political ideology.

5

Action and Engagement: Europe

Valuable as our case-study of the conflict in Northern Ireland has been in our search for the character and motivations of the modern terrorist organisation, its strong historical background, broad-based working class identity and readily identifiable sub-goals, together with the wide-spread illegality of both major terrorist factions in their need to finance their operations, are all in marked contrast to the more monolithic structure of terrorism in mainland Europe, fuelled by its ideological fight against international capitalism and its search for a socialist Utopia, to which we must now turn.

An incident in Amsterdam

At around 11.30 at night the light in the fifth floor apartment was switched on and off several times. Even in the dark November night, the signal could be clearly seen from the front of the apartment building and all around the area of Baden Powellweg. A few moments later a man could be seen indistinctly on the walkway in front of the apartment entering it. This apartment was under the surveillance of the Dutch Security Services, who had become aware that it was probably used by Rolf Clements Wagner, a wanted German terrorist. It was also thought likely that it was used by other *Rote Armee Faktion* (Red Army Faction – RAF) members. They were right. Amongst those using it at that time were two other RAF men, Christof Wagernagel and Gert Schneider.

The Dutch police became aware of the presence of this terrorist base during the course of investigations into the abduction of the Dutch businessman Maurits Caransa in late October, 1977 (although Caransa does not, in fact, appear to have been abducted by terrorists). German terrorism, indeed more general European terrorism,

129

was extensive at that time. Fuelled by left wing protest, waves of abductions and shootings had taken place, mainly directed against US and Israeli interests, but also including German officials and industrialists. Prominent in this activity was the RAF. The group had come to prominence in the early 1970's, emerging from a period of extra-parliamentary activity which swept across Europe. Although with a relatively small active membership, RAF members were involved in a wide array of arson attacks, bombings, kidnappings and assassinations, and became widely known. They were either feared or admired, depending on one's perspective. The RAF was an explicitly left wing organisation, which saw its activities in Marxist terms of class warfare. Its aim was to undermine the German State, and precipitate a proletarian revolution.

The fifth floor apartment in Baden Powellweg in Amsterdam was placed under observation by the Dutch police in November 1977. On the night of 10 November, that observation yielded fruit. At around 1800 hrs, two men were seen on the walkway in front of the apartment. One of the men entered it, the other was seen to walk away. After about fifteen minutes, a man left the apartment. These movements alerted the police, and members of the Amsterdam Anti-terrorist squad were deployed around the area. At about 2300 hrs, two more men left the apartment and walked down the walkway to the stairs. Shortly afterwards, a man wearing a grey overcoat and another wearing a dark brown suit left the building, and walked towards a nearby major road, Pieter Callandlaan. They were quickly out of sight of the police observation post, but were seen in a telephone booth on Pieter Callandlaan by a passing police car. These police officers reported the presence of the men, but did not stop.

Four unmarked police cars converged on Pieter Callandlaan each containing armed police officers. The commander's car stopped about 10 metres from the telephone booth, and whilst the driver gave cover, another of the car's occupants approached the telephone booth. The policeman had his hand in his right coat pocket, holding an unlocked pistol. Speaking to the men in the telephone booth, he asked in Dutch '*Will you be long, I must call a doctor*'. A voice from the booth answered in German '*Einen Moment noch bitte*' (Just a minute please).The policeman returned to his car and reported to his commander '*They're Germans!*'.

' "*Now or never*" *I thought*' recalls the commander. '*The three of us got out and walked over to the booth. We had our pistols cocked. When we were at the telephone booth, I opened the door and called out in German "Polizei, Hände hoch!" I was wholly focusing on Schneider, for I noticed that he reached with his hand under his coat. Once again I said "Hände hoch!"*'.

'*Then there were a number of impressions in a split second. Schneider did not obey my command and continued his movement, which I took to be the drawing of a weapon. I then shot Schneider straight in the body. More shots rang, everything was so unreal; my colleague fired through the window of the booth at the terrorists; I was hit in the wrist. The first thought that flashed through my brain was that he had hit me.*

'*It may sound hard to believe, but I felt it was almost a relief that we were fired at from the booth. My fear that I had possibly made an error of judgement when I shot at Schneider was over. It was a weird sort of feeling. At the same time, I thought I had been hit in the head or neck, for it hurt there. We took cover in the bushes behind the booth. By then the terrorists were lying on the ground . . .*'

Wagernagel shot at least four times at the three police officers with his SIG Sauer pistol. His first shots hit one officer in the right hip, and hit the commanding officer on the left forearm. Whilst Wagernagel was still firing from the telephone booth, the uninjured officer stepped to the left side of the booth, broke the window with one shot, and fired four times at Wagernagel. This officer, and one of his injured colleagues took cover at this point behind bushes, and the remaining officer, who was also injured, took cover behind some parked cars.

In the meantime, Wagernagel and Schneider had crawled from the telephone booth, and lay to its left and right. Schneider reached to his trouser belt, and an officer shouted '*Liegen bleiben*' (do not move). But Schneider continued to move, and was shot twice. Schneider pulled the safety pin from a hand grenade and threw it in the direction of the uninjured police officer. When it exploded, that officer received serious shrapnel injuries. It was at this time that other police officers arrived.

'. . . *I walked around to the cars parked in front of the telephone booth in order to contact the other colleagues who had arrived in the meantime. Then there was a tremendous explosion. My first thought was that my colleague's pistol had burst. It wasn't until later that I learnt that the terrorists had thrown a hand grenade.*

'*Right after the explosion, I heard a cry from the bushes behind the booth. My name was shouted, and I heard the cry "I'm injured. Help me". I realised this had to be my colleague, and I called back that we were coming, and that he should stay where he was.*

'*Immediately after the explosion of the grenade, an awful amount of shots were fired . . . when I saw the men were lying still, I called out "Stop". 'Everything happened very quickly . . . they were down, I was down as well, I was injured . . . it all happened very quickly.*' '*All of a sudden it was deathly quiet.*

'*So the shooting happened, you rolled down on the ground . . . it was over and you were taken to hospital . . . you came home, then you went back to work the following day. That's how it happened.'*

This brief incident resulted in serious injuries to all concerned. Three police officers were injured, the most serious being from the hand grenade explosion. This resulted in grenade splinter injuries to his right eye, right temple, chest, left leg and right foot. Both Wagernagel and Schneider also received serious injuries. Wagernagel had bullet wounds in his right elbow, grazes to the head, and bullet wounds in the right foot; he was hit by four shots. Schneider received nine bullets, resulting in gunshot wounds to the back of his head, two next to the right shoulder, and further wounds near to the pelvis, loins, right armpit, right buttock, left knee and left foot.

Both Wagernagel and Schneider were subsequently convicted in 1980 of membership of the RAF and of attempted murder, and received sentences of 15 years from a court in Düsseldorf. At the time of their arrest, both Wagernagel and Schneider were politically mature. They knew they had entered into an underground lifestyle that was dangerous. Like most of the membership of the RAF, both Schneider and Wagernagel were relatively well educated people who came to terrorism out of ideological and political commitment. Schneider in particular had a long involvement in political activity, and had by his own account moved into terrorism out of frustration at the lack of progress towards political change.

In contrast, Wagernagel had enjoyed early success as a child actor. At the age of 15, he had major roles in two West German films, and had appeared in television films. In his early 20's, he moved into a Stuttgart commune, and established an alternative printing press. But after some years, his enthusiasm for this waned. '*The commune was the first Utopia that shattered. It was a great disappointment to find out that one can't build an island apart from society*'. He became more and more engaged with the radical left movements in Germany at that time, and in 1977 he went underground with the Red Army Faction. His aim, as he described it, was to discover '*whether you can find freedom if you completely break with society*'. This freedom, if such it was, proved to be illusory and short lived. The shooting on Pieter Callandlaan occurred only a few weeks after his decision to go underground.

After their conviction in 1980, it might have been expected that both Wagernagel and Schneider would simply fade into the statistics of terror. A brief hunger strike by convicted terrorists held in West German prisons in 1981 resulted in better conditions, and Wagernagel and Schneider benefitted by being moved to the same prison, and allowed to see each other three times a week. In all respects both proved to be unremarkable prisoners. Moving them together, however, in fact proved to be an important development, although not apparent for some three years.

In October, 1984, the senior policeman involved in the shooting at Pieter Callandlaan and the subsequent arrest of Schneider and Wagernagel, Herman Van Hoogen, was approached by a Dutch lawyer acting for them both. Under Dutch law, convicted offenders can apply for early release if new circumstances come to light. In the case of Schneider and Wagernagel, they wished to claim these new circumstances involved a change of heart. Whilst held together in prison, they had both begun to reassess their political involvement in terrorism. Allowing them to live together in the same prison '. . . *started our critical thinking. Together we could examine whether we had done anything wrong*'. They began to read authors such as Lenin and Marx '. . . *on which our fight was allegedly based. The more we read, the more difficult it became to justify our armed struggle . . . It just didn't work*'.

Schneider and Wagernagel's lawyer approached Van Hoogen to tell him that they were offering to make a public renunciation of their RAF involvement, and as one of the main people involved in their arrest, how did he feel about this, and would he co-operate?

For any police officer, co-operation with someone whom you have caught can present both moral and ethical dilemmas. It certainly goes against police traditions and culture; even more so, when the people you are being asked to co-operate with have shot and injured you, and two of your close colleagues. Van Hoogen realised that this was an unusual request to say the least, but he agreed to re-examine the situation. '. . . *I had no hate or feelings of vindictiveness towards them. Even though cynicism is not foreign to me after 30 years in the profession, I regard Wagernagel and Schneider's renunciation of RAF allegiance with less distrust than a similar statement made by a gainseeking criminal. Besides, . . . apart from the fact that I harbour no hate or desire for revenge, in my experience long sentences hardly ever have a beneficial effect on . . . later . . . behaviour. . . .*'

Schneider and Wagernagel did indeed publicly renounce their membership of the RAF in 1984, and wrote to newspapers saying the RAF should stop its violence and seek an amnesty for convicted members. But the results of this appeal disappointed them. '*On the one side we were called deserters. On the other side, even people who had been leftist sympathisers in the 1960's and 1970's did not want to talk about an amnesty.*' Their appeal, using Van Hoogen, also failed in German law, but as a 'thank you' to Van Hoogen for his good will, Wagernagel sent him a collection of short stories which he had published whilst in prison. There the matter might have ended.

In 1986 both Schneider and Wagernagel benefitted from West German laws that allow prisoners to engage in useful work under special circumstances whilst remaining in prison. For Schneider, that involved attending a university, but for Wagernagel, it involved working as an actor in a local theatre. At this point, both again approached Herman Van Hoogen through their lawyers to seek a meeting with him, but this time the aim was to achieve reconciliation with Van Hoogen as the policeman who had commanded the group that arrested them. That meeting took place on the 6th of December, 1986 in the local theatre in Bochum where Wagernagel was allowed to work.

In describing this meeting, Van Hoogen presents a diffident account. But its peculiarity and significance should not be underestimated. Neither Schneider nor Wagernagel have renounced their ideals. Van Hoogen notes that '. . . *their view of the world has remained the same*'. But the discussions between the ex- terrorists and their former arresting officer yielded interesting reflections on their reason for renouncing terrorism. According to Van Hoogen, what seems to have happened to both is '. . . *that they came to the conclusion that weapons as a means to achieve their goal will not work. It was contrary to their goal, and they realised that their efforts would only strengthen and sharpen the activities of the security forces in opposition to them. The expected public mobilisation of support in their favour as a result of this had not happened.*'

In November, 1987 both Schneider and Wagernagel were released from prison after serving seven years of their original 15 year sentence. Both benefitted from laws which allow clemency to repentant prisoners, under Article 57 of the West German Penal Code. Schneider has sought to retain his privacy, and has largely dropped from public view. Wagernagel has sustained a successful career in acting, on the fringes of left wing German theatre, and has tried to put his former notoriety as a terrorist behind him '. . . *I am not only that man. I am an actor, I ran a printing press, I have written books. I am not only him*'. Their friendship with Van Hoogen continues, and that it does is a reflection of the unusual qualities of all three. Paradoxically, they all share in some measure a similar moral view of the world, where values such as justice and freedom are more than just clichés. Wagernagel and Schneider sought to achieve those values through violence, bringing themselves into conflict with the State, as it happened quite literally in the form of Herman Van Hoogen. The renunciation of violence by Wagernagel and Schneider enabled the fundamental affinity between the three men to emerge. Their extraordinary meetings have, for all of them, given a sense of completeness to the past, captor and captives reconciled to both their violent encounter and their congruent perspectives on society.

European Terrorism

The series of events that culminated in the imprisonment of Wagernagel and Schneider had parallels throughout Europe in the 1960's and 70's. Their movement into terrorism, capture, imprisonment, and eventual reassessment and release is typical of what might be termed the life-cycle of the European terrorist. Different individuals of course experienced different circumstances and differences in detail, and a residual core of terrorists never recanted their views. But as we will see later, this cycle of optimistic involvement followed by defeat and eventual reassessment of violence seems to represent an authentic quality of the European terrorist experience. The significance of the effect of imprisonment in this example is different from that we have noted for the Irish terrorist, but this may be related to the relatively greater ideological sophistication of the European terrorist at the outset.

Almost all European countries experienced a wave of political protest in the 1960's and 1970's. It most often took the form of frustration with normal democratic processes, and a gradual movement towards violent confrontation with society to stimulate the movement towards social change. This, plus protests against the war in Vietnam, anti-nuclear protests, and civil rights agitation, were a heady mixture that exploded in the 1960's into a period of youth power; a breaking of post-war social conventions that had powerful and enduring political implications. In a sense, there was great optimism in the air, in that change in society, and the creation of a more just world seemed attainable through concerted and challenging action. The notion of 'propaganda of the deed' became dominant, and the various fringe political groups of the time saw themselves in leadership roles, providing the catalyst which would ignite the proletarian revolution.

Unlike the situation in Northern Ireland, or the Basque regions of Spain, the primary motivation of those involved was relatively abstract idealism. Political change, and a desire to attain abstract ends, drove a whole generation of politically committed young people towards violent confrontation with the State. Our concerns here are exclusively with *left wing* terrorism, but it should be noted that *right wing* terrorism was also greatly in ascendance during this period, and made a significant contribution to the extent of violence. Indeed, to an extent, each fed off the other, with actual or imagined threats from one providing the justification for violence by the other.

The principal focus of much of this activity of both the left and the right was West Germany and Italy, although France, and to a lesser extent the United Kingdom, also experienced unrest. Various terrorist groups existed in both Germany and Italy, often simultaneously and sometimes with overlapping membership, but two main left wing groupings have become associated with the events of those times. In Germany, the Red Army Faction (*Rote Armee Faktion* – RAF) and in Italy the Red Brigades (*Brigate Rosse* – RB).

The Red Army Faction (RAF)

The RAF, of which Schneider and Wagernagel were members, was an extreme left wing German terrorist group which was established in 1970. It took its name from the Japanese Red Army with whom it formed an association, although the specific event that is often referred to as creating the organisation was not that association, but the rescue from police custody on May 14, 1970, of Andreas Baader. The origins of the RAF lay in the extensive extraparliamentary opposition which mounted non-violent demonstrations against both the West German State, and what it regarded as agents of Imperialism (especially the United States and NATO) during the 1960's. Two leaders of the radical left emerged who became associated with the whole era: Andreas Baader and Ulrike Meinhof. They, typical of others of that time, made the transition from peaceful protest to violence and terrorism that characterised the RAF in their impatience at the lack of swift political change.

Setting a pattern for later left-wing European terrorists, the early RAF terrorists were largely of either comfortable working class or middle class origins, and came to terrorism through an intellectual commitment to radical politics, rather than social deprivation or nationalist fervour. Early RAF attacks showed a caution and restraint that later activists came to despise, and in the development of the group, we see an increasing escalation of violence associated with an increased withdrawal from normal society. The early command of the RAF lay with essentially four people: Andreas Baader, Gudrun Ensslin, Ulrike Meinhof and Jan Carl Raspe. All four were arrested in 1972, but the command of the organisation remained with them whilst they were in prison. The presence of the leadership in prison shifted the focus of protest, and much of the attention of the RAF after 1972 was focused on the release of the prisoners in some measure, to the exclusion of broader political aims. Indeed, a whole series of kidnappings and bombings occurred where the primary aim was the release of the prisoners.

Perhaps the most dramatic of the actions undertaken to gain the release of the prisoners was the hijacking of a Lufthansa jet travelling from Palma de Mallorca to Frankfurt on 13 October 1977. The Boeing 737, flight LH181, had in all 86 passengers, two aircrew and three cabin crew. Somewhere over the Mediterranean Sea, two men and two women took control of the jet by bursting into the cockpit, dragging the co-pilot from his seat, and threatening to blow the plane up by exploding hand grenades held by the two women. The leader of the hijacking called himself 'Captain Martyr Mahmud'. The plane diverted to Rome, and on landing, Captain Martyr Mahmud announced that he demanded '. . . the release of our comrades in German prisons. We are fighting against the imperialist organisations of the world'. The comrades referred to were principally Baader, Ensslin, Meinhof and Raspe, but included a further 5 other prisoners. A day later whilst the hijacking was still in the air, the kidnappers attempted to increase the pressure on the German authorities. They offered not only the release of the hijacked aircraft passengers and crew if the 9 RAF members in German prisons were freed, but also to release a kidnapped German industrialist, Hans-Martin Schleyer, who had already been held for 40 days. Schleyer was in fact subsequently murdered by his captors.

Captain Martyr Mahmud was the assumed name of Zohair Youssif Akache, a student with a history of association with Palestinian protests. He was a member of the Popular Front for the Liberation of Palestine (PFLP). He was probably responsible for the assassination of the ex-Prime Minister of Yemen in London in April, 1977. Those with him were also PFLP members

The hijacked Lufthansa aircraft left Rome, and landed briefly at Cyprus, Dubai, Yemen, Saudi Arabia, until on 17 October it landed at Mogadishu airport in Somalia. During the course of the journey, the hijackers murdered the pilot of the aircraft, Jürgen Schumann. Whilst negotiations with the terrorists on the ground, and between Baader and other German prisoners were being conducted by the German authorities, a German Special Services Force launched an attack against the hijacked aircraft; the attack team having been surreptitiously flown to Mogadishu. The two male hijackers and one of the females were killed in the attack, and the remaining female hijacker was badly injured. One of the air hostesses was also injured in the leg, the remaining passengers being freed.

On 18 October 1977, both Baader and Meinhof died in Stammheim Prison. Their deaths can be directly linked to the failure of the Mogadishu hijacking to achieve their release.

But significant as their deaths may have been, the RAF continued in existence, with new active personnel replacing those imprisoned. From this point, several phases can be seen in the development of the RAF, as it sought to sustain its credentials as a leader of the revolutionary fight in the light of the loss of its original leadership. In 1977, the first of these changes had occurred, when what the Baader-Meinhof leadership termed the 'Military-Industrial Complex' (MIC) became the new focus of attention, and representatives of the 'apparatus of repression' became the principal targets for bombings and assassination. The period of kidnappings which had characterised the pre-1977 period came abruptly to an end with the failure of the Mogadishu hijacking.

Although remaining focused on the MIC strategy, in 1982 a broader ideological programme began to emerge, more explicitly relating the terrorist violence to broader ideological and organisational goals. An RAF strategy paper of the time refers to the development of a new organisation based on a series of circles expressing functions at different levels. At the centre remained the prisoners. Operations were to be carried out by the so-called commando, command level units, consisting of some 10–15 people. This group was encircled by some 200 or so 'Illegal Militants', who were themselves encircled by another level, the 'political fighters'. These were the legal arm of the RAF, numbering in the early 1980's some 400 people.

This document reveals the organisational sophistication of the movement. Its structures had evolved into a complex system designed to protect its clandestine active members, and to provide them with logistical support to continue their terrorist violence. Its operations were well planned, and frequently carried out with considerable daring.

This period in the life of the RAF was characterised by a series of attacks against NATO personnel and bases, and against the manufacturers of weapons and munitions. But despite a high level of activity, the actions of the RAF began increasingly to be seen as unrelated to the major preoccupations of the German left. The RAF began to become isolated from the mainstream of political thinking, which found less and less sympathy with the heavy emphasis on violence, and the propaganda of the deed. One act more than anything seemed to crystallise the isolation of the RAF – the murder of an American soldier, GI Edward Pimental. On 7 August 1985, two RAF members murdered Edward Pimental by shooting him in the nape of his neck. He was shot and killed so that they could merely steal his ID card. This followed on the controversial death of Ernst Zimmermann, a prominent manager in the German armaments industry on 1 February 1985. Both deaths led many members of the radical left to question the moral and ideological justification behind the RAF attacks. Eventually, the attack on Pimental was described as 'a mistake', but a rift had emerged between the radical left and the RAF which to a large extent remains today.

The effects of these doubts was to question the legitimacy of the RAF. As a response to this, and also as a response to the changing political circumstances in Europe, a further new direction began to emerge within the RAF in the mid to late '80's. The focus of attention shifted from the strategy of the Military-Industrial Complex, to that of the United Europe. Attempts at that time to create a transnational 'West-European Guerilla' had failed, and had left the RAF in something of a strategic vacuum. This vacuum they sought to fill by focusing attention on the idea of 'European global power' as the new emergent agent of exploitation to be opposed by the radical left. As far as can be seen, this currently remains the objective focus of the RAF's activities, but there seems to be evidence of increased isolation of their activities from contemporary concerns. In particular, there seems to be little evidence that the modern RAF have come to terms with a United Germany. Its contemporary leadership is now too young to have played a part in the student movements of the 1970's from which the RAF grew, and a fixation with seeking a clearly defined enemy seems to have been substituted for the more sophisticated ideological analyses of the earlier founders of the movement. Despite the history of the RAF, and its origins within the radical left, RAF members are now seen paradoxically as outsiders in the eyes of the extremist left. Strategy failures, such as the failure to establish an international movement, and the continuing emphasis on violence, emphasises the isolation of the RAF from contemporary concerns.

In summary, it can be seen that over the past 15 years, terrorist activity by the group has tended to be consistent but sporadic, with a residual but small core of intellectual and activist support for them within Germany. Whilst recent revelations have linked the RAF to the now defunct East German Security Services, there seems to be little reliable evidence of actual collusion between the East German State and the RAF. A number of ex-RAF terrorists have been found living in East Germany; for example during the period between the 6th and 9th of June, 1990, nine former RAF members were arrested in various parts of East Germany having lived under assumed names for up to 10 years. However, East Germany appears to have only offered a safe base for those terrorists who wished to renounce the armed struggle without facing the possibility of imprisonment in West Germany, rather than a base from which they might operate.

The demise of East Germany, and the reunification of Germany will place even greater pressure on those who wish to renounce their RAF membership, but is unlikely to affect the current activities of the RAF. Despite its decline, the organisation of the RAF remains largely intact, if diminished. Its capacity to strike fear in the authorities, however, remains, and the fear of the RAF initiating contemporary terrorist violence is such that it resulted in April 1992, for example, in five suspected RAF sympathisers being detained by the British authorities for four days on entry into Wales from Ireland. In so far as can be seen, they were suspected of having links with the Provisional IRA. The RAF remains a terrorist group with the potential to inflict considerable damage and destruction, although its claim to leadership of the revolutionary movement lacks credibility, as indeed does the whole notion of the propaganda of the deed leading to mobilisation of the masses in the new Europe.

The Red Brigades (RB)

The Red Brigades emerged in Milan in 1970 in broadly similar circumstances to the RAF. This organisation too sought to mobilise the working classes through propaganda of the deed, and it too saw itself as leading the masses towards revolution and social change. During its period of maximum activity, it had a surprisingly small membership of about 500, with only some 50 or so full-time clandestine members. Its size, however, should not lead to an underestimate of its significance. In the period 1970–80, it carried out over 440 terrorist attacks, including 55 murders and 18 kidnappings.

Like the RAF, the origin of the Red Brigades lies in the turmoil of the late 1960's. A number of extremist left wing groups, who looked to the Latin American experience as a model, emerged in Northern Italy, especially in the industrial areas around Milan. They largely grew from Trade Union bases, but took a broader ideological view of their role, agitating against capitalism rather than for better working conditions. Progressively, these groups moved from actions that would damage 'capitalism' without particularly alienating the workers, such as sabotage, picketing, etc. to more explicit violence. Concurrent with this, attention moved from the work place to broader social concerns. Groups in particular factories, such as the *Comitati Unitari di Base* in Pirelli, and the *Gruppi di Studio* in Sit Siemens and IBM came together to form the *Collettivo Politico Metropolitano*, which gradually emerged through linkage with other groups such as the Red Brigades. This process of organisational development was associated with an increased commitment to violence, and to the armed struggle. Members of the initial groups who remained went through a slow process of increased involvement in violence, testing their commitment to the ideals of the movement, and their confirming ability to survive the stresses of terrorism.

The early Red Brigadists looked to the South American guerrillas; especially Carlos Marighella, as their role models. They followed, sometimes almost exactly, the procedures of groups such as the Uruguayan Tupamaros. But as the momentum created by the Red Brigades grew in the early 1970's, so it became necessary to develop more formal organisational structures. Two broad categories of members emerged: the regular forces, who were completely clandestine and had '. . . severed every tie with legality'; and the irregular forces, who lived legal lives, and operated at a broadly political, rather than 'military' level. Both the regular and irregular forces were organised in *cells*; groups of cells made up a *Brigade*, which collectively made up *columns* formed in cities or particular areas. In addition, strategic decisions at a national level were co-ordinated by a number of *fronts*. What emerged was, in organisational terms, a pyramid structure. At the apex of the pyramid stood an Executive committee of four. Below that Committee, and subject to its authority, were the various Fronts and Brigades. The more important Fronts were the Logistical Front, which dealt with the supply of arms, etc., and the later Prison Front, which co-ordinated the armed struggle within the prisons.

This relatively sophisticated organisation was initially premised on principles of collectivity and democracy. However, as the early membership of the organisation became depleted through arrests, so movement through the various structures to positions of command became less democratic, and more related to length of membership, and experience. As one of its early leaders Alberto Franceschini said, '. . . *in fact it was the enemy who dictated the rules, and whoever survived was in command*'. Allied to this relatively formal structure, Red Brigades members were subject to strict internal codes of discipline. This discipline became of great importance when members moved into clandestine lives, and undoubtedly contributed at one level to the effectiveness of the organisation, although where these rules impinged on personal issues, their value is less clear. For example, the code of conduct was extended in 1976 to forbidding couples who had a relationship from living together if both were clandestine. This may have been organisationally useful (limiting the possibilities of partnership compromising terrorist action) and ideologically correct (the concept of the couple was a petty bourgeois institution). But it placed clandestine members, already under great stress, under even greater emotional strain.

The nature of the clandestine lives adopted by Red Brigades members, and the strict security structure in which the members lived, created great tensions. Lives were organised, social contacts were greatly diminished and controlled, and members lived in a self-created world far removed from the workers whom they claimed to represent. An inevitable result of this was a spiral of increasing loss of contact with social conditions.

This form of isolation is a necessary feature of increased disengagement with society. Adopting a clandestine lifestyle may be a pragmatic response to pursuit by the security services. But such a lifestyle also has profound psychological consequences that create a major psychological paradox for the terrorist. Adopting a clandestine lifestyle necessarily diminishes contact with the society in which the terrorist lives. The dynamic forces within the group to which the terrorist still has access then become greatly magnified, further reinforcing the individual's dependence on the group, and enhancing his or her distance from normal society. The disassociation from society and its moral values, so often referred to in accounts of terrorists, undoubtedly has this as one of its causative factors, and it is probably in these terms that we should look for one major source of the blurring of moral and social boundaries that characterise terrorist violence.

The most dramatic and infamous attack of the Red Brigades was the kidnapping of the Italian politician, Aldo Moro, in 1978. On 16 March, Moro was abducted on his way to the Italian Parliament, and held for 55 days whilst the Red Brigades attempted to bargain his freedom for the release of their members in prison. Arguably, his captors always intended to kill Moro, but the refusal of the Italian Government to negotiate for Moro's release was the ostensive reason for his death on 9 May 1978. Paradoxically, this successful operation (in their own terms) probably heralded the eventual decline of the organisation. The Italian State was galvanised into action, and dissent within the revolutionary left wing movements about the appropriateness of Moro's murder led to increasing fragmentation. Steadily, Red Brigades activists began increasingly to be apprehended successfully by the Italian security forces, removing those early members who helped to shape the organisational and ideological bases of the movement. Whilst initially this seemed to have little effect on the level of terrorist violence, fragmentation and dissent grew within the ranks of the Red Brigades. By 1983, that dissent had resulted in defection and arrest to such an extent that the organisation had lost much of its moral authority amongst the radical left. In 1984, and again in 1985, the Red Brigades were reorganised, but the result of this was the emergence of two competing factions. These proved relatively ineffective, however.

As with the RAF, the RB had a large intellectual membership. Their working class aspirations did attract into the movement young workers, but their appeal seems to have been much greater amongst students and professionals, especially teachers; this was especially the case amongst those who emerged in leadership roles. The organisation adopted a frankly Marxist-Leninist position, and attracted a large number of passive supporters in addition to its activist membership. Its more prominent early leaders were Renato Curcio, who was imprisoned in 1976, Margharita Cagol who was killed in 1975 and

Alberto Franceschini, its chief ideologue, who was captured in 1974 and who in 1993 was still in prison. Unlike the RAF, ex-activists agree that the RB as such no longer exists in its original form as a terrorist organisation, although intellectual support for its aspirations remain. As with the RAF, the Red Brigades failed to mobilise the working class support they claimed to represent, and through their process of confrontation with the government, alienated other extraparliamentary opposition groups. Nevertheless, the name of the Red Brigades continues to emerge from time to time associated with violent protest. Several attacks during the late 1980's, for example, have been claimed by the Red Brigades. If it does exist at all, it seems likely that this contemporary organisation is a pale shadow of its earlier namesake lacking any structured ideological base from which to justify its violence.

In something so varied as terrorism, it is of course impossible to identify a 'typical' member of a terrorist group. 'Leaders' may differ from 'followers', and the varied social contexts from which terrorists emerge limit the extent to which generalisations can be made. It is possible, however, to identify some general qualities, and in Chapter 4 we discussed some of the distinctive qualities of Irish terrorism. The underlying ordinariness and rationality of the people involved, for example, is undoubtedly shared by the European terrorist. But some of the qualities of the Irish terrorist would not so readily be found in Europe.

In terms of broad generalisations, a conventional distinction is often made between the working class origins of most Irish terrorists, compared to the more middle class or intellectual origins of European ones. A further dichotomy is often identified in terms of nationalist vs ideological aspirations. This dichotomy is clearly recognised by European terrorists themselves '. . . *the IRA was a nationalist movement; we were Marxist-Leninist; we were on two opposite sides . . . We never had contacts with ETA for example, because it was another nationalist movement. We had contacts with French and German movements because they were more similar to us in ideology. To me the IRA could very well have been a fascist movement, at least to judge it with the same mentality I had then . . .'* A further distinction can be made at a social and psychological level in terms of the nature of the lives lived by individual terrorists. This is apparent from the relative ease with which Irish terrorists can remain part of their community, compared with the rigorous demands of clandestine living experienced by the European terrorist. This, in turn, has important implications in the extent to which the terrorist remains sensitive to the community which he claims to represent.

Alberto Franceschini

In what follows we will now examine in greater detail an individual who was involved in European terrorism – the prominent Italian Red Brigadist leader, Alberto Franceschini, not as a representative of European terrorism, but as someone who will help to illustrate some of the forces that influenced a whole generation of Europeans to adopt a violent route to the resolution of political problems. The social forces which characterised the 1960's are reflected in Alberto Franseschini's life, and his account gives a tangible sense of how these were experienced. The following is based on an extensive and lengthy interview with Franceschini, which followed the framework of the structured interviews referred to earlier[1] which has been used with a number of Irish terrorists.

Alberto Franceschini was interviewed in 1991, in the offices of a prisoners' publication where he works on day release from prison. He is small, stockily built and looks quite muscular. The sharp features of his face are emphasised by gold metal glasses. He was at that time 44 years old, having been in prison for 17 years. His resilience and general demeanour belied the extraordinarily long prison sentence he had already served; he was alert, articulate and aware of events. He showed no signs at all of the institutionalisation that might be expected in so long serving a prisoner.

He was born on 26 October 1947 '. . . *in Reggio Emilia. My father used to be a [trade union employee], my mother was a housewife. It was a normal family; not too poor, but not rich either. It was the average worker's family* . . .' The Franceschini family were in one sense unusual, however, in that both his father and grandfather were heavily involved in the communist movement. Of his immediate family, his grandfather in particular seems to have been a significant figure in the young Alberto's political development. With evident pride, he recalls his grandfather fought ' . . . *as a partisan during the 40's against the Nazis. But before that, he spent about 10 years in jail, during fascism. He was in fact one of the first founders of the communist party . . . to me he was a fascinating figure, because of his adventurous life . . . he used to talk about it quite often . . . maybe in a romantic fashion*'.

'*It wasn't a religious family at all . . . well, my mother was mildly Roman Catholic . . . There was an atmosphere of atheism . . . my father and grandfather were not religious in any way. They even discouraged me from going to church. They were atheists. They used to practise the so called "militant atheism." . . . to me communism was like a religion. . . . I learnt politics from them. For my parents my interests and involvement in politics was a fundamental part of life.*'

His father and grandfather were both involved in left wing political activity, and this seems to have laid the foundations for much of Franceschini's later life. '*Politics for me was the world I used to live in because we used to live near the Trade Union Office where my grandfather used to work. In fact our apartment was part of the same building. My father used to work there as well as a clerk.*'

A childhood anecdote reflects this linkage between the family situation and politics: '*When I was 4 or 5 . . . in fact I wasn't going to school yet and it was about 1952 or 1953 . . . the military police occupied the building where the Trade Unions were and where we were living as well. We had an apartment there. The fall of fascism in Emilia Romagna happened before the Americans arrived. People occupied all the houses and buildings built by the Fascist regime. In some of the buildings the Communist Party and the Trade Unions set up offices and the office of the Trade Union was in the same building where we used to live. That building was the original site of the Fascist Party. During the year of 1950 or 1951 a minister whose name was Scielba issued a law which stated that these buildings had to revert to the State. Therefore those living or occupying those houses or buildings were charged with unlawful possession. So the minister sent the military police (they were called Scielbini or 'soldiers of Scielba' after the minister!) to get people out of the buildings and out of the Trade Union offices. And I remember that all the clerks and staff locked themselves inside the offices and they occupied the building to resist the police. Can you imagine a child in the middle of all that chaos? We had to move, anyway, afterwards. Then, the Trade Union bought a new building where we went to live.*'

This political commitment was also evident quite early in his school life and colours his accounts of that time. But school is remembered as a happy time, and young Alberto seems to have been popular with his classmates. This is a significant point, for as we will see later, the friendships formed then remained and became significant in his early development into terrorism. '*I was one of the few communists in the school . . . in a way, I was a leader in negative, the leader of a minority. It was a school for people who had money, although it wasn't private . . . for those who wanted to enter those schools there was still an entrance examination in order to guarantee the quality of the student and certainly their social level. The number of students that belonged "to the working class" was very low in my school . . . I remember that we used to have a "representative organisation" for the students . . . one person from each list of students was elected as representative . . . I was head of our list . . . I had already started politics in school*'.

The ambitions of the young Alberto do not seem to have been directed towards academic success as such. But Alberto clearly was not lacking in aspiration. '*To me school was something useful. I never had the ambition to be first in the class. I only wanted not to fail and, most of all, to get out of it what I was interested in most . . . There were a few subjects l was interested in most of all . . . philosophy and mathematics.'*

He went to the University of Palma, and then Bologna, to study engineering until 1968, when he left University without completing his degree to devote himself full-time to political activity. The influence of his father and his general family background seems to have coloured the initial choices he made at University. '*My choice was conditioned by my passion for mathematics and scientific subjects. I think it was my father who drove me towards engineering, because he was a worker in a factory. Therefore to him the engineer was a self-actualised person, a person who had everything – a good job, money and power. He always taught me that there couldn't be a better job . . . I came to a point that for me engineering studies were too hard though. It was a very heavy and tiresome kind of study'.*

The catalyst that seems to have prompted Franceschini to leave University was the beginning of student protest in Italy during 1968. '*When everything started I gave up studies, I did my last exam in 1967. Until then things were very quiet here in Italy. It wasn't like America where movements and chaos began in 1963–64. Here everything began in 1968. When the student's movement began, I stopped doing exams'.*

The significance of the early political commitment he showed at school, the friends he made at that time, and the sense in which politics and friendships were bound together and permeated his early life becomes at this point even more evident. '*. . . Friendship has always been I'd say a fundamental thing, in fact most of those people that organised the Red Brigades with me were friends of mine. This was the so-called "Apartment Group" of Reggio Emilia[2] . . . we were about 7 or 8, all from the same suburb of Reggio: and we knew each other since we were 10 or 12 . . . to me politics meant being together with the others, with people you liked . . . To me politics had the value of being together. It was the reason for being together.'*

Franceschini and his friends learned of events in the world in the normal way through newspapers, radio and television. But the significant element in his *understanding* of those events was his ideological commitment '*. . . our great informer was the Communist Party. Being all communists we used to meet everybody within the Party, and that was our main source of information.'* Friendship, community and politics – these totally dominated his life from the formation of the Apartment Group to his capture in 1974. '*. . . I would never have made certain choices without this group of friends. . . . I was certainly one of the most sensitive . . . [to the international dimension of their protest] . . . but it was something that was growing in a collective spirit anyway . . . Nearly all our friendships during those years were progressively limited to the group'*

The political origins of what emerged as the Red Brigades were firmly Marxist-Leninist. Their aim was '*. . . to educate, organise and encourage the working classes to throw off the oppressive rule of*

capitalism by an armed proletarian revolution'. Throughout its existence, the Red Brigades held to those broad objectives, and it is in the
failure to achieve them that we can see the reasons for the eventual
decline and ultimate defeat of the movement. Alberto Franceschini
became the chief ideologue of the Red Brigades.

The choice to follow violence and terrorism (the '*lotta armata*')
emerged during the occupation of Bologna University. Not only was
the occupation a major act of defiance, but it also resulted in significant changes in Alberto's life style. '*From April to June we wouldn't
allow anyone to do exams . . . during the three months of occupation, I
always stayed in Bologna at the University . . . the relationship with my family and friends was much more distant. I also changed friendship. . . . And
that was the time I started changing my life. After the occupation I missed a
whole session of exams, and I felt there was something profoundly changed in
my life. Another decisive event during that period was the bombing of the
Piazza Fontana[3], an event of very strong emotional impact.*'

'*The thing about the occupation of the University was my own existential
moment that started changing my life. Before the occupation in fact I used to
dress with a suit and tie like all other students of engineering . . . After the
occupation I had long hair and a beard and I started dressing cheap; we used
to wear blue jeans and some sort of Eskimo coat that we bought at the second-
hand American market.*'

'*. . . it represented a fundamental change in my way of living. To live away
from the family . . . for instance. We were about a hundred students occupying the university. We used to live together and we also used to sleep together
with no distinction between boys and girls, although there were few girls who
were allowed by their families to spend the nights out. And for those years in
Italy, it was quite an unusual thing . . .*'

This change of life style, and all that went with it, was a significant
factor in Alberto's breaking from society. Up to this point, he had
lived at home, and it is quite clear from his account that his family
continued to exercise considerable influence on him. Contact with
his parents in later life, especially during imprisonment, seems to
have been important to him. The reference to clothes and long hair
are, in their context, the significant outward signs of his social break
from his early background. Alberto's experiences echo those of an
earlier German terrorist, Michael Baumann, founder of the West
German terrorist group the '2nd of June Movement'. Baumann left
his job as an apprentice because he couldn't face the monotony of it.
'*I did all sorts of shit jobs until around 1965 when my story began to be not
so conformist any more. Actually, with me it all began with rock music and
long hair*'. Clothes and hair were the outward sign of rebellion, the
symbol of rejection of the bourgeois society.

The occupation of the University can be clearly seen, therefore, as a critical personal event for Franceschini. The images of that time, the sense of community and shared purpose recur in Franceschini's reflections of the *positive* qualities of his life as a terrorist. In his later terrorist career, he seems to have looked back on this time as one of especial significance, and it seems to have provided a model against which he judged his later life. He describes the significance of this time as the 'existential moment', and he and his group tried to recreate that moment after the ending of the Bologna University occupation. Before the forming of the Red Brigades, the group moved to Milan, and went through a transition period of some 7 to 8 months where they tried to recapture the existential significance of the University occupation. *'Before starting the clandestinity, the first thing we did was to form "le comuni", as we used to call them. We were two groups of people and we rented two houses in Milan where we lived together'*

Allied to this, and at around the same time was a further breaking away from orthodoxy when he left the Communist Party. This break was of primary *political* significance, as distinct from the *social* break occasioned by the occupation of the University of Bologna. More than anything else, it made possible the development of the armed struggle. The Communist Party provided a facilitating ideological environment for the aspirant revolutionaries, but it also exercised control and restraints on its members. As far as Franceschini was concerned, this control limited the nature and extent of violent protest, and it was this more than anything else that led to the Franceschini group splitting from the Communist Party of Italy. *'. . . we were realising step by step that our aspirations and ways of thinking were totally opposite from the Party's policy. For instance, on the issues of the war in Vietnam and Che Guevara we had a certain position that was different from the Party's. For instance, remember that they always had a poor opinion of Che Guevara, he didn't represent much to them. This disagreement then became progressively more and more profound, because the Communist Party to us were always more pacifist and reformist, whereas we wanted to make revolution!'*

'. . . it was a gradual process, but the moment and the excuse came with one of these demonstrations. It was in 1969 that we officially went out of the PCI because it was the year of the renegotiation of the "Atlantic Pact", when the membership of Italy to NATO had to be renewed. The PCI itself was against this renewal, but said that we had to demonstrate peacefully. On the other hand, we were of the opinion that we should have assaulted the NATO bases in Italy, we wanted to react violently – such things were already happening in Germany and other places. We belonged to the Communist Youth Federation, and the Federation organised a demonstration against one of the NATO bases located in Rimini, a military airport. The first great crash happened with the PCI because we wanted to assault the base! . . . there were about three hundred

people with us . . . that demonstration was the excuse and the occasion to leave the Party.'

'*The explosion of the bombs in the Piazza Fontana was another decisive political event that drove us towards certain conclusions. Some people thought it was the comrades who put the bombs. We thought it was the State, and that there were fascist forces in Italy that wanted to make a coup; so we started wondering if it was not just a matter of words and discussions concerning the revolution; we thought it was better to put our hands on our guns.'*

As Franceschini's engagement with violence increased, and as the Red Brigades became more involved in lethal actions, so it became necessary to adopt a clandestine life style. The heady days of the University occupation and mass protest changed to the more constrained but dangerous routine of the wanted terrorist. The Red Brigades developed a sophisticated cell structure, which limited the possibilities of exposure through arrested members who might talk, or through infiltration by informants. But the cell structure also has the effect of further isolating the activist, diminishing the range of contacts he might have with his fellow terrorists in other cells. '*. . . there was the problem of clandestinity and the division of the groups. We always used to try to find the time when we could live together. For instance there was a place called "La Cascina Spiotta Dove Morta Mare" . . . that was a place where from time to time we used to meet and eat together even against the rules of clandestinity'*

'*The rules of clandestinity had an extremely depressing effect on each of us I believe. The clandestinity reduced naturally the quality of our lives. It was an ugly living, it wasn't a nice life. We accepted it . . . I don't remember it as a period of my life when I learned something. I see it as a time of my life when I lost something, because the type of life I lived was ugly and extremely poor . . . even if I saw fifty people in a day, I was always on my own . . . it was a very solitary life.'*

At one level, living a clandestine life diminished the quality of his life. On the other hand, one striking feature of his discussion of his terrorist life during this period is the sense of personal agency he felt. He felt himself to be in control – not only of himself, but also of the political climate of Italy at that time. The actions of the Red Brigades commanded immense media attention, and there was indeed a sense in which he personally was in control of events. This, allied to the sense of common bond that emerged between the members of the group transcended the negative features of a clandestine life, and resulted in an intense sense of camaraderie and sharing between the group members. It seemed to him that the ideological and political objectives of the movement were almost attainable through their continuing actions.

'*My distinct feeling was that I was really making a deep mark on the*

*reality of the country, and this sensation was given to me by the newspapers
and magazines, through the mass media. When you do certain things, and
these things turn into big paragraphs in the papers; and when you see that
because of the things you explode, fights and chaos happens between the politicians; all this summed up gave me a sensation of great power. It gives you the
feeling of being powerful.'*

'*It ended at the end of the '70's. I realised at a certain stage that all this
sensation of power that I felt was some sort of delirium, that it was ephemeral.
At a certain stage you realise that probably it wasn't you who guided the game,
that there must have been somebody else that guided the game for you! . . . You
feel you have been cheated by someone. At that stage you understand, and you
don't feel powerful any more*'.

On the 8 September 1974, Franceschini's direct involvement with
the Red Brigade struggle changed. Renato Curcio[4] and Franceschini
agreed to a meeting with an ex-priest, Silvano Girrotto. Girrotto had
a reputation for revolutionary activity in Bolivia and had indicated a
desire to join the Red Brigades. Girrotto was known in Bolivia as
'Father Machine-gun'; but he was in reality a police collaborator, and
acted as the bait in a trap set by the security forces. Both Curcio and
Franceschini were captured after putting up only a token resistance.
'*This was the biggest trauma of my whole life. After living a clandestine life for
four years I entered such a state of mind that thought I was uncatchable. Four
years is a long time . . . and you always think it happens to others and not
yourself. When it happens it is a trauma. I was astonished . . .*'

After his capture, and subsequent trial, Alberto Franceschini's
career as an active terrorist in one sense came to an end. He, and
thirteen other Red Brigadists and other left wing activists were eventually found guilty of eight murders, and were sentenced to three life
sentences plus 172 years of prison. Franceschini received a life sentence. But in another sense imprisonment merely meant a shifting of
the arena of conflict, rather than a withdrawal from conflict.

The arrest of many of the early leadership did not diminish the
activities of the Red Brigades. New leaders emerged, who sought to
carry on the struggle. One such leader was Giovanni Senzani. Under
the leadership of Senzani, a new avenue of struggle was opened
through a process of engaging the prisons in the political protest (the
Fronte delle Carceri). Senzani was a criminologist of some distinction,
and he recognised the potential within the prison system for effecting
further political protest. The Moro kidnapping in one sense heralds
this development, in that one of its ostensive purposes was the release
of prisoners. But more significant origins to this development can be
seen in the conditions of the prisons themselves. In 1977, a series of
top security prisons were created to house the increasing flood of Red
Brigade members. Conditions in the prisons steadily deteriorated,

giving rise to considerable tension amongst the prisoners. The deteriorating conditions both motivated the inmates, and provided a propaganda focus around which protest could be organised and legitimised. Franceschini was involved in a number of, at times, audacious protests within the prison system, which resulted in ever increasing sentences for him. In terms of the effects on Alberto Franceschini, however, the most significant protest which occurred in this period, and which marked a further turning point in his political development, was the hunger strike.

The Red Brigade hunger strike took place in the autumn and winter of 1983.

The Irish experience of hunger striking was very evident in the thinking of the seven hunger strikers, including Franceschini. '*I said that in my opinion we should have followed their example. Of course, we as opposed to the Irish had different reasons to do it. Basically it was because we did not like our conditions in jail, and we could not resist . . . This was our protest . . . Therefore we started discussing the possibility of hunger strike. I decided that I was going to bring the thing to its extreme conclusion.*'

'*I never wanted to die . . . I always hoped not to die. I did not want to play the part of the martyr either. I wanted to live. In fact I remember we sent a letter to a newspaper where we said our protest was a fight for life. We were talking about life not death . . . One day, I remember I got really scared because I looked at myself and I had a vision, I recalled the picture of Olgar Meinz, who had been a prisoner from the RAF, who died of hunger strike in prison. There was a photo which was going around in Italy at the end he '70's which showed his body. He was a very tall and thin comrade, after the autopsy was made. And all you could see practically was this skeleton, he was incredibly thin, with an enormous beard and the cut which was sewed up. And I remember one evening when 1 looked at myself like that, I had the vision of the image in that photograph of the comrade . . . and I had the impression that I was like that. That was a moment of heartache, nearly of terror, the only one. It was about 10 days after we had started the hunger strike.*'

The hunger strike seems to have started in a real sense of despair with the prison conditions, and frustration with the prisoners' inability to effect any change. Drawing on the Irish experience, however, showed how a well-managed protest could turn defeat and subjection into victory. '*You start from desperation and defeat, then slowly it turns into peaceful inner serenity. I remember exactly a feeling of great tranquillity and serenity. At a certain stage, you're afraid of nothing.*'

'*We were quite sure of what we were doing because after all this time we weren't asking for the revolution or communism or all that stuff. We were only asking for banal things such as spending more time outside, permission to see our parents more often . . . In fact then you could only meet and talk to other people through thick glass, so we did not want this glass. Therefore I never*

really felt a martyr. We knew we could have won, we could have obtained pos-
itive results. But I was also determined to keep going to the end.'

'*The real difference between us and the Irish was that until that moment we*
had always protested in a violent way. We nearly destroyed the prison twice,
and twice it was rebuilt always more carelessly. So our conditions didn't
improve at all, they even got worse each time. Therefore we realised that destroy-
ing the prison was no use and that we were going against our own interests.
The problem was to find a form of peaceful protest that could not have been
manipulated politically, to claim rights not just for ourselves, for political pris-
oners, but also for all other prisoners . . . because in the 'special prisons' there
weren't just the terrorists, but also for all the other prisoners. And this was the
real difference . . . the Irish did the protest just for the benefit of IRA members'.

Their hunger strike served its purpose, and attracted wide support
outside the prisons amongst influential political and church leaders.
The Bishop of Nuoro in Sardinia for example, where the prison was
located, even cancelled Christmas mass in protest at the conditions
the prisoners were enduring. The hunger strike lasted some five
weeks, after which the prison authorities relented and promised
improvements in conditions.

Prison life undoubtedly changed Alberto Franceschini, and forced
him to re-evaluate his position. But events in the world outside also
played a part in his movement away from violence. He himself dates
the beginning of his change in the way he thought about violence
from 1980. At that time, there were lay-offs of 23,000 workers from
the Fiat factories in Turin. Instead of reacting with violence to this,
however, the workers accepted compensation, and turned towards
minor forms of capitalism by opening shops and small businesses
with their compensation money. The dream of a proletarian world
without capitalism seemed to turn cruelly to a reality of increasing
capitalism amongst the workers. Franceschini also began increasingly
to feel that the Red Brigades had been used by the workers to fight
battles they themselves would not undertake; and with this came the
realisation that the Red Brigades had not been 'leading the fight' at
all, but had in reality been used. '. . . *You feel that you've been cheated by*
someone' captures the sense of disappointment and betrayal he felt.

The process of re-evaluation of his former life eventually led
Alberto Franceschini to became a '*dissociato*'. Amongst the responses
of the Italian State to terrorism, two innovative laws, (discussed more
fully on page 156) were enacted to encourage voluntary collaboration with the authorities, and help in the renunciation of terrorism
and violence. The first, enacted in May 1982 was the Penitence Law.
In return for a reduction in sentence, the '*pentito*' had to both make
a full confession of all crimes committed, and make a contribution to
the prevention of further acts of terrorism through collaboration

with the authorities. The second, enacted in March 1987, was the Dissociation Law. To benefit from this law, the convicted terrorist had one month from the appearance of the law on the statutes to confess all his or her terrorist activities, formally abjure from violence as a form of political struggle, and demonstrate in prison behaviour consistent with a renunciation of violence. Both these laws have made a significant contribution to the Italian State's capacity to deal with its terrorist problem, although they have given rise to considerable moral and legal disputes about their appropriateness and legitimacy.

Unlike the '*pentiti*', the '*dissociato*' only makes a personal assumption of responsibility for his previous life. But for Franceschini, this step was the critical and significant moral point in his movement away from terrorism. It marked in a sense a very personal admission of defeat, from a life where he felt himself in the leadership of the political revolution to one of acknowledging error and mistakes.

Other Red Brigade members have found the step to '*dissociato*', or even '*pentiti*' less traumatic and significant than Franceschini. Whilst the fire of commitment still burns for Franceschini, it no longer is evident in political activism. '. . . *today's politics in Italy do not arouse any enthusiasm; they are not politics made with ideals or with things that might be particularly involving . . . I personally live today's politics as an observer. There's nothing interesting in them. Politics for me was a great passion, therefore it was good whilst there was strong feeling. Otherwise I don't know what to do with politics. . . . For me politics are an ethical commitment*'

Franceschini made a number of poignant reflections on his life of political violence, that extend beyond the circumstances of his own life. He is an articulate and intelligent man, who has reflected on his own state through a series of traumatic changes. '*I became a terrorist because my life had been too normal and plain. I did not become a terrorist because something traumatic happened, but because I was looking for something traumatic. I know that people think if somebody becomes a terrorist probably that person must have experienced something strange. For me that did not happen.*'

Reflections on his life reveals the personal trauma of his failure, and also the way in which he has adjusted to this. '*The thing I'm least proud of is to have chosen violence and terrorism (the lotta armata), because it is the most stupid way to face certain problems, talking rationally. The worst and most stupid idiot way. Everything that to me was culturally important and prominent in my life happened before I made the choice of the "lotta armata". When I think back to those years, I realise that they took a lot out of me, they didn't give me anything; they did not enrich; they were years when I consumed what I had before.*'

'. . . *it's hard for me to say I'm proud of something because of the way the story ended. It really ended in the worst way possible, so it's difficult to be proud of something that ends tragically. But I've got to say . . . I feel proud of myself again. Even in the middle of all this chaos, I didn't lose my self esteem, I mean that despite the disaster of everything I do not have a low esteem of myself . . . because I'm sure I always did the right things ethically, at least from my point of view. I could have been completely wrong, but I did everything in good faith. In other words, I absolve myself from an ethical point of view!'*

 'My good faith is what makes me keep my self esteem: even if now I reckon I did a lot of bullshit, then I did it convinced that I was doing good things. I did not do anything with a second aim. If I'd done some terroristic acts for money I could not keep my self respect . . .'

The strength of his own self respect contrasts with his views of those who have, in his own terms, betrayed the cause, especially those who acted as informants, the *'pentiti'*. *' . . . amongst those [ex Red Brigades members . . .] I met again, the ones who seem to have little respect are the pentiti, I think. . . . there's one of them that I knew vaguely . . . I know that one of them became a drug addict; now he lives in a community for drug addicts, trying to detoxicate himself . . . From the stories I hear anyway, certainly the pentiti are those left with little self esteem, because they sold themselves and did things which were against their own code of moral rules and belief.*

After a long and varied, and perhaps tragic, career in terrorism and political protest, Franceschini can claim in his own terms to have retained his own personal integrity. Is this more than the use of clichés that we have encountered earlier? Perhaps so, but at least Franceschini appears to believe in his own rationalisation, which he expressed with frankness and confidence. It seems that this, more than anything else, has enabled him to withstand the pressures of 17 years of unremitting imprisonment with so little overt effect. If this is so, it seems that this may be all that he has left after so great an investment.

Indeed, there is a very real sense in which Franceschini's account of his life is tragic. He has undoubtedly retained his self-esteem, and this is no doubt related to the original strength of the ideological commitment he had. But by remaining true to his principles, by engaging in the struggle whilst in prison after his arrest, he had effectively enormously increased the duration of his sentence. It may be a testimony to his strength of character, or it may be a reflection of the strength and rigidity of the control ideology exercised over him. More positively, this may account for his lack of institutionalisation, but he has paid a heavy price for this.

* * *

Both the RAF and the Red Brigades created relatively sophisticated structures to control their activities. Both also required of necessity those members actively involved in violence to adopt clandestine lifestyles. Both organisations were initially in their own terms very successful, and both undoubtedly felt that during the late 1970's, they were within sight of attaining their objectives. Their organisational structures created a world which shaped and conditioned the lives of active members. But whilst providing security and apparent success, these structures restricted movement and social interaction and in a sense contained the seed of their own decline.

Franceschini illustrates the tensions and necessary paradoxes this produces in the individual. The essence of violence for the individual who commits a violent act is the immediacy of response. Exploding a bomb, or killing an individual immediately attracts media attention. Indeed, it can even be suggested that there is a simple equation relating size of damage to media effect; the greater the damage, the greater the media impact. However illusory it may prove in the long run, violence gives to the perpetrator a sense of personal agency, which when allied to strong ideological commitment results in a very powerful self-sustaining psychological force. The effects of bombings or shootings are necessarily traumatic, and when the fermentation of social trauma is a fundamentally important ideological weapon, a vicious circle of regenerative conditions are created which become very resistant to other influences.

As we saw in the case of Joe Doherty in Chapter 4, an interesting quality of many of those interviewed in the Irish context is a disregard for the *individual* victim. This same disregard emerges amongst the German and Italian terrorists. Such residual empathy the terrorist might feel for the victim of his attacks seems to be overlaid, or at least diminished, by the immediate effectiveness of violence in capturing media attention.

All of this takes place within an intensely narrow social context. Illegality and clandestine living necessarily limits the extent of social interaction available to the individual, forcing social contact with others sharing the same dangers and holding the same views. Given this, challenges to their views are therefore rare and limited. Indeed, in the intense world of the clandestine terrorist, any challenges may well be perceived as traitorous, calling into question the sacrifices made by comrades. Democratic involvement and collective decision making, which was a quality of decision making within the Red Brigades, as with other radical left wing groups, offers no balance against these effects. Indeed, we know from Social Psychological evidence that group decision making in these circumstances can tend towards a group collectively adopting even more extreme decisions than originally held by members.

This way of living produces profound psychological effects. It isolates the individual from normal social pressures and constraints, allowing the boundaries of appropriateness of behaviour to become blurred. The success of violent action, mediated by media coverage, becomes amplified, further diminishing the boundaries to behaviour. Allied to this, the sense of imminent attainment of ideological goals further drives the individual ever onwards. A self-sustaining cycle becomes established which is largely impervious to the world outside, fuelled by the inflexibility of an ideology almost attained.

The unpleasantness of clandestine living is clearly expressed by Franceschini. But so is the sense of personal agency he felt. The significant factor which sets the balance in favour of continuing engagement in violence in this complex situation is ideological commitment. This provides the direction, focus, goals and consequences to behaviour that result in continuing engagement in terrorism.

Penal Policy

In both the German and Italian situation, probably the single effective factor that has significantly affected the long term reduction in terrorist violence lies not in high profile security force operations against active terrorist groups, but in the policy adopted with convicted terrorists. In both countries, initiatives addressed at the level of penal policy seem to have materially contributed to the reduction in terrorist activity. Especially in the Italian situation, the 1982 Penitence Law (law 304 – 'Measures in defence of the constitutional order') and the 1987 Dissociation Law (law 34 – 'Measures in favour of those who dissociate themselves from terrorism'), as we have just seen, created a situation in which convicted terrorists could gain material benefits, in terms of reduction of sentence, for example, through cooperation with the authorities and the provision of information (in the case of the *pentiti*). These laws are probably unique in the Western World.

Under the Penitence law, for crimes committed prior to 31 January 1982, for a period of 120 days penitent terrorists could enjoy effective amnesty. For terrorists who prior to final sentencing would confess their crimes and dissociate themselves from violence and their companions, sentences were substantially reduced. For those who in addition provided information which led to decisive proof of identity or capture of terrorists, further reductions in sentence were available. In many cases, the dispensations were such that provisional liberty became available, subject to a judge's discretion and opinion that the ex-terrorist no longer presented a danger to the State. This law effectively depenalized serious terrorist crime through offering incentives to terrorists to accept their defeat, admit their guilt and inform on others so that the dangers of terrorist violence could be diminished. The strict focusing of this law on terrorism can be seen by the fact that significantly, these dispensations were only available in the case of political crimes.

The 1987 Dissociation Law offered less incentive to those who benefitted from it, but it also required less of them. It applied to those who had 'definitively abandoned the organisation, the terrorist or subversive movement to which they belonged', who engaged in behaviour which was incompatible with such membership, and 'who repudiated violence as a method of political struggle.' Franceschini has benefitted from this law, and its significance in his case is that it does not compromise his own view of himself as a 'moral' person. By not insisting on his acting as an informant, the State has enabled Franceschini to formally step away from violence, whilst retaining what he describes as his 'self respect'.

The German authorities have made use of somewhat similar provision under Article 57 of the West German Penal Code, rather than enacting special legislation as such. The provisions of this Article offers the possibility of reduction of sentence or suspension or deferment of sentence when convicted terrorists renounce terrorism. Dierk-Ferdinand Hoff, for example, a notorious bomb maker in the early years of the RAF, served only half his sentence; Norbert Kröcher, Horst Mahler, Heinz Dellwo, Gerold Klöpper, Till Meyer, Siegfried Haag and Manfred Distelrat all served two thirds of their sentence; and, of course, Christoph Wagernagel and Gert Schneider received premature release.

The effect of these laws has been to diminish significantly the capacity of both the RAF and the Red Brigades to struggle. In both countries, individuals have been both given the opportunity publicly to renounce their involvement in violence, and to benefit from that renunciation. Significantly, it does not require the terrorist to renounce ideological commitment, but only a commitment to violence to achieve ideological ends. The effect of this is probably enough in itself, but in some cases the State has gained further benefit by the actions of informants, who have collaborated with the authorities in apprehending their ex-colleagues, thereby also renouncing their ideological commitment. Not all convicted terrorists in either Germany or Italy have wished to avail themselves of these legal provisions, however. In Italy, for example, there is a group of convicted terrorists termed the '*irriducibili*', who have refused to collaborate with the authorities in any way. They continue to occupy the role of moral and political authority which the early Red Brigade leadership held.

Approaches along these lines have not been particularly explored within the context of Northern Ireland. There was a period of what were termed the 'supergrass' trials, which were extensive trials based on the evidence of informants, but these became largely discredited because of dependence in the trials on uncorroborated evidence of the informer. A category of prisoner equivalent to the '*dissociato*' does not exist in any formal sense, although presumably decisions about parole might, in a sense, reflect similar kinds of evidence. What is lacking, however, in the Northern Ireland setting is a mechanism that allows of formal renunciation of terrorism.

It is difficult to judge whether such a mechanism would have any effect in Northern Ireland. An important difference may lie in the close relationship between the various Northern Irish communities and their paramilitary groups, in contrast to the much looser relationship between the German and Italian terrorist groups and their ostensive communities, and the ideological origins of the various groups. Whilst nationalism is in one sense an ideology, it has distinctive features which bind the adherent closely to a particular and specific community. Political ideology, in contrast, equally binds the individual to a community, but one which is more conceptual, rather than geographical. For the nationalist, the consequences in terms of exclusion from the community which might follow from a renunciation of its ideals (as expressed by its paramilitary groupings) are likely to be much more severe than in the case of the political terrorist.

In fact, experience in Italy does largely confirm this view. Whilst not in any accepted sense a political movement, the Italian Mafia has many qualities in common with nationalist political movements. In particular, in a psychological sense, the way in which it permeates its own geographical areas seems to be significant. It is worth noting that attempts to apply penal provisions somewhat similar to the Penitence and Dissociation laws to convicted Mafiosa have largely failed, in particular with respect to the emergence of informants. An example of this can be seen with respect to the incidence of ransom-kidnappings. In Sardinia, waves of ransom-kidnapping of foreigners during the 1980's were successfully brought under control by the use of provisions like the Penitence Laws. But these laws have failed to effect a similar situation in Calabria. One reason for this may lie in the extent to which the Mafia extensively permeates Calabrian life, in contrast to the organisations' relatively small involvement in Sardinia.

On the other hand, in Chapter 4 we noted the significance for ordinary members of a terrorist organisation of the sense of 'trust' in the organisation and in the cause. The emergence of individuals who formally and publicly renounce their terrorist involvement, without necessarily renouncing their ideals and long term aspirations, has undoubtedly served to gain a sense of moral initiative for the authorities in both Germany and Italy. The quality of voluntary renunciation, as distinct from 'turning informant' is a critical distinction which appears to have never emerged, or at least never been exploited, in the situation in Northern Ireland. Informants may have an operational role, but their benefits may be short term; as we have seen in the UDA, the emergence of the double agent Brian Nelson has served to revitalise rather than diminish.

Reflections

Despite the differences in location, ideology and aspiration, the general conclusions that emerged from the earlier chapters appear relevant to this one also. The strength of community support (albeit in a narrow form in the situation of European terrorism), the exclusivity of social relationships and settings, the significance of the terrorist organisation, the illegality of actions, the militancy of ideology, and the very real sense of personal agency create the psychological context for the European terrorist just as much as the Irish terrorist in the attainment of their goals. These factors result in psychological processes which whilst they are complex, are inherently rational and coherent. When translated into behaviour, they exercise enormous control over the individual, creating and sustaining the awful forces which result in terrorist violence.

The single factor that seems to structure the lives of both European and Irish terrorists is ideology. It provides the purpose and framework in which they live, and it determines their behaviour. The terrorist contributes to the attainment of his or her objectives through the special knowledge they have, received from their ideology. Furthermore, in their view the attainment of those objectives becomes quicker through their actions. This, and this alone, seems to be the enabling factor that allows what are otherwise quite normal people to become engaged in the most barbarous acts. Charming and friendly as Alberto Franceschini was, pleasantly companionable as many Irish terrorists are, they have killed and maimed people; they have irreparably damaged the lives of individuals, their families, their children. In the next chapter, we will pursue this theme further. We will now turn to examine an example of terrorism that even in its world, stands out for its barbarity, cruelty and callousness.

6

The Ends Justify the Means: Arab and Islamic terrorism

Place names often strike a resonance, create images, form expectations. Sallynoggin, a part of Greater Dublin, seems to be such a name – a romantic and intriguing Irish name, suggesting at the least an attractive old Dublin community with pubs and old shop fronts, full of 'characters' who entertain with quick repartee and jokes over a Guinness in the bar. The reality of Sallynoggin is, regrettably, very different. It is an area of low price and public housing to the South of Dublin. In architectural style, it is typical of many areas of public housing on both sides of the Irish Sea – a settled working class community, rather run down in parts, and with a generally seedy air. It has had its fair share of trouble with vandalism and delinquency, and suffers high unemployment. For all its failings, its depressing familiarity makes it far removed from the turbulence of Islamic and Middle Eastern politics.

In a quiet close in an area of run down council property live a mother and daughter. Their lower maisonette is of undistinguished appearance, poorly maintained, with red paint peeling from the window frames. Its front door is battered, and the garden neglected. To the front, in a parking space, is their aged car. This is not a particularly bad house to live in, and many single parents live in similar or worse circumstances. The mother is pretty; dark-haired, sunburnt with freckles, but not well dressed. She and her daughter eat fish on Fridays, as do many ordinary Irish Roman Catholic families. But neither she nor her daughter are ordinary. Their story captured the world's headlines, and takes us to the very heart of one of the most chilling ever terrorist exploits.

Ann-Marie Murphy and her daughter Caoimhe live with the

terrible knowledge that Caoimhe's father deliberately conspired to kill them both with a bomb which Ann, unknowingly, attempted to carry on board an aircraft whilst she was pregnant. '*I was so in love with him. I'd never had a boyfriend before and when he said he loved me I believed him.*' Her boyfriend, the father of Caoimhe, and the man who attempted to kill Ann-Marie Murphy, his unborn daughter and some 375 passengers of an El Al Jumbo jet was Nezar Hindawi.

A Family Plot: The Hindawi's

Nezar Hindawi was born in 1954, the son of a Jordanian family who had been forced to flee to Jordan from a relatively prosperous farm in the district of Bet She'an during the troubles that accompanied the formation of the State of Israel. The family was regarded as once being wealthy, having moved in 1922 to the Trans-Jordan from Libya. Their social standing appears to have remained high, and indeed in the 1960s and 70s, two uncles were members of the Jordanian Cabinet.

Nezar Hindawi was born in the village of Baqra at the base of the Golan Heights where the family settled. Amongst his immediate family, Hindawi seems to have been close to his older brother, Hasi. In 1967, the village they lived in is said to have been attacked during the Arab–Israeli war by Israeli aircraft, and the family home razed to the ground. It is only possible to speculate on the effects of his family background on the young Nezar, but the attack on his village seems to have fuelled the already burning resentment felt by the 13-year-old boy and his brother towards the State of Israel.

Whilst Hindawi's mother, some brothers and sisters continued to live in Jordan, one brother and his father eventually moved to the United Kingdom, where they took up permanent residence. When he was 26, Nezar visited England. He enrolled on various English language courses in London, and became the London correspondent for a number of Arab journals. He may also have been employed in 1980 or '81 by the Libyan Intelligence Service, selling to the Libyan People's Bureau in London the names, addresses and car number plates of opponents to the Libyan régime living in London. Whilst attending English language classes in Kensington in 1980, he met and later married in December, Barbara, the daughter of a Polish farmer, who was also attending the language classes. After a short stay in London, they left for Poland, where Natasha, their daughter, was born in 1981. It seems that Nezar continued this relationship. Interviewed in 1986, Barbara claimed that her relationship with Hindawi had continued, but that Hindawi would disappear for long periods on his journalistic assignments, returning suddenly and often without warning.

The fateful first meeting between Ann-Marie Murphy and Nezar Hindawi occurred in late 1984. Ann-Marie Murphy was 29 when she first arrived in London from Dublin in October 1984. She lived with a friend, Theresa Leonard in Earls Court, and obtained a job as a chamber maid at the London Hilton Hotel. Ann-Marie was introduced to Nezar Hindawi by Theresa, who was friendly with a Jordanian who shared a flat with him. Nezar was described by people who knew him at that time as an arrogant and flamboyant man, who enjoyed good living. For a girl like Ann-Marie Murphy, whose experience of life extended little beyond the factory in Dublin where she had worked, Hindawi must have presented a dashing and irresistible figure. Her brief relationship with him lasted until Christmas, 1984, when Hindawi abruptly disappeared. By this time, Ann-Marie was pregnant, but by the time Hindawi re-appeared in February 1985, she had miscarried. He seems to have proposed marriage to her around this time, telling her that he was divorcing his wife in Poland. He also apparently asked her if she could put him in touch with the Provisional IRA for what he described as a journalistic interview. In the light of what we now know of Hindawi's activities at that time, this may be a revealing insight into his thinking. During this period, Hindawi was frequently absent, but shortly after he re-appeared from a long absence in November, Ann-Marie found she was pregnant again.

Ann-Marie clearly found the news of her pregnancy traumatic and difficult to deal with in view of her previous miscarriage. Eventually she told Nezar of her pregnancy. '*He was abroad at the time and had telephoned me at the Hilton. But I couldn't tell him over the phone there that I was expecting because nobody knew. I'd kept it secret because I had to keep working. I was sick every morning – I was carrying heavy Hoovers up and downstairs and lifting mattresses to change beds. . . . Anyway he gave me a number to ring him back on and I went out to a call box. I remember it was freezing cold and pouring with rain. I asked the operator where the number was and she told me it was West Berlin.*

'*I was shivering pushing 10p pieces into the slot. I told him about the baby and he just kept saying "Throw it, you don't want that, throw the baby". He told me to ring his brother who worked in an embassy in London and he'd arrange it for me. I was so confused. I didn't really know what I was doing. I had no one to talk to.*

'*I rang the brother and he said he'd make arrangements but I don't believe in abortion, it's like murder to me. Anyway I went to meet him. I told him I wouldn't do anything – I'd keep the baby myself. He seemed annoyed. I think he'd already made arrangements.*

'*Then suddenly Nezar was at the door of my flat. He said we'd marry and that everything would be alright. It was like a big weight had been lifted from*

*me. He was very tender and loving . . . He was very tender and loving and
told me of his plans to marry in the Holy Land'*.

Nezar seems to have been anxious to make the arrangements for
marriage as quickly as possible. To Ann-Marie it must have seemed
that her troubles were over. But her naivety seems with hindsight
appalling – she seems to have given little thought to the practical
issues involved, and Nezar seems to have given her little encourage-
ment to explore them. This offer of marriage occurred in April 1986.

We now know from immigration stamps in Hindawi's Jordanian
passport which we found in his brother's flat after his arrest, that during the period 1985 and 1986 Nezar Hindawi undertook extensive
journeys across Europe and the Middle East, visiting Poland (where
his wife and daughter lived), East and West Berlin, Egypt, Syria, Italy,
Bulgaria, and Rumania. It seems that these travels were related to
Hindawi's attempts, with his brother Hasi, to generate support and
funding for terrorist attacks on Israel.

Amongst other places, this effort to gather support took the brothers to Libya in late 1985, using the contacts with the Libyans that
Hindawi had already established in London. They may also have
been accompanied by a cousin, Awni Hindawi. But Colonel Gadaffi's
régime seemed to be unimpressed by them. They received some ideological instruction, but their apparent inexperience seems to have
deterred the Libyan authorities from trusting them, and all they
received was a very modest handout of US$5000, with no specific mis-
sion but a suggestion that they return when they had proved
themselves.

Undeterred, Nezar Hindawi and a further person, Farouk
Salameh, visited the Syrian capital of Damascus in January 1986,
where they were made much more welcome. They were met at the
airport by a senior Syrian Intelligence Officer, Colonel Haitham Said
of the Syrian Airforce. This in itself is some indication of how seriously the Syrians took Hindawi, and the link that he formed with the
Intelligence sections of the Syrian Airforce is itself highly significant
in subsequent developments. The Syrian Airforce, under the leadership of General Mohammed Khouli, had a long history of
sponsorship of terrorism. Khouli was at that time a close confidant of
the Syrian President, Hafez el-Assad, and Colonel Said who met the
Hindawi's is said to have been one of Khouli's most trusted aides.

Hindawi claimed to represent a terrorist cell in Europe who, in
return for cash and equipment, would make their services available
to the Syrian Government. A request of this kind to the Syrian
Government would not have seemed unusual nor was it unique. Most
Arab terrorism at this time received sponsorship from one or other of
the national Governments in the area, and in turn acted as a

surrogate for the sponsoring state, generally attacking targets that were identified by that state. Syria has a long history of using terrorist organisations to pursue through violence its foreign (and sometimes domestic) policy ends, and one of the most notable terrorists having links with Syria is Abu Nidal. Syrian embassy staff, and members of Syrian Arab Airlines were often the agents through whom the Syrian government operated to move funds and weapons to groups receiving Syrian sponsorship.

Colonel Said was impressed by Hindawi. He and Salameh appeared to have good credentials and, above all, appeared sophisticated and westernised and therefore able to move around in Western Europe without attracting much attention. Nezar's cousin, Awni Hindawi, may have played a role in facilitating his contacts with the Syrians. Awni was unusually well connected within the Arab terrorist world. Said discussed potential targets and activities with Nezar and Farouk Salameh, and showed them bomb making plans. They agreed that the Syrian authorities would contact the Hindawi's and 'activate' the organisation when the time was right.

The organisation that Nezar Hindawi claimed to represent was the Jordanian Revolutionary Movement. It seems that this organisation was formed by Nezar, his brother Hasi and Farouk Salameh, during discussions in Hasi's Berlin flat in March 1985. Nezar's cousin, Awni, was also probably involved. Nezar seems to have claimed to them that he was already a member of a terrorist organisation, and also seems to have used his modest relationship as an informer with the Libyans in London to support this claim and impress Hasi and Farouk. Both Hasi and Farouk had previous criminal records, but no known substantial terrorist associations, and they appear to have believed that Nezar was recruiting them into what they thought was the well established Jordanian Revolutionary Movement. There is no independent evidence that this organisation had existed outside Nezar's imagination and it appears likely that Nezar, up to this time, had operated only on the fringes of Arab terrorism. The first target Hasi and Farouk were 'recruited' to attack was the German–Arab Friendship Society in Beriin. Nezar was convinced that this organisation was thoroughly infiltrated by Israeli agents. It seems to have been this plan to attack the German–Arab Friendship Society that Hindawi proposed to the Libya authorities, and later more productively to Damascus.

Shortly after Nezar Hindawi and Farouk Salameh's return from Damascus, Hasi Hindawi was contacted by the Syrians. Hasi and Farouk were instructed to drive to the Syrian Embassy in East Berlin where Colonel Said was waiting to show them how to prime a suitcase bomb with which they were to attack the building of the

German–Arab Friendship Society. The bomb was smuggled into West Berlin through Checkpoint Charlie in a Syrian Diplomatic car. In early March, Hasi and Farouk attempted to detonate the bomb against an outside wall of the Offices of the German–Arab Friendship Society, but the bomb failed to explode. They tried again a week later, and again the bomb failed to detonate. This inauspicious start to the Jordanian Revolutionary Movement's career in international terrorism clearly concerned Nezar, and from London he contacted his brother Hasi to find out what was happening.

Nezar appears to have then contacted the Syrian intelligence authorities and told them that the bomb was defective, because a few days later a Syrian agent appeared at Hasi's flat in Berlin, and adjusted the wiring of the bomb to make it operational. Just after 2100 hrs on 2 March 1986, the bomb did successfully detonate outside the German-Arab Friendship Society, causing substantial damage to the building and injuring seven Arabs.

In November of that year, Hasi Hindawi and Farouk Salameh were both tried and convicted in a West Berlin Court for this bomb attack. Hasi was given a 14 year prison sentence, and Salameh received 13 years. The court also issued an international arrest warrant for a man described as a Syrian military intelligence officer, Colonel Haitham Said, who had brought the bomb into West Germany from Syria. This Said was, of course, the Hindawi's contact in Damascus. Both Hasi and Salameh confessed to the attack, and they implicated Said as the Syrian agent responsible for the provision of the bomb. They also implicated Nezar Hindawi as the man who both planned and organised the attack.

The creation and activation of the Jordanian Revolutionary Movement through the bombing of the German-Arab Friendship Society, all coincide with the time of Ann-Marie Murphy's second pregnancy and Nezar's swift offer of marriage to her. Given Nezar's central role in the bombing attack in Berlin, as events unfolded after the bombing of the German–Arab Friendship Society it becomes increasingly difficult not to see a malign and cynical manipulation of Ann-Marie Murphy into Nezar Hindawi's terrorist plans. In particular, Nezar Hindawi's hurried plans to marry Ann-Marie in '*the Holy Land*' gain new and dreadful significance, suggesting a degree of forethought and cynical manipulation of Ann-Marie.

We now know that in February, before the bomb successfully exploded in Berlin, Nezar Hindawi had made a further visit to Damascus to meet Colonel Said, this time accompanied by his cousin. Awni is thought to have had existing links with the terrorist organisation of Abu Nidal, but although he was arrested several times by the Italian authorities in 1986 and 1987, he was never charged with terrorist offences. What does seem clear, however, is that he had contact with a number of significant Syrian officials and others with connections to terrorist organisations. This visit to Damascus appears to have concerned Nezar's plan to bomb an El Al aircraft, using Ann-Marie Murphy as his unwitting accomplice to place the bomb on board in a bag. It seems likely that the target selection, and possibly the means of passing the bomb on to the aircraft, were decided by the Syrians; in any event, the target was confirmed at this meeting, and Nezar was shown the sophisticated timing device and the bomb, located in the false bottom of a bag, which was intended to destroy the aircraft.

At this time, Nezar was also given by Said a false Syrian passport in the name of Izzam Shara, which he used to return to the United Kingdom on 12 February. This passport had in it a legitimate visitor's visa to the UK issued by the British Embassy in Damascus on 11 February. Izzam Shara was described on the passport as a mechanic in the Syrian Army's supply unit. On 11 February a messenger, apparently from the Syrian Foreign Ministry, applied for the visa at the British Embassy in Damascus, a quite normal and unremarkable occurrence. The application was accompanied by a letter from the protocol department of the Syrian Foreign Ministry. In the afternoon of the 11th, the visa was processed in the normal way by local and Embassy staff, and signed by Arthur Balfour, the vice-consul. Using this passport, Nezar travelled to London. On arrival at Heathrow, Nezar Hindawi, as Izzam Shara, was passed through immigration and given a stamp in the passport authorising him to stay in the United Kingdom for six months. The value of this passport to Hindawi was that it was expected that he would use it to escape from the country after the bomb had been placed on the El Al aircraft, given that his real identity might become compromised in later investigations. Shortly after his return, Nezar Hindawi made a practice run to collect the aircraft bomb in London.

Nezar made a second trip to Syria from London at the end of March, probably accompanied by his cousin Awni and possibly by his brother Hasi, and apparently received further training in the priming and use of the bag bomb. This training reportedly took place in the Bekaa Valley in Lebanon, and was conducted by three Syrian security officials, including Said. In particular, he was shown how the priming device for the bomb was located in a pocket calculator, which was activated by the insertion of the calculator batteries. The bomb arrangement was unusual and creative; the detonator and timer disguised by the calculator were located in the body of the bag, whilst the explosives were hidden in the bag's false bottom. The detonator needed only to be placed close to the main charge to cause an explosion. This made detection of the bomb by airport X-ray machines much more difficult. Raw explosive is difficult to detect on X-ray and may not be discovered in security screening, but the tell-tale wires and batteries of the detonator are the usual sign of the presence of a bomb. As we have seen the detonator and timer in this case were hidden in a quite legitimate and normal small electrical device, a calculator.

Either on this occasion, or on his earlier visit, Nezar also received an amount of money (thought to be US$12,000 from a total 'reward' of US$250,000) from Said in payment for the planned attack on the Israeli aircraft. Hindawi also made use on this second occasion of the passport in the name of Izzam Shara to return to England. The Syrian authorities again went through the formalities to obtain the necessary visa stamp, but described Shara's occupation this time as an assistant accountant in the Syrian Foreign Ministry. Why the Syrian authorities should have done this is unclear, because it might clearly invite suspicion if the second application was checked by Embassy Officials against the first. To minimise this, it seems that the date of the visa application was deliberately timed to coincide with the absence from the Embassy of the vice-consul, Arthur Balfour, who had signed the first visa, and who might possibly have become suspicious.

As events subsequently developed, major weaknesses in the way the British Embassy worked in Damascus emerged, particularly in the management and control of the issuing of visas. It seems likely that the processing of the visa applications for the passport in the name of Izzam Shara was facilitated by a member of the Embassy's local staff who was himself a Syrian Agent. He appears to have manipulated procedures to avoid the kind of cross-checking which might have been expected to take place. After Nezar's eventual arrest, this member of the Embassy staff disappeared, taking with him records which included the visa applications and accompanying photographs for Izzam Shara. He also took a number of other records which presumably relate to people who have received visas to the United Kingdom on false passports.

Nezar's second visit to Syria ended on 5 April, when he returned to London. On his arrival, he booked into the Royal Garden Hotel with Colonel Said's brother, Ghassim Said. Both posed as crew members of Syrian Arab Airlines. The following day, 6 April, Nezar was met by another Syrian agent, Adnam Habib, who gave him the bag containing the hidden explosives and the calculator detonator. The bag contained about three and a half pounds of Semtex explosive. Nezar left the bag at his father's flat for some 10 days, and moved into the Palace Hotel, London, using the name of Izzam Shara. Another

Syrian agent then contacted Nezar through his father, and at a meeting outside the Cumberland Hotel, gave Nezar a Browning
semi-automatic pistol and two clips of ammunition.

Whilst Nezar Hindawi was engaged in the development of his
planned attack using Ann-Marie Murphy, there was a second terrorist attack in Berlin which may also have had links to Hasi Hindawi.
On 5 April 1986, a bomb was detonated in the La Belle discothèque
in West Berlin. It killed a US serviceman and a Turkish woman, and
injured some 230 people. It seems that the bomb was placed by
Christiana Endrigkeit, a drug addict and prostitute. It is likely that the
bomb was supplied to her either by Hasi Hindawi or Farouk Salameh,
who again obtained the bomb from the Syrian Embassy in East Berlin
as in the case of the attack on the German–Arab Friendship Society.
Incriminating documents were eventually found in Hasi's flat when
searched by the police, and there are similarities to the other bombs
used by the Hindawi's, in terms of the types of explosives used. Hasi
however denies involvement in this bombing.

Ann-Marie Murphy had no knowledge of all of these events. After
he returned from Damascus, Nezar Hindawi suddenly reappeared in
Ann-Marie's life, and not only proposed that he marry her but that
he should do so immediately, and that the marriage and honeymoon
should take place in Israel. Over dinner in Julie's Pantry, a cheap fast
food restaurant in Oxford Street, London, Ann-Marie agreed to
travel to her wedding in Israel on her own, as Nezar already had a
ticket to Jordan because of his journalistic work. A few days later,
Nezar took her to Superstar Travel agents in London's Regent Street,
a subsidiary of El Al. He gave her the money to buy a ticket to Tel
Aviv; he took care, however, to stay outside the travel agents so that he
could not be connected with Ann-Marie's ticket purchase.

Ann-Marie Murphy began to plan her pregnancy and her marriage in Israel to Nezar Hindawi in the short time she had left before
her departure. '*He gave me £100 to go and buy a wedding dress and he
wanted me to wear black shoes and black tights. I went to a chain store first
but I couldn't find anything. Then I saw this dress in another shop. It was
perfect. It was pale blue silky with a drop waist . . . I was really excited. I
thought it was beautiful.*

'*My passport had run out so I had to go and get another one. I remember
it was the same day that I had first seen my baby on a scan at the hospital.*

'. . . *He gave me another £100 to buy some more dresses and underwear
and then he came with a new bag for me. I remember being a bit puzzled about
him buying a new one because I had a suitcase already – but he insisted. He
wanted to pack it for me so that I wouldn't have to keep bending down and I
was pleased he cared. He insisted so I let him. He packed the bag and told me
not to touch it or go near it.*

'He didn't stay with me that night – our last night in London. I was a bit surprised but he said he had to see someone and would stay in a hotel.

'When he came for me the next morning I was ready. I'd decided to wear my wedding dress so I'd look nice for his family when I arrived. He'd told me he wouldn't be able to travel with me because he had to go to Jordan to do something for the newspaper he worked for as a journalist. Nezar insisted on caring the bag downstairs to the taxi because he thought it would be too heavy. And he'd bought me a little set of wheels so I wouldn't have to carry it at the airport.

'When we were in the taxi he seemed a bit nervous. He was smoking and it made me feel sick. But I didn't want to say anything to spoil the day. He took out a calculator which he said he'd had repaired for a friend of his over there and I was to take it with me. He put batteries in and placed it back in the bag, I think towards the bottom.'

Unbeknown to Ann-Marie, but well understood by Nezar, by putting the batteries into the calculator he had set the timer on the detonator. It was scheduled to explode exactly 5 hours, 1 minute and 1 second later, triggering the explosives hidden in the false bottom of the bag, by which time, if everything had gone to plan, Ann-Marie's flight, El Al 016 on 17 April, should have been at its cruising height of 39,000 feet somewhere over Southern Europe. The result of an explosion at such a height would have been similar in its effect to that which destroyed Pan Am flight 103 over Lockerbie in Scotland in December 1988. The 375 passengers on El Al flight 016, including Ann-Marie Murphy and her unborn child, would have been killed.

'Then we got to the airport and he put the bag on a trolley. I wanted to go to the toilet and he was annoyed. I asked someone where the Ladies' was. It was just at the top of the escalator. I said I would only be a minute but when I suddenly turned round on the stairs he was right behind me carrying the bag. I thought he was being really nice and attentive.

'When I came out we got onto one of those moving walkways and Nezar was in front of me. When we got to the end of the walkway, he kissed me on both cheeks and said "Good Bye".'

'But after he left me, I realised I was in the wrong place . . . I didn't want to take the bag with me on the plane – I wanted to put it through the luggage desk. But I went by accident through the place where you show your passports and put the bag on the security belt thing. It went right through all right but then I had to go to the El Al security desk.'

El Al security staff decided to subject the luggage to a thorough search. It seems likely that they were in a heightened state of alertness at this time as a result of a warning they had received of an attempt to blow up an El Al civilian aircraft. All the contents of the bag were removed in her presence, including the calculator, but nothing suspicious was found. A member of the El Al staff even made a simple calculation on the calculator to check that it worked, which it did. It was only when a member of staff picked up the bag to repack it that he felt it was rather heavy for an empty piece of baggage. The bag was then taken to a nearby office, and taken apart. Underneath the interior cardboard base was a flat blue plastic package measuring 16 inches by 9 inches by 3/8 inch which was shaped to the contours of the bag. On unpacking, this proved to be 3 lbs 4 oz of the Czech made high explosive Semtex. Initially, the find caused some surprise to the Security Officers because there were no detonators attached to the explosives. The role of the calculator as the timer and detonator was subsequently discovered by the bomb disposal expert called to the scene. Ann-Marie was detained by Heathrow police, and subsequently handed over to Anti-terrorist squad police officers. It was quickly established that she was the innocent dupe of Nezar Hindawi.

'*The man looked in my bag then took it away. I waited about 20 to 30 minutes, then he came and took me to a room. Two British policemen with guns and tracker dogs came in. I kept thinking "Oh my God what is it?". Then one of them showed me a brown taped parcel and asked if I knew what it was. I said I'd never seen it before. I was sobbing. One of them told me the parcel contained . . . explosive. My world fell apart.*

'*I thought: "Oh my God, he wanted to kill me and the baby. He wanted to get rid of us."*

'*It didn't enter my head at that time that all those other people would have died. The officers took me to another room and told me to take everything off. It was terrible, awful . . . They cut a piece of my hair and scraped under my nails. They gave me a white paper boiler suit to put on. Then they handcuffed me and led me through Heathrow to a police car and took me to Paddington Green Police Station.*

'*They put me in a cell and kept asking what I knew about politics and where I'd met Nezar . . . I'll never get over what he tried to do.*'

Whilst this was happening to Ann-Marie, Nezar Hindawi following a pre-defined plan, returned to the Palace Hotel, collected his luggage and went to the Royal Garden Hotel to get a lift back to Heathrow with Syrian aircrew to catch the 1400 hours Syrian Arab Airline flight to Damascus. But shortly after 0900 hours, the discovery of the bomb was made public through the media, and a man called Mohammed Raja Zidan, a Syrian agent, who was travelling with the aircrew, gave Nezar an unaddressed envelope and told him to go straight to the Syrian Embassy at 8 Belgrave Square.

When he arrived at the Embassy, Nezar presented the letter, and was welcomed by a Syrian diplomat. He later was more formally and warmly greeted by the Syrian ambassador, who in Nezar's presence telephoned Damascus to get further orders. The Ambassador told Nezar that Damascus was very pleased with his actions, but that it had been decided to hide him in a safe place in England for a few days, before helping him to leave the country. Nezar was then given over to the charge of two Syrian Embassy officials, Mounir Mouna and Ahmed Abdul Latif, who took Nezar to Mouna's flat at 19 Stonor Road, West Kensington. Whilst in the flat, Nezar's hair was cut and dyed.

At around 0530 hours on the following morning, Mouna and another man, Zaki Oud, arrived at the flat, and told Nezar that he was to be taken away back to the Syrian embassy. Nezar became suspicious of this, and refused to go. Oud then attempted to force Nezar into the car, but after a brief scuffle, Nezar broke free and ran away. Oud and Mouna jumped back into the car and drove away. Nezar's suspicions appear to be well founded, and it seems likely that he was being taken on orders from Damascus to be killed.

He wandered around Kensington a little, and eventually went to the Visitors Hotel which lies between Notting Hill and Earls Court. This hotel was owned by a Jordanian Nezar knew, Niam Al-Oran. By this time, Nezar's role in the attempted bombing was well understood by the police and his picture had appeared on television and in the press. As part of their investigation, the police had also sought the help of Nezar's family to capture him. The staff of the Visitors Hotel became suspicious when Nezar tried to book in using a Syrian passport in the name of Izzam Shara, and the hotel manager telephoned the owner. Al-Oran realised this must be Hindawi, and in turn contacted Nezar's brother Mahmood, who had already been approached by the police. Both Al-Oran and Mahmood rushed to the hotel and tried to convince Nezar that he should surrender himself to the police, promising him that they would seek assurances from the British police that they would not hand Nezar over to Mossad, the Israeli security service. At the same time, a member of the public also alerted the police to Nezar's whereabouts. As a result, he was arrested at the Visitors hotel, and taken into custody. He made no attempt to resist arrest, and onlookers reported that he was led unhandcuffed from the hotel to a waiting police car.

'*I was so in love with him. I had never had a boy friend before and when he said he loved me I believed him*'. There is little doubt that Ann-Marie Murphy was innocent of any involvement in Nezar Hindawi's attempt to blow up the El Al aircraft on 17 April. Ann-Marie Murphy was used in a way which is almost unimaginably evil and barbaric, and the inescapable conclusion is that she was an innocent abroad in a world which she simply did not understand. This combined with her openness and naivety, and perhaps her desperation on finding herself pregnant again and the release Nezar Hindawi appeared to offer her through marriage, allowed her to be used in a plot involving herself and her unborn child as a human time bomb.

At his trial, Nezar Hindawi showed no regret or remorse at what he had done. During the trial, when Ann-Marie was giving evidence, she broke down in the witness box and shouted across the court at him 'You bastard you. How could you do this to me. I hate you, I hate you . . .' Throughout this outburst, as in most of the trial, Hindawi remained impassive, showing no emotion. After the jury returned a verdict of guilty, he was sentenced to 45 years imprisonment.

The Hindawi trial brought to the surface what must be one of the most callous acts of attempted terrorism ever undertaken. Given the general barbarity of terrorist behaviour, this is a quite significant comment. It is not clear, however, whether Nezar Hindawi's terrorist career was confined to the series of events described above, or whether it extended further. Some comments at his trial suggested that he had a broader background in terrorism than emerged at the trial, and there was some press speculation of links with a range of Arab and European terrorist groups, including the Red Brigades and even the Provisional IRA. Certainly his family involvement enabled contact with a range of terrorist groups, and it seems, in particular, that his cousin Awni was a significant point of contact, if not anything more. Hindawi's acknowledgement of the significance of Awni's role can be seen in a letter published in the British Press[1] and reproduced below which was smuggled out of Brixton prison, written by Hindawi to Awni during the trial.

'Dear Brother, many greetings, it is time to act. This is your time. I write to you hoping you won't disappoint me.

Go to Damascus and talk to brother Abu and Ahmed-Haithan of the following: Ahmed Gebril has two Israeli prisoners. Haithan has his word. Thatcher will be visiting Israel next Saturday. He has two Israeli prisoners. Abu has their word as well.

A prisoner exchange should be organised which must include my brother Hasi. If necessary this can be accomplished in Thatcher's visit. Tell Haithan if necessary to include some foreigners from Beirut in the exchange. Have them give you 15,000 Deutschmarks for my brother's lawyer and the same amount for my family..

You are authorised to study any solution. Time is running out quickly.'

This letter was intercepted before reaching Awni, but it seems clear that Nezar saw Awni as someone with contacts that could help him. Clues to these contacts can be seen from the world in which Awni Hindawi lived. Awni lived in Genoa, which at that time was a major base for Arab and Palestinian terrorism. There seem to have been two major Palestinian groups operating in Genoa, one centred on Abu Abbas, the other related to a splinter group from George Habash's 'Popular Front for the Liberation of Palestine', the 'Abu Ibrahim' faction. It seems likely that the Hindawi's were associated with this latter grouping. A member of the Abu Ibrahim faction arrested at around the same time (but for reasons unrelated to Hindawi's) was thought to also have close links with Abu Nidal's 30th June Group, for whom he acted as an arms supplier for attacks in Europe. Specifically, this person has been implicated as the supplier of arms for attacks in Italy. These links give a further connection with Syria. Awni came to the attention of the Italian authorities because of his extensive travels and frequent phone calls to the Middle East. Awni was known to have been in contact with someone close to the Abu Nidal group that carried out the Fiumicino attack in Italy in 1985.

Suspicions about Awni appeared to be confirmed when Nezar's letter to him was intercepted as it was being smuggled out of Brixton Prison in London. This letter was written on non-regulation paper and, as can be seen from the translation reproduced above, suggests a prisoner exchange, drawing on two captives held by Ahmed Jibril and on two other captives held by someone else of importance. Of some significance, omitted from the translation above, is the sentence '*You have the capacity to do all this and your word will carry weight with the others*'. The Italian police arrested Awni, but later released him because of lack of evidence. Awni was subsequently re-arrested twice in 1987 on charges related to association with terrorism, but released later on both occasions. The conditions of his release required him to report to the Carabiniere twice a week, but in June 1987 just as a decision about his future liberty was to be taken, he got on a flight from Genoa to Rome and, despite the fact that his passport was not valid for leaving Italy, he did so. It is only possible to speculate about the role Nezar Hindawi might have played with Awni's contacts.

A top grade terrorist?

Whilst the precise details of the Hindawi family's involvement with terrorism might be unclear, the events surrounding Nezar Hindawi do show us how terrorist networks can be formed, especially within the Arab or Palestinian context. Under the impetus of an initiator, a small group is formed which is relatively isolated from other similar groups, but connected to a central 'core' of terrorism through the initiator. A significant strength of the group often lies in clan, family or long standing friendship. Close ties of this kind both bind people together, enhancing a sense of loyalty, and also protect against the insertion of informers. Such groups present themselves to embassies seeking sponsorship, and through the diplomatic intelligence links of an embassy which is attracted to what they can offer, the group finds

itself linked in to the mainstream of what is essentially State sponsored terrorism. The group may be used for courier work,
information gathering, or action, but it may also be allowed to 'sleep'
until the right opportunity comes along. Such groups may even be
'traded' between friendly embassies as needs for political violence
arise or change. The Hindawi's were attractive to the Syrians because
they were urbane and westernised, and had roots in Western countries that facilitated their residence there. They also came along at a
time when the Syrians were actively seeking a means of retribution
against the Israelis, after the Israeli Air Force had intercepted a
Libyan executive jet in February 1986, and forced it to land at Tel
Aviv airport. The jet was en route from Tripoli to Damascus, and was
thought by the Israelis to contain Dr George Habash, leader of the
Popular Front for the Liberation of Palestine. Instead, travelling in
the plane was Mr Abdullah Ahmar, Assistant Secretary-General of
Syria's ruling Ba'ath Socialist Party, who was probably the most important man in the Syrian Government hierarchy after President Assad.
This was taken by the Syrians as a great affront, and demands for retribution against the Israelis were vociferously made. These events
seem to be the likely broader context in which the specific Syrian
funding and support of the Hindawi's to bomb the El Al plane
should be understood.

But was Nezar Hindawi a 'top grade terrorist' as was stated at his
trial? He certainly had links with significant figures in the Palestinian
terrorist world, and his actions and those of his family placed large
numbers of people at risk. He acquired significant support from a
major sponsor of State terrorism, Syria, whose officials undoubtedly
provided the inspiration, guidance and material assistance for both
Hasi's and Nezar's terrorist activities.

But Hindawi's behaviour does not seem to be that of a cool calculating top grade activist. He certainly had little regard for his victims,
as evidenced by his treatment of Ann-Marie Murphy and his unborn
daughter. But his actions do not give the impression of a man commanding a group that followed his plan or strategy. He appears to
have worked to a script devised for him which gave little room for
improvisation, and when things began to go wrong, he showed little
ability to take charge of events himself and effect his escape. Indeed,
he seems to have made a number of panic decisions that led him
back to familiar locations and people, which inevitably made him
accessible to the police. His flight to the Syrian Embassy betrays an
extraordinary measure of naivety and seems at best to have been an
ill-judged response from the point of view of his own safety.
Subsequent events early in the morning of 18 April may well have
confirmed this. From the perspective of his Syrian supporters, as

things began to go wrong, Hindawi must have appeared to be a major liability, leading them into a diplomatic crisis of major proportions.

The weaknesses shown by Nezar seem to have been shared by Hasi Hindawi, who also showed little capacity for 'creative' terrorism. Both seemed to have had a limited capacity to withstand interrogation. Indeed, only Awni seems to have shown much talent for escape from justice, but there is, in any case, no public evidence directly linking him to any specific acts of violence. Reports at the time emphasised Nezar's mercenary motivations, rather than political, and this seems to be much more in accord with his behaviour, despite his evident hatred of Israel. People who knew him in London give the impression of an avaricious, boastful and deceitful man. Despite his apparent certainty and confidence that a deal would be done to arrange his early release, so far he remains in prison, emotionally volatile and showing a degree of deep suspicion of those around him, verging on the paranoid.

Yet Nezar Hindawi keeps returning to the surface of public consciousness. In 1992, he claimed that the British Government had reneged on a deal to release him and three others in return for the release of Terry Waite and other hostages held in Lebanon. He reportedly threatened the British Prime Minister, John Major, with retribution if this alleged deal was not honoured. As with his letter to Awni smuggled out of prison, this seems to have gone unheeded.

As an act of terrorism, what Nezar Hindawi did was not particularly unique. Other terrorist organisations have from time to time deliberately used people as 'human bombs', creating conditions in which the person carrying the bomb would almost inevitably be killed as the bomb reached its target. The Provisional IRA, for example, have from time to time used this tactic. Vehicles and drivers have been hijacked, and with the driver tied into the vehicle carrying a remote controlled bomb, the driver has been told to drive to some sensitive location, where the bomb has been detonated. Ironically, given the circumstances of the Hindawi affair, the Syrians were the target of similar attacks by Christian Militia Forces in Lebanon. In November 1987, a young woman was used to carry a booby-trapped suitcase bomb into Beirut Airport, which was then controlled by the Syrians. The suitcase blew up just inside the main terminal, killing her instantly. At about the same time of day, a second woman carrying a booby trapped box of chocolates was killed just inside the American University of Beirut. Reports at the time suggest that both young women were drugged, although that would be difficult to establish in the circumstances. In a similar incident in 1982, the influence of drugs can be more clearly established. A young woman under the influence of drugs parked a car filled with explosives in an underground car park beneath the Ministry of Information in West Beirut; but she was caught and the bomb defused.

What is unusual in the case of Nezar Hindawi is not so much the use of a woman to carry a bomb, but the abuse of what Ann-Marie Murphy thought was a personal relationship to deceive her into carrying it. His cynical use of Ann-Marie from his own perspective and that of his Syrian paymasters had many positive aspects. Women are often used by terrorist organisations to move bombs, or gun parts around. Women are frequently (but wrongly) seen as non-threatening, and able therefore to carry weapons more readily; they tend to attract less suspicion when entering shops for example. Women accompanied by children, or pushing prams, or pregnant, are often viewed by police officers or soldiers as unlikely assassins, and are therefore even more attractive in their capacity to smuggle explosives. Experience in Northern Ireland, for example, shows how misplaced is this view. From the point of view of delivering a bomb, a pregnant woman offers many attractions. Even more attractive is someone who does not know they are doing so, and who when the event occurs, will be killed, thereby effectively destroying any evidence that might lead to the terrorist. Regrettably, Ann-Marie Murphy met all of these conditions.

Islamic Terrorism and *al-Jihad*

Nezar Hindawi attacked a target that was attractive to Arab and Palestinian terrorists. He himself was an Arab, and there is no doubt that Syrian funding of his activities was related to broader Syrian efforts to attack and undermine the State of Israel, whatever the immediate context of Hindawi's actions might have been. In the public imagination, his attempted bombing of the El Al aircraft probably typifies many of the qualities of Islamic and Arab terrorism. It fits into other fanatical and extreme forms of terrorism that have been associated with Islam, such as the suicide bombings of American and French forces in the Lebanon in 1985 and 1986. Like the instigators of those attacks, Hindawi showed an extreme lack of regard for human life, and like them showed a determination to attain the target regardless of the consequences.

But Hindawi's actions strike little sympathy with Islamic extremists, and they show little regard for what he did. What he did to Ann-Marie Murphy is not typical of Islamic political violence, and many Islamic activists find the moral basis of Hindawi's actions offensive.

'*We value human life, as the Prophet taught us . . . Relationships matter in Islam, and knowledge and choice in what we do are gifts from Allah to his people. Death in jihad is appropriate, even necessary, but not in this way . . .*'

'His actions desecrate the name of Islam. Yes, we have a philosophy of confrontation . . . it is a political and Islamic analysis . . . it gives us an Islamic base to confront the secular government . . . political violence is a reaction. We are committed . . . to the benefit of our religion . . .'

* * *

Over the past few years, Cairo seems to have changed very little, at least at a superficial level. The traffic is as bad as ever, the fumes and smoke and dust as pervasive as ever. In poorer parts of the City, like Imbaba, the degree of poverty is as striking as ever, and the contrasts between rich and poor remain as evident as ever; but above all, it is the sheer press of people that strikes the Western visitor. The bustle and movement of people in the *souks* seems to come from an apparently endless flow of people, and even away from the main areas, people are everywhere. This weight of people serves to emphasise the fact that Cairo remains the centre of the Islamic world in the Middle East. It is still the largest and most populous city in the Arab world, and Egypt continues to provide the impetus that sets the agenda for Arab thinking.

But there are changes in the city. Disorganised and complex as it is, there is a discernible change in the moral and political climate affecting the lives of its people. This change relates more than anything to the growing influence of Islam, and perhaps the most striking visible indicator of that is the growing number of women wearing Islamic style dresses and head dress. Whilst the majority of the population of Cairo adhere to Islam, its observance has always been less than strict. Cairo has always been a city where the influence of the West was felt, but the modernisation of Egypt in the 1950's and 60's seemed to accelerate the degree of Western influence to a much greater extent than before. The middle classes had greater access to wealth, and the influence of Western industry, foreign travel and foreign media seemed to be producing profound changes in Egyptian society.

Clear signs that this process of Westernisation was neither inevitable nor particularly welcomed by significant sections of the Egyptian community were seen in October, 1981, when President Sadat was assassinated by a group of army officers. The group that assassinated Sadat, known as *al-Jihad* (sacred combat), were largely unknown at the time, and the Egyptian security services initially made determined efforts to ensure that little emerged of the group's political and ideological agenda. But it is quite clear that the conspiritors were motivated primarily by a kind of belief in Islam that reflected a major strand of contemporary Islamic thinking. The assassins of Sadat were undoubtedly Egyptian nationalists in one sense, concerned about the current state of Egypt; but their concern was drawn from a broader Islamic perspective which offered a critique of the evils of modern society not only as they occurred in Egypt, but throughout the whole Islamic world.

We know something of the beliefs of the al-Jihad Group, however, from the work of the chief ideologue of the group, Mohammed Abd al-Salam Faraj, who produced a pamphlet describing the aims of the group. Faraj was executed, along with four of the principal plotters of the assassination of Sadat on 15 April 1982, but his work, 'The Neglected Duty' (*Al-Faridah al-Gha'ibah*), survived him. Initially, partial and incomplete copies of the work circulated underground, some probably printed in Amman. In 1983, however, the full text was published in Cairo. In the West, we tend to describe these people as 'fundamentalists', but as in the case of the term 'terrorism', we are often confused and unclear about what we mean. Appendix 2 examines in greater detail the concept of fundamentalism with particular reference to Islam, exploring how we might make some psychological sense of it. A clearer understanding of the aspirations of organisations such as al-Jihad as Islamic fundamentalists will help us to appreciate better what is often seen in the contemporary world as one of the major sources of political violence, and which presents itself as a challenge to the West.

The assassination of Anwar Sadat was in one sense a failure as far as the al-Jihad Group was concerned. It did not prompt a mass revolution nor a return to the Shari'a (Islamic law), and the Egyptian State has continued along broadly similar paths under the present leadership. On the other hand, there have been perceptible concessions towards Islamic thinking in the area of criminal justice, and perhaps more importantly, there has been a discernible shift in the Egyptian public's views on the implementation of the Shari'a and the general processes of Islamisation. Empirical evidence on this is difficult to find, but in 1985 The Egyptian National Centre for Social and Criminal Research conducted a survey on public views on the implementation of Islamic law. This revealed very large percentages of respondents (in excess of 95 per cent) to be in favour of '. . . the implementation of Moslem law (*al Shari'a*) in relation to crimes against the bounds set by Allah (adultery, false accusation, drinking alcohol, theft, brigandage, apostasy)'. However, when the respondents are broken down by religion, some 33 per cent of Christians included in the survey disagreed with the implementation of Shari'a. As can be seen in Sudan where the process of Islamisation has made considerably more progress than in Egypt, the position of a dissenting Christian minority significantly deteriorates as Islamisation progresses, and is a source of major social strains.

Those four members of al-Jihad directly involved in the assassination of Anwar Sadat, plus Mohammed Abd al-Salam Faraj, were eventually executed. In retrospect, none of them appear to have been politically sophisticated. Khalid al-Islambuli was the leader of the assassination team, and he appeared to have made the decision to assassinate Sadat. He was a lieutenant in the Egyptian Army artillery, and was 24 years old at the time of the assassination. Khalid appears to have planned the attack. He had been placed in command of an armoured transport vehicle which was to take part in a military parade reviewed by Sadat to commemorate the eighth anniversary of the launching of the October War against Israel. He had managed to replace the other occupants of the vehicle by members of the al-Jihad Group (excepting the driver, who was not involved). In the middle of the parade, in full view of television cameras, the four conspiritors left their vehicle in front of the reviewing stand, and sprayed it with automatic fire. Khalid al-Islambuli was seen by the world firing at Sadat and shouting 'I am Khalid al-Islambuli, the leader of a group of assassins, I have killed Pharaoh, and I do not fear death'.

But the execution of the assassins did not end the al-Jihad group. The group continued in Egypt, but took two different forms. One group continued under the leadership of the mufti of the original group, Sheik Umar abd al-Rahman. The other group continued under the leadership of one of the original conspiritors who escaped the death sentence, but remained in prison, Colonel Abbud al-Zumur.

Sheik Umar abd al-Rahman was a blind professor in the Azhar Faculty in Asyut. He had long established links with radical Islamic groups in Egypt, and had developed his own distinctive following amongst Islamic students. He could rightly be described as a fundamentalist in the sense used here, in that he translated into behaviour the ideological and theological priorities of Islam as he understood them. For example, whilst his blindness protected him from the crime of fornication (*zina'*) of the eyes (by looking at women), to avoid the risk of fornication of the ear he refused to allow female students to ask him questions in discussion, requiring their male colleagues to read their questions to him. After the assassination of Sadat, Sheik Umar abd al-Rahman left Cairo and moved to the United States, where he established himself and a small group of followers in New York. He continued to develop the radical and violent agenda described by Faraj, and it was his group that was probably responsible for the attack on the World Trade Centre in New York in 1992.

The group that continued around Colonel Abbud al-Zumur are probably the more significant inheritors of Faraj in terms of political sophistication and opportunity to influence the Islamic movement. In particular, Abbud al-Zumur seems to have a political stature that distinguishes him from other radical fundamentalist leaders. Whilst

Abbud was involved in the discussions with Khalid al-Islambuli about the attack on Sadat, he seems to have had grave reservations about the effectiveness of the assassination, in terms of the preparedness of the organisation to mobilise and sustain a general uprising. Abbud was 35 at the time of the assassination, and showed a much more mature approach to the political analysis of their actions. There is no doubting Abbuds' Islamic fervour, but his pragmatic recognition of the realities of revolution place him in a different category to the other conspiritors.

Whilst Abbud al-Zumur has remained in prison since the assassination of Sadat, a group of radicals has emerged around him. This group, adopting the name of Islamic Jihad, seems to represent a significant element in the current terrorist violence in Egypt aimed at both the Egyptian Government and at Westernising influences, such as tourism.

* * *

'... *political violence is a reaction. It is not an action against some other incident ... Abbud al-Zumur and his followers are committed to debate for the good of the country, and to prevent bloody violence. But oppression is the main policy of the (Egyptian) Government. These violent actions are a reaction.*'

These are the words of an Islamic activist and leader of the al-Jihad group in Cairo who is closely connected to Abbud al-Zumur. We met on a number of occasions, in Cairo and elsewhere. For many hours, we discussed at length the issue of terrorism and political violence within the Islamic movement in Egypt. For reasons of his own security, it is not appropriate to give any further personal details of him, other than to note that he was relatively young and from a professional background. But the abiding impression he gave after long discussion was of integrity and dignity. He, and others like him, are clearly motivated by a cause that they believe in. Their struggle is as much a moral as a political struggle, and they take religion seriously, in the sense that they strive to put in place in society what their religious beliefs dictate. In this sense they are fundamentalists. But to suggest that their fundamentalism narrows their view of the world is too simplistic. The stereotyped image of a rigid unbending and humourless puritan of protestant fundamentalism is far from the truth in this case. The views of this particular fundamentalist expressed to me were not so much narrow as different from ours, starting our from different assumptions about the nature of life, and about the relationship between life and religion. The sincerity with which he expressed his views left me impressed, not so much by the views themselves, but by the unassailable strength and confidence of commitment.

'... *al-Jihad have a military plan, which we will implement when the time is right. We are powerful in the military, we still have the roots of our support there . . . The military wing are informed by the political structures . . . We see the organisation from three sides; the military, the political and the media. The leaders of al-Jihad work on all three sides, and our revolution will use all modern means available when the time is right . . . Yes, it will soon be right . . . but who knows when? The general base of our movement is set by Abbud al-Zumur . . . We can generally communicate with him well, but more recently sometimes with difficulty.*

'*The attacks on tourists are unnecessary. They are carried out by Umar abd al-Rahman"'s group . . . we reject that, but now we are starting to hit and bomb the Government, not the people, not the tourists. We now confront the police and the Government . . . we seek a political change that will bring Islam to our country . . . ours is a continuation of Islamic revolutionary activity, this is how the Islamic revolution continues. We develop our military strategy from the Qu'ran.*'

The recent changes in Sudanese society have had a major effect on the Islamic world, both by way of moral and political example and as a channel through which more substantial assistance to Islamic movements can be developed.

'*. . . We do not have any links with the Sudanese. We see them as brothers, but their fight is not ours at this moment. Indeed, we believe that the analysis of Turabi (the principal architect of the Sudanese Islamic State) is wrong in important ways . . . it is not an Egyptian way . . .*

'*The Government does not have a mature view of political change . . . Yes, al-Jihad has some problems because of the Government's security actions which depend upon the violation of human rights, on torture . . . but we work within the Islamic movement, within Islam . . . the military courts will pass . . .*'

Islamic Jihad recognise their relationship with Umar abd al-Rahman's group in the United States, but from the following it is quite clear that they see themselves as having developed a clearer and more sophisticated political and ideological base for their activities.

'*The two groups (Umar abd al-Rahman's and Abbud al-Zumur's) grew from one base, from one source. The difference between them concentrated on how to change the social and political government in Egypt. In detailed ideology, there is no difference between them . . . there is a common thinking in relation to principles, there is complete agreement between the two groups. There are differences in membership of the two groups, and because of these differences they have some differences in implementing their policies . . . only differences in implementing . . . It is very hard to prove that Umar abd al-Rahman was responsible for the bombing of the World Trade Center in New York, but what if he did. It was in my opinion a nonsense and useless act . . . it lacks the strategic thinking, the broader view of the political situation from the military side . . .*'

In discussions, what emerges is a sense of the inevitability of the outcome of achieving an Islamic State, and a sense of desperation in that violence seems now to be the only way in which that can be achieved.

'*Look what has happened in Algeria. What else is left to us except violence . . . . ? We must purify and deepen the attitude of the military and social elements of the movement . . .*'

On one occasion, the person whose voice is heard above brought to me a variety of documents from and about the group, including a document smuggled from prison to the cell leaders of Islamic Jihad by Abbud al-Zumur. The document was written in 1993, probably for a Western audience, and is a short summary of previous discussions between cell leaders and Abbud al-Zumur[2]. This is both an interesting and important document, illustrating how the kind of analysis developed by one of the major authors of the Islamic movement, Qutb, and later strengthened by Faraj, continues to influence Egyptian Islamic movements. Its analysis of the evils of Western life clearly echo those offered by Qutb some 30 years ago, pointing to the decadence and the lack of moral success of the West. Its use of events on Bosnia-Hercegovina to illustrate how untrustworthy the West is when it comes to Islamic interests strike a powerful contemporary chord in the argument. The contrast between the West's energetic involvement in the Gulf War, and its lethargy in Bosnia-Hercegovina does not escape the authors. 'Muslim blood is not worth to the West more than the equivalent weight of petrol which it is extracting from our wells at a very cheap price .

In the final paragraphs, the document extends a measure of friendship to the West through offering a way forward out of its image of '. . . pirates and armed robbers'. But the way forward is through Islam, and the threat of not following this advice is that '. . . they will . . . gain more and more huge investments of enemies as a result of what its hands have done'.

Another document from the same source, dated 1992, describes 'The Basis for Tomorrow's Battle'. This document betrays Abbud al-Zumur's military training, and is much less conciliatory towards the West. It is a rigorous and thorough manual on how to prepare for confrontation; that confrontation is necessary, however, is clearly taken for granted:

> . . . It is the duty laid on the shoulders of the Islamic movement world wide. They have to rise to the inevitable confrontation level. . . . The enemy is vicious and malicious, and has great capabilities. The Islamic nation has no choice, except to raise the banner of the frontier and be prepared for the decisive battle.

This document stresses the need for information and intelligence in the development of the Islamic revolution. It is principally a discussion of how intelligence can be gathered, and in what ways it can be used. Using examples from the Qu'ran and the time of the Prophet, it illustrates how significant intelligence is, and offers advice on how to gather intelligence, collate it, and use it in tactical and strategic planning. To the Western reader, it gives a decidedly odd look to the document, with modern discussions of good practice in surveillance technique using 6th Century examples of the life of the Prophet and his followers to elaborate or emphasise points.

A further document discusses and elaborates on 'The General Principles of our Ideological Programme'. This document, dated 1993, bears many similarities to the discussion by Mohammed Abd al-Salam Faraj in 'The Neglected Duty'. It discusses the need for struggle within the context of the debilitated state of Islam, and the strength of Western secularism. It quite clearly and formally establishes the Qur'an and the Sunna as the basis of the programme, offering a logical and compelling (if the assumptions are accepted) account of the inevitability of violent confrontation.

Arab terrorism and Islamic political violence

The discussion in this chapter illustrates two quite opposite aspects of Middle Eastern terrorism. The Islamic movements, of which the al-Jihad organisation is an example, belong to a sophisticated and well established tradition. Meeting activists, the overwhelming impression given is of people who are dominated by an idea. That idea, that ideology, relates to the need to further the cause of Islam. To achieve this in the present circumstances will necessarily involve confrontation, either directly, or through a process of destabilisation. But the violence is not in itself of primary significance to the analysis. It is firmly located within an ideological context that condones extreme violence both to others and to the activists themselves as a means to a greater achievable but above all necessarily better state. The ready acceptance of martydom by Islamic militants should not be equated with the desperation of the suicidal; rather it is the acceptance of the religious logic that *necessitates* and condones violence both against others and sometimes against one's self. Words like 'integrity' and 'morality' spring to mind when thinking of the individuals involved.

In psychological terms, this results in extreme control over behaviour by ideology, a control augmented by millenarian influences[3]. There was an intensity about the activist whose account is given above that conforms to this view. On one occasion whilst with him on a visit to the West, dietary restrictions presented something of a problem in eating out in an environment not accustomed to cater for Islamic dietary practices. His response to problems – '*Man does not live by food alone, there are other more important sustainers*' – was not simply a way of passing over a potentially embarrassing social problem when food proved to be unacceptable; it properly reflected an approach to life which was in a large measure 'other worldly'. But what is surprising to the cynical Western view is that this does not occur in any sanctimonious context. The strength of feeling was a natural part of life, which both challenged and enriched it.

This does not seem to be the world of Nezar Hindawi and the Jordanian Revolutionary Movement. The actions of Hindawi gained little sympathy from Islamic activists who used the term 'terrorist' in a pejorative sense to describe his behaviour. It has to be said, however, that the irony of their use of 'terrorist', when we would undoubtedly also regard them as terrorists, was to a large extent lost on them!

What Hindawi did seems to have little place within an Islamic analysis, nor does his behaviour conform to that of the Islamic activist. Hindawi drank alcohol, he clearly had little regard for Islamic restrictions on sexual behaviour, and seemed to regard his responsibilities towards Ann-Marie Murphy in a very un-Islamic way. At one level, Hindawi was undoubtedly calculating and manipulative, but it seems that this was largely for his own ends, rather than some greater ideological end. Hindawi's actions seem to belong more to the realm of criminal behaviour, rather than political terrorism, although his behaviour was *used* within a political context. The Islamic activist may well merit the term fanatic, in the sense of an individual fired with religious enthusiasm. Such people may well make uncomfortable allies, and they no doubt view the West with suspicion and disdain. But however misplaced it may appear, they do have a sense of righteousness which allows of a measure of regard. This cannot be said of Nezar Hindawi.

It would be wrong to characterise Palestinian political violence as necessarily being like that practised by Hindawi. For many Palestinians, the spartan ideology of nationalism finds many parallels with the Islamic Movement, and indeed there are considerable areas of common cause between them. The vision of Islam which lies behind the Islamis also lies for many behind the aspiration to a Palestinian State, and this is, of course, emphasised by the historical basis of conflict between Jew and Arab. It seems likely that Hindawi to a large extent, stands aside from the broader Palestinian movement. His marginality in this sense seems likely to be confirmed as changes in the relationships between Israel and the Arab States occur.

7

A Drawing Together

Never has our future been so unpredictable, never have we depended so much on political forces that cannot be trusted to follow the rules of common sense and self-interest – forces that look like insanity, if judged by the standards of other centuries . . .

. . . there prevails an ill-defined, general agreement that the essential structure of all civilisation is at breaking point. Although it may seem better preserved in some parts of the world than others, it can nowhere provide the guidance to the possibilities to the century, or an adequate response to its horrors . . .

. . . everything seems to have lost specific value, and has become unrecognisable for human comprehension, unusable for human purpose. To yield to the mere process of disintegration has become an irresistible temptation, not only because it has assumed the spurious grandeur of 'historical necessity', but also because everything outside it has begun to appear lifeless, bloodless, meaningless and unreal.

(Hannah Arendt. *The Origins of Totalitarianism.*)

The above quotations from Hannah Arendt's important analysis of the origins of totalitarianism were written in the immediate aftermath of the Second World War. The book was published in 1950, and reflected Arendt's fear of a resurgence of what she regarded as the twin evils of Stalinism and Nazism. In much of her work, she attempted to understand, and therefore help to avoid, the consequences of their recurrence. She was not alone in that ambition and at that time, many academics, intellectuals and politicians shared a similar fear. As a result, there was in the late 1940's and

'50's a determined effort to try to explore at both the personal and social level the determinants of extreme violence. The imperative was to understand, and therefore perhaps avoid, future wars and atrocities. Parallel with this, there was an attempt at the international level to put in place, through the United Nations, worldwide social and political structures that would render violence unnecessary in the relations between states.

Looking back from our present position at the end of the twentieth century Arendt's pessimism seems well founded. With regret, it seems that a good case can be made for saying that nothing has really changed. It also has to be said that, despite the optimistic push for knowledge that characterised much effort at that time, it achieved relatively little.

The problems of extreme violence can, of course, be viewed from a variety of perspectives. There is, however, a sense in which the problems relate not simply to the society in which we live, but also in the more complex issue of what men do. This places the problem clearly within the realms of psychology, a location Arendt herself would have acknowledged. Yet we still know relatively little at a psychological level about the forces that give rise to extreme violence.

Dictatorships, civil disorder and war has continued unabated in the period since the Second World War. The late twentieth century has seen a series of bloody wars, admittedly generally on a more limited geographical scale than the World Wars in the earlier part of the century, but nevertheless embracing large parts of the world. Of particular concern to Europeans, we now see the resurgence of old ethnic tensions as events in Bosnia so tragically illustrate. One issue of great concern is the international communities' apparent inability to influence the course of events in a war arena such as Bosnia, events which bear a more than passing similarity with the excesses of the Second World War. This inability to control events perhaps more than anything else lays bare the last vestiges of pre-war optimism. Weapon developments have made the capacity to inflict damage in war much greater, and there seems to be increased targeting of uninvolved civilians as part of the process of war. Indeed, the war in Bosnia is as much about the deliberate targeting of people as it is about geography.

The late twentieth century has seen a new psychological dimension added to warfare, in what we have referred to in this book as 'terrorism'. Terrorism in the sense in which we know it today was not recognised as a particular problem in the aftermath of the Second World War. At that time the concern was mainly with the development of mechanisms of control of the excesses of State activities, such as the concentration camps. But our appreciation of the power of terrorism is something which has grown steadily as the century has progressed, as we have gained more experience of it. Many people have argued that terrorism is warfare by another name, a democratic form of warfare enabling the weak, the disaffected and the small to wage effective war against the massive superpowers that have dominated the international arena. It may well be that the collapse of the Soviet Union will make this form of warfare even more prevalent, as small impoverished ethnic communities strive through force to define their own identity and territory.

What this book has presented is an overview of some of the individuals and organisations engaged in this form of warfare, if that is what it is. The individuals interviewed whose voices lie behind the accounts given are not systematically chosen to 'represent' terrorists. They are the people the author has met, talked to and tried to understand. It is of course not possible to know if they are in any way representative in any scientific sense, and it is not the intention of this book to offer an account in that sense. What does emerge, however, is some sense of the individuals who are behind the dreadful attacks we read about or see in the media, and why they become involved in the way they do.

Assumptions

It is clearly the case that our understanding of the psychology of terrorism is incomplete, but given the accounts presented earlier in this book, what conclusions can we draw? There are a number of broad themes that have emerged. To give some order to the discussion, we will present these themes in terms of a series of assumptions and assertions. From our discussion in earlier chapters, the first thing we can do is identify some three false assumptions that are made about terrorism and the terrorist.

False Assumption 1

This assumption concerns the way in which we use the term 'terrorism'. If we review the kinds of situation described in this book, it is clear that terrorism is a collective word that embraces a wide variety of different activities. Furthermore, there is wide agreement from most authors that the concept of terrorism is complex and imprecise. Yet *because* a single word is used to describe a range of activities, we may well assume that there is some common single or limited quality underpinning the concept of terrorism that helps to bring together the varied activities we label as examples of it. Sometimes this view is expressed in terms of assumptions of a single 'cause' of terrorism.

We can of course distinguish between different kinds of terrorism. Distinctions are conventionally made, for example, between state terrorism and other forms of political violence. State terrorism is extra-legal political violence sanctioned and sponsored by a state against its opponents. What is regarded as state terrorism can sometimes be controversial however, and problems focus around the concept of the legitimacy of state violence. Supporters of a state may not recognise or necessarily accept that actions against what are, to them, illegitimate subversive groups can be thought of as acts of terrorism. The example of South Africa is one very obvious example of a situation where large numbers of people outside South Africa saw its activities to control its enemies as an example of state terrorism. As we have encountered elsewhere in this book, more complex distinctions can be made between nationalist and political terrorism, or the relationship between terrorism and criminality.

Whatever kinds of distinction we choose to make about types of terrorism, however, we need to recognise that the situation is complex and our understanding partial. It is clear that within the *social and political* arena, terrorism and the broader problem of political violence cannot simply be understood by drawing on a homogeneous set of causal concepts. The varieties of terrorism, the heterogeneous backgrounds of terrorists, and the multitude of political (or criminal) aspirations espoused by terrorist groups, seem to argue against this view. Paradoxically, however, this may not be quite the case at a *behavioural and psychological* level of analysis. Single cause explanations of so complex a phenomenon as terrorism are clearly inappropriate, but we may be able to identify commonalities in *processes* rather than causes. In many ways, this is one of the clearest messages to emerge from this book. Despite different settings, backgrounds and ideology, individual terrorists show considerable commonality of process in terms of development into terrorism, and once in, maintaining membership. To understand this further, we need to be sensitive to the nature of the activities involved in terrorism, and to avoid being beguiled by the term.

False Assumption 2

Following on from this, we can identify a *second* assumption that needs to be examined. This concerns how people become and remain terrorists. From a psychological perspective, one way in which the issues related to this can be simply posed is 'are terrorists made, or are they, in some sense, destined to become terrorists because of their inherent psychological qualities?'

Because the acts of terrorists are so barbaric, we tend to consign them to those categories of behaviour which are the result of abnormality or infirmity. Explanations of this sort assume, sometimes without realising this is the case, that there are identifiable abnormal or pathogenic psychological states that in some sense 'cause' terrorism. Those individuals whose voices are recorded here do not seem to conform to this assumption in any obvious sense. None show the attributes of abnormality in any technical sense, despite the fact that a number have been involved in clear and unambiguous atrocities involving death and injury to innocent third parties.

The individuals that we heard in earlier chapters described situations that created their behaviour, rather than suggest people in the grip of inner mental distress. Because of this, a more reasonable approach seems to be that terrorists and terrorism represent a response to the psychological and social environment as experienced by the individual, rather than the expression of some inherent quality within the terrorist. The implications of this are that whilst some terrorists may well be abnormal, and certainly the acts they do are abnormal, we cannot accept the comforting and unchallenging assumption that equates this aspect of their behaviour with mental illness. Nor can we accept the equally comforting assumption that if it is necessary to identify fault, then the problem lies with society rather than the individual.

If these points are accepted, then it stops us from assuming that, in some sense, the terrorist is out of control of both society and themselves. It reintroduces into the analysis the sense of individual action which so frequently seems lacking in contemporary debate, and because of that a sense of responsibility. Certainly, in one sense, the terrorist has been created by the experience of society, and is in turn sustained by it. But equally, it is the terrorist who commits atrocities, and in doing so exercises choice of some kind.

A more fruitful approach is to recognise a series of dimensions in terrorism. To begin with, we can identify developmental dimensions to both the individual terrorist and terrorist groups. These might be profitably characterised in terms of psychological (and perhaps social) *processes* rather than psychological *states*. Individuals join terrorist groups through exposure to certain kinds of events. Experience of disadvantage or oppression may be one kind of event; economic or social disadvantage in some sense, for example, is a common theme of the terrorists own descriptions. Explanations in these terms have a certain common sense validity, and certainly fit some social and political analyses. But they seem not to be so obviously the case when the detailed lives of individual terrorists are examined. The preponderance in Western Europe of middle class, relatively well educated terrorists suggests that personal experience

of socio-economic deprivation is a limited factor in the events leading to a life of terrorism. Ideology, a 'rational' awareness of
conditions, and even fashion or peer group pressure might be much
more influential factors here.

There is however a contrast here between politically and national-
istically orientated groups which is striking. Prominent nationalist
terrorist organisations, such as ETA and the Provisional IRA have
quite different profiles of membership than more explicitly political
groups such as the Red Army Faction. The dynamics of membership
are presumably quite different in each broad situation. Yet even if
there are no simple explanations, we can say that something happens
to individuals to ease their passage into lives of terrorism. Sometimes
this may be individual and idiosyncratic; but only systematic and
essentially empirical studies of the processes of terrorism will provide
the answers to those questions.

It may well be the case that adequate answers to these questions
may not emerge from analyses of large data sets, such as global
descriptions of the membership of groups. Accounts of individual terrorists, or individual incident analyses may be a more appropriate
starting point. We are used to the idea that a multitude of circumstances affect more 'normal' life choices. Why should we regard the
terrorist as something different?

The sense of development into terrorism described above might
be extended to embrace not only an initiation phase, but also a maintenance phase (*remaining* a terrorist) and a terminal phase (*ceasing* to
be an active terrorist). This is consistent with analyses of other deviant
behaviour (like criminal conduct) and reflects the overall organisation of the early chapters of this book. At one level, these distinctions
may seem rather obvious, but characterising terrorism in this way
has one very important implication for policy makers and others
who have to respond to it. The factors that may give rise to someone
becoming a terrorist may be very different from those factors that
maintain terrorism once someone has embarked on that lifestyle.
Furthermore, it may be possible to distinguish between factors in a
general sense that maintain an individual's involvement with terrorism, and the particular circumstances which determine and select a
particular terrorist activity, such as planting a bomb, or setting up an
ambush. There is no necessary reason why any of these factors should
have any relationship to those factors that result in a movement away
from active involvement in terrorism. Confusion about this cluster of
distinctions may lead to both inappropriate political initiatives and
attempts at control. We can systematise these distinctions further, by
outlining the factors associated with them.

Becoming a terrorist. The process of becoming a terrorist is no doubt complex and obscure. But we can assume that for many individuals involved in terrorism, aspects of such things as socialisation or family history, are significant factors. These might combine with ideological commitment and real or imagined insults or disadvantage, in individual and distinctive ways, to place someone in a position where the attraction of terrorism as protest, a sense of personal agency, or simply a means towards an end of friendship and camaraderie become powerful enough to lead someone to increasing involvement with violence, and eventually a violent act. This deceptively simply analysis hides many complex forces, but it is, in fact, supported by the reports from terrorists themselves described earlier in this book, and from what we know about how terrorist groups operate. As in the voices heard earlier, most terrorists describe a process of induction into a terrorist lifestyle, rather than immediate involvement, which supports the notion of a developmental process.

One factor to consider briefly further in this process of growing or confirming involvement is imprisonment. The influence for some individuals of imprisonment as a source of enhancement and confirmation of a movement towards ideological commitment and terrorist involvement complements the analysis presented above. The importance of this as a contributory factor in the process of becoming a terrorist should not be underestimated. We have already noted in earlier chapters the paradoxical situation of apparent punishment confirming involvement in the activity supposedly being punished. This is not confined to terrorism, of course and is an all too common quality of our criminal justice system. Imprisonment may be an occupational hazard of extreme political involvement, but the role of imprisonment in confirming extreme ideological commitment seems to be important.

This is not clearly understood and certainly is not always recognised by policy makers. The number of embryonic extreme political and terrorist leaders, for example, who report that prison was a formative and confirmatory experience is considerable and cannot be ignored. For example, all but one of the clerical leaders of the revolution which led to the founding of the Islamic Republic of Iran, have spent periods of time in prison. The effects of this, and the extensive exile experienced by Ayatollah Khomeini and his followers, were of considerable importance in the totality of influences which determined the shape of the Islamic revolution in Iran. A more explicit example we have noted is the way in which Provisional IRA prisoners in Northern Ireland have developed discussion groups within the prison to explore their own ideological motivation, producing an extraordinarily effective environment for the distillation and refinement of ideological control over behaviour. Relatively minor terrorists who, as prisoners, have experienced this say they 'now know' why they did what they did – a telling comment on the success of this method of ideological formation (and of course on the factors that led to their original involvement with terrorism). Processes akin to those popularly known as 'brainwashing' might characterise what happens.

Similarly, support groups which surround prisoners also offer highly effective means of both developing and disseminating terrorist ideology. Legitimate welfare activities can blend into part of the process of sustaining terrorist involvement. For example, the various prisoners' support organisations in Northern Ireland play an effective role in sustaining community support and in explaining terrorist activity to the community at large and to themselves. In times of extreme stress, such as during the 1980–81 hunger strikes, these organisations played critical roles in mobilising support. In a slightly different context, the influence of Sayed Qutb, the Islamic fundamentalist theorist, was significantly enhanced by the role played by Mrs Saynab al-Ghazali as a member of the Society of Muslim Ladies, a support organisation for prisoners' families. She became the principal source of communication between Qutb and his followers, and the discussion groups held by her, at her home, on Qutb's writings (which eventually became the influential book 'Signposts'), significantly contributed to the regeneration and sustenance of the Muslim Brotherhood in Egypt during a period when many of its leaders were imprisoned.

Remaining a Terrorist. In contrast to the above, once somebody is already an active and committed terrorist, a quite different array of pressures may drive continuing involvement in terrorism. Peer pressure, group solidarity, and the widely known phenomena that characterise the psychology of group processes may become very powerful agents sustaining continuing involvement despite the moral contradictions, to which a life of terrorism must inevitably give rise. Again, the exposure in prison to intense political and ideological influences may serve to enhance and confirm existing terrorist commitment.

Other additional forces that may generate continuing involvement in terrorist groups can be identified at a different level of analysis. The discussions in earlier chapters have explored the significance of organisational pressures, as opposed to ideological control, as forces that drive terrorist action. A well established terrorist group (such as the Provisional IRA) has a great deal in common with a large commercial organisation. We know through analyses of business organisations, that a number of forces towards organisational cohesion and collective decision-making can be identified that impinge on the individual. The interaction of these forces in the internal dynamics of such organisations are as much a source for action in the situations of concern to us as gaining profit or commercial advantage. When applied to terrorist groups, this analysis suggests that internal dynamic pressures, such as the fundamental need to sustain the organisation, can, in some circumstances, become an important determinant of action along with, and indeed sometimes substituting for, ideological and broader political objectives.

In these circumstances, whilst the terrorists' rhetoric may emphasise attainment of broad political objectives, the actions of the terrorist group may be much more related to maintaining organisational integrity and cohesion, and providing incentives for its members to continue. The implications of this can be far reaching, and if this is correct, some examples of terrorist activity may have as their primary focus an internal agenda, rather than the overt political programme of the terrorist group. This may be especially the case in examples of international terrorism, or in situations where the need to raise funds becomes a critical issue, resulting in involvement with other parties (governmental or otherwise). We may need to look for 'inner meaning' of this kind if we are to understand the logic of terrorist actions, as the events surrounding Hindawi's efforts to bomb the El Al aircraft suggest. Much terrorist propaganda can be understood in the same terms.

This leads to another important implication for policy makers. Because of factors like this, it may be that attempts to address the overt political context in which terrorist groups function may have little effect on the actual activity of a terrorist group, especially if it is well developed and organisationally cohesive. This may be one reason why initiatives like the Anglo-Irish Agreement, for example, have had little effect on the continuing viability of the Provisional IRA.

A useful further critical distinction can be made here between the role of the leader, the active follower and the passive supporter. Evidence suggests that the lifestyle and activities of all differ greatly. Factors that sustain the involvement of leaders, for example, may be very different from those that sustain active followers and passive supporters. The need to accommodate conflicting and perhaps contradictory needs of a broad membership will itself be an additional factor determining the leaders' responses, which eventually translate into terrorist action.

Indeed, in our thinking about terrorism, we may need to distinguish more clearly between factors influencing leaders and followers.

This distinction has not been made to any great extent in this book, mainly because those interviewed tended to be actively involved in action rather than policy making. In the case of Islamic terrorism, for example, most attention focuses on the need to understand leadership factors in the Islamic movements more clearly. On the other hand, it seems likely that the Islamic suicide bomber, or the front line Islamic terrorist in general is probably motivated in quite different ways from the leadership. Our knowledge in this area is limited in the extreme, but we need to understand these central issues.

A critical factor to emphasise here may bring us back again to the notion of ideology, and the nature and extent of control it can exercise. In the active terrorist (as opposed to the leadership), we may see a person under explicit control of ideology expressed as behavioural rules which operate in different ways for terrorist leaders depending upon the individual's position within the organisation. Martyrdom, for example, is much more a feature of the Islamic follower than the terrorist group leader. Religious ideology sustaining such behaviour presumably impinges on the suicide bomber in quite different ways from his political leadership. We might make further distinctions here in terms of ideological control between the active and passive supporter.

Ceasing to be a terrorist. The factors that contribute to a moving away from terrorism for an active terrorist are poorly understood. There is very little reliable systematic evidence on which to draw. However, it does seem to be the case that direct government intervention is not a critical factor in the decline of terrorist organisations. The situation appears to be very complex, and organisational, social and psychological factors play more important roles than direct action by the security services to 'defeat' terrorism.

Conventional wisdom (on which policy is often based) suggests that increased risk of apprehension or injury, increasing family commitments, and simply growing older, are relevant factors. The necessary isolation of the terrorist from the broader community is also thought to be a factor. Whilst isolation may enhance security, it also impedes normal social interaction, thus reinforcing and sustaining an involvement with terrorism which becomes very difficult to break. To complicate the issue further, such evidence that does exist also suggests that currently active terrorist organisations actively victimise members who seek to drop out. Whatever the merits of these views, we do know that, for whatever reasons, once an individual embarks upon a terrorist career, it seems to be very difficult to prise him or her away from it. This is a critical area for further investigation. Recent suggestive evidence from Italy on the role of legal initiatives is very relevant here, and the discussion in Chapter 5 of the role of amnesties and the '*pentiti*' may offer a way forward.

Despite the uncertainties, recognising that there are different developmental phases of terrorism, and that different phases related to different (and possibly unrelated) causal factors is the thrust of the above discussion. Specific targeting of initiatives towards particular elements in the process of development of a terrorist group are the clear operational implications in this discussion if efforts to contain terrorism are to move away from simply reactive managements of incidents. International and comparative dimensions are critical further elements in this, and we badly need to extend our research and analysis to embrace these factors.

False Assumption 3

This leads to a *third* and final assumption that needs to be examined. Terrorism and political violence frequently involve violent and sometimes gruesome death and injury of people, with little or no connection with the terrorists' cause. Our newspapers are full of the almost daily horror of atrocity somewhere. Because of the truly revolting events, there is an assumption that the local community, which the terrorists aspire to serve and perhaps represent must necessarily also share the revulsion which the broader community feels at such acts. The argument seems to be as follows: members of communities where terrorism is endemic, (such as in some parts of Northern Ireland) are not discernibly different in human attributes to members of other communities. Surely, therefore, they must be sensitive to the appalling tragedy and moral depravity such acts show.

All the evidence suggests that this is not the case, at least in any straight forward way. Analysis of public opinion data on these matters is complex. To make sense of the situation, we need to differentiate between particular support for specific acts, and a sense of more general diffuse support for the aspirations and ideologies of the terrorist. The latter is probably the more important in assessing the extent of public support. It seems to be the case that amongst already supportive communities, generalised support for the political objectives of terrorist groups seems to be largely unrelated and insensitive to the particular actions of terrorists.

We can assert with confidence that terrorism never thrives in an unsupportive environment. For a terrorist group to mount actions, it has to draw on both the explicit and tacit support of a lot of people. Furthermore, a group has to recruit and renew itself. Unfortunately for the broader community, such support continues to exist in the main areas where we find contemporary endemic terrorist activity, regardless of outrages or clearly horrific massacre. Such continuing support, despite moral outrages, allows us to assert with some confidence that terrorism is not just a security problem, nor even a political problem. Analyses must extend beyond these narrow confines to embrace the broader social and psychological context in which terrorism exists, and to identify the bases of such apparently uncritical, resistant and loyal support.

An example will serve to illustrate this. Despite a history of barbaric repression amongst its own community and a striking lack of achievement in terms of its political agenda, the Provisional IRA continues to command the invariant electoral support of somewhere between 50,000 and 70,000 people in Northern Ireland (out of a population of about 500,000). Such electoral support seems to be largely unrelated to the specific activities of the movement and might be argued to reflect a general cultural aspiration related to national identity, rather than a vote for a particular set of policies. Because of this, a hinterland of broadly insensitive passive support, verging on active support, exists. In this hinterland the Provisional IRA sustain themselves and their activities.

We have already noted the sense in which a terrorist group might become divorced from its ideological agenda, and become focused on organisational factors such as survival. At times, the Provisional IRA clearly fits this analysis, but this should not distract analysts from a concern with the social context in which they exist. Even if the Provisional IRA could be contained, the factors that give rise to its more general support will remain, and these most certainly are not conveniently relegated to 'security problems'. At one level, they relate to such factors as relative social disadvantage and national identity. It must be acknowledged that, in social terms, there are reasons for a community to support terrorism, however, uncomfortable or inconvenient this may be for policy makers. But to add to that discomfort, the reason for that support may well also lie within the realms of psychology and sociology, rather than politics and economics. Policy makers, security force personnel and academics all need to learn to work together better to a broad agenda to meet the common objectives of understanding and containing terrorism.

Assertions

Following from our discussion of assumptions, we can make more positively a series of four assertions about terrorism. Whilst they are speculative in character nevertheless they are all supportable from existing evidence and to a large extent emerge from the interviews printed in this book. If they are broadly correct, they may lead to a rather different analysis of the nature of terrorism from that conventionally made.

Assertion 1

Our first assertion is that *the active terrorist is not discernibly different in psychological terms from the non-terrorist.* In other words, terrorist membership is drawn from a population that, in psychological terms, describes most of us. Having said that, there can be no doubt that continuing membership of a terrorist group produces adverse effects on the individual. The things terrorists do, the isolation from the broader society, the sense (and reality) of danger all conspire to produce effects on the person concerned. But we must recognise that these effects are, in essence, no different from those experienced by non-terrorists subject to occupations that produce social isolation and stress. Paradoxically, some of the effects on the terrorist of being a terrorist may be similar to the effects on the member of the security services charged with his apprehension!

Assertion 2

Related to this we can make a second assertion: *in psychological terms, there are no special qualities that characterise the terrorist.* This is not quite the same as the above. This assertion implies that the processes or reasons why the terrorist behaves as he does are broadly similar to those that affect all of us. At any given time, we can analyse the various life choices that an individual makes. There are no necessary reasons, however, why people who have reached a similar position in life (in terms of career choices or social contacts), necessarily have psychological elements in common. Exactly the same line of argument can be applied to the terrorist. That terrorists do similar things (in terms of seeking to influence the political process through violence) does not necessarily imply that they have anything in common other than the fact that they are involved in terrorism. Thus recourse to explanations of terrorism in terms of constructs such as personality seem inappropriate.

We also need to distinguish between factors that lead a terrorist to behave as he does, and the broader moral context of his acts. The depravity of many acts by terrorists may lead us to despair of ever understanding them. They seem so out of the context of those things which normal people do, that the only way we can understand them is to place them within the context of abnormality, as we have noted above, where we have already recognised the inappropriateness of

this. But if they are not abnormal, and they are subject to the circumstances that control the rest of our behaviour, how can we come
to terms with understanding them? Does this mean that many of us
in the right circumstances could become terrorists? Depressingly,
the answer to this may well be 'yes', although it is unlikely in the
extreme that most of us will experience the rather unusual circumstances that lead to terrorism and political violence.

   The fact that many people experience the social conditions that
seem to be correlated with terrorism but do not become terrorists
does not invalidate the comments above. Indeed, in this context
focusing on the exceptions (the terrorist) may be less useful than
addressing the problem of why *so few* individuals become involved in
terrorism, given the widespread social and political problems in
potential terrorist environments.

Assertion 3

The term 'terrorism' is unnecessarily complex. *Political violence*
might be a better generic term which could include terrorism, but
also embrace other violent acts (as in forms of self-injury and suicide, for example, as acts of political violence). Using this
terminology also enables us to separate out criminal violence from
political violence. If we embrace this perspective, we can then
address what might prove to be a more meaningful issue – what in
psychological terms leads to the expression of political violence? In
thinking about this, we can make our third assertion: *political violence (in contrast to other kinds of social violence) is the result of a complex
interaction of social and psychological forces which in some sense relate to the
effects of ideology.*

   Political violence (as opposed to familial or criminal violence)
obviously has political objectives that guide the individual. How do
these political objectives, frequently expressed at a general level,
come to influence the behaviour of individuals in detail? In the discussion above, we have frequently stressed the significance of
ideology as the critical and distinctive factor in political situations.
But how can we characterise ideology in psychological terms? In
Appendix 2, a somewhat technical discussion of ways in which we
might begin to understand ideology in the context of Islamic fundamentalism is presented for the reader who has an interest in the
details of these issues. The Appendix identifies a number of processes
that serve as a bridge between the political expression of ideology,
and the forces that control and shape our behaviour, so helping to
explain, at a behavioural level, how the politically violent person
develops. We can conceptualise these forces in terms of behavioural

rule following. Conceptualising the problem in this way also enables us to see how social psychological forces come to bear on the terrorist, in terms of sustaining and guiding his behaviour.

Assertion 4

One further and final assertion we can make is that *political violence is a learned behaviour, and as such subject to the forces that control all our behaviour*. This follows from the discussion above, but has important implications. If terrorism (or political violence) is controlled by those forces that control all our behaviour (violent or otherwise), we do not need to invent special explanations to account for terrorist behaviour. Furthermore, if this is correct, we know that the most powerful forces that control terrorist behaviour will, in some sense, relate to its positive consequences. In terms of political rhetoric, terrorism may be portrayed as an ideological duty, but to the active terrorist it is an occupation that has positive consequences. What these may be may well be idiosyncratic. However, we do know that some of the consequences (easy access to sex, social approval within the supportive community, excitement, a sense of personal agency) are acknowledged to be important by terrorists themselves. We also know that for terrorist organisations, as distinct from individuals, the 'oxygen' of publicity constitutes perhaps the most significant positive factor determining terrorist policy, planning and action.

Recognition of this may help us to explain some of the very puzzling features of contemporary terrorism. For example, the idea of martyrdom for the cause is a pervasive theme in many terrorist obituaries, but of late, martyrdom has gained a new meaning in the 1980–81 hunger strikes in Northern Ireland, and the more recent suicide bombings undertaken by Shi'a militants in the Middle East. Whilst for most of us the ultimate consequence of martyrdom (death) might be assumed to be highly aversive, in particular cases this does not seem to be the case. It may be helpful if we see martyrdom as a form of victimisation which is paradoxically inflicted on the individual by himself for positive reasons. One explanation of the positive power of self-victimisation in this form may lie in the particular qualities of ideological control and its consequences. But even at the more mundane level of victimisation, however, we can see how recognition of this in an operational context lends further justification to the need for a more sophisticated approach to terrorism in order to avoid counter-productive acts by both the security forces and policy makers.

Terrorist Lives

Terrorism is a disturbing and frightening phenomenon. Terrorist bombs or shootings kill and injure people who have no connection with the terrorist's cause, offending all our notions of justice. What is more, the threat of terrorist action can influence the political process significantly, distorting and undermining democratic processes. It is a political tool of immense force and is clearly recognised as such by the leaders of terrorist organisations.

The reality is that terrorism will remain a part of the political arena for the foreseeable future. It is an effective form of informal warfare, a way for the poor and disadvantaged to exert influence on the political process, but equally – a way for an oppressive minority to press its case and achieve what, in democratic terms, is seen as a disproportionate amount of influence. But terrorism is not an abstract phenomenon. It is produced by individuals who do certain things – such as placing bombs or setting up sniper attacks. The chilling and frightening conclusion is that those people who do these truly frightening things are themselves largely like everyone else.

The individuals whose voices are heard in this book have killed and injured many people. They are not the voices of madmen or women, they are not the voices of serial killers in any criminological sense (although a number have been responsible for more than one death). Their voices are indistinguishable from the voices of ordinary people. They do the things ordinary people do, and they are essentially indistinguishable from them. So they should be – they are ordinary people, products of ordinary environments, sharing the interests of their community.

What then makes the terrorist different? This is a very difficult question to answer. In some senses, the difference lies in chance – the chance friendship, the chance influence of parents and families, the unpredictable encounter – the list is lengthy and will probably always remain incomplete. But after that critical series of steps that leads to initial involvement, we can see a clearer psychological pattern emerging. We can identify the difference between individuals described here and those not involved in terrorism in terms of what might be characterised as a 'psychological equation' comprising a series of factors. These include the influence of a militant and essentially millenarian ideology, the psychologically imminent attainment of the ideological end, and a life 'lacking in public space', a closed world where criticism and the influence of ideas from outside the particular ideology are restricted or even non-existent.

In some combination that we don't necessarily always understand, these factors seem to be associated with, and perhaps to give rise to extreme violence in the form of terrorism. For the individual already engaged on the fringes of the terrorist world, these factors seem to serve as the magnet that draws the individual further and further in towards violence. The individuals we have heard in the earlier chapters of this book seem to broadly fall within this framework. The world they enter is not a fantasy world unrelated to reality, but a world that is almost selectively engaged and disengaged at the same time. Most of their world is like that which exists for everyone in their community. The areas where their world is disengaged relate primarily to what we might regard as constraints on behaviour. But what we see is not a lack of constraint, but a different form of constraint. Behaviour remains controlled, but in a different way from the rest of us. It is in this central quality of control that we see the influence of ideology.

Observing terrorism leaves the observer with a deep sense of unease. Terrorists always have a logic, which from their point of view is compelling. Indeed, it is so compelling that they *have* to commit the most awful crimes to achieve some greater good. Sometimes the logic is so beguiling that you can even begin to half believe it, to join in with the process and to be carried along by its momentum. We do so at our psychological and social peril.

Appendix 1

Abbud al-Zumur's Communication (1993)

This document is an internal communication to the cell leaders of Islamic Jihad Egypt by Abbud al-Zumur, former Colonel of the Egyptian Military Intelligence Service. The document is dated 1993. It was smuggled from the military prison in Cairo and is a short summary of previous discussions between the cell leaders and Abbud al-Zumur.

'In the name of Allah, the Merciful and Compassionate. Thank Allah and pray, and peace on the Allah Messenger.

These are the summarised conclusions of our discussion about our attitude towards the West; we are able to consider our attitudes from the following perspectives:

First What is the West's attitude to Islam?
To answer this question we have to remember the long history of hatred and conspiracy from the Crusades until the slaughter of the Islamic Khelafa (succession) in 1924. But the matter did not stop at this point, and the West aggressively continued to keep the Islamic world under its control so that it could suck its wealth and resources, and keep it as a market for its consumer products. Imperialism did not leave the Islamic world until it implanted the devil's seeds and put into power the secular rulers, guiding them to follow the path which was drawn by the West. This is because the forces of the West create the feeling of readiness of the Muslims to fight against the foreign enemy. Whilst this happens, the rulers who have a skin like ours are able to achieve the immediate goals of the West which are concentrated on westernising the Islamic world and secularising it, and crushing anything Islamic and putting it in the forgotten past.

The West has tirelessly insisted on killing Islamic ideology and standing against all the attempts at Islamic renaissance.

The oriental scholars and missionaries were and are a continuation of the Crusades at the ideological level. They opened the insulting door against Islam and have distorted the facts and history. The Western hatred of Islam reached such an extent that their leaders say 'Destroy Islam and eliminate its people', and a well-known Englishman – Gladstone – said 'We have to destroy the Quran and purify Europe from the Muslims', and what is going on in Bosnia and Hercegovenia, where the Serb forces are involved in raping women, destruction and bloodshed, is without a doubt the mere Crusader's black hatred of Islam and his people.

Second What has the West provided humanity with, and what remains of its qualifications to lead the world?

We can clearly say that the West has not provided humanity with anything except the means of self-destruction and collapse at the scientific and moral level . . . The West presents a dark picture of rotten morals with the absence of dignified values, the large-scale and unprecedented Aids epidemic, alcohol and drug addiction.

Therefore Western civilisation has deformed man's morals and made inferior his natural disposition. Let anyone who would like to be more enlightened read the following book: '*The Man that is the Unknown*' by Lalexis Carl: what is the family's situation in the West and what happened to the family from loosening, breakdown and prostitution which went too far?

Arabic poem: 'Nations exist with their morals, they will be gone if their morals have gone'.

The West also has not succeeded in utilising advanced Science and Technology for the welfare of humanity, but it is concerned with the arms race and owns a destruction capability to destroy the earth tens of times!! It spends huge amounts of resources on that, whilst hundreds of deprived and hungry people die every day in poor countries of the world. The West lost its basic qualifications of leadership when it failed to get rid of its racism, and the way it looks at others in a haughty and arrogant way . . . a look of the unjust to the victim . . . a look of strong arrogance towards the weak and impotent. That was why the South was convinced completely and voluntarily rejected the Northern leadership. The West has no respected and appraised values and morals. The West no longer has any qualifications to lead, except through military might which they always use to serve their own interests, not those of justice and dignity, and history is the best witness . . . has the West used its military power to force Israel to withdraw from the Arab occupied land? Has the West intervened to lift the suffering of the Bosnian and Hercegovenian people in the same way it initiated the intervention in the Kuwaiti war?

Third How have the outlook and beliefs of Nations been formed towards the West?

The West has been shown to be lacking in trustworthiness in front of the Muslim people across the world. None of us feel at any day that the West has acted for anything except its own interests which were the only reason for its acts, even at the expense of the lives and blood of Muslims, men, women and children. How could anyone respect the Western call for principles when they do not respect them unless they serve their own aims. They claim for deepening democratic principles and the wishes of the peoples, expressed through the ballot boxes, but in the results won by the FIS Front in Algeria for example, the West initiated support for the secular government, and did not oppose the coup which aimed to prevent the Muslims gaining power. Despite this behaviour, a stab in the heart which falsifies their claim to democracy, we see the West as blind, it cannot see this fact, and we force them to uncover their real and shameful attitudes. How can we believe the West in its claim that they respect human rights when they violate the human rights of man in Palestine, and deport the Palestinians at will from their homes and land. The West is blind to see how the Arab governments oppress the Islamic Movement in an ugly and unprecedented way . . . How can we believe the West without them taking any decisive action on the crimes and formidable acts committed in Sarajevo? The West exceeded the limit when it exploited the severe hardship of some African countries, and practised Christianity there, raising the slogan of 'Believe in the cross and you will eat bread and drink milk!' The real picture has formed in the heart of the Islamic Nation and it very clearly reflects how the West hates Islam and Muslims. We cannot see them more than in fighting us in our earnings and food. Muslim blood is not worth to the West more than the equivalent weight of petrol which it is extracting from our wells at a very cheap price.

Fourth Future relations between the West and the Islamic World.
We can say this will be determined by the Islamic movements. The shining future will be for Islam at Allah's will. If the West continues in its policy of neglect of the rising Islamic force, and continues to support the pro-Western governments in which its share of support is declining day after day, and to lose its support hour after hour. If the West stays like this, without a review of its accounts, it will lose the area of the Islamic world, with the help of Allah.

Therefore the West must improve its image and get rid of its ugly racism, and weigh the issues on one scale, and it should have one policy standard, and close the curtain on its anti-Islamic stance, and stop its aggression to Muslims, and it should not put its weight alongside governments that are going to vanish.

It was a great lesson for the Americans to learn when they supported the former Iranian Shah, and stood against the Iranian people's wishes. The US did not gain anything except the anger and hatred of the masses. We do not require to improve our image in front of the West as others do.

From the beginning, we believe that we have not done anything wrong, but the West's practices and attitudes are still below the acceptable level. It would be better for them to accept the Algerian people's attitude when they proved their stand through the ballot box. But the West disowned its own known principles and gave its support to the unlawful government which pounced on power. The West was able to gain some respect and trust in Egypt, when it endeavoured to force the Egyptian rulers to stop torturing the Muslims and implemented the courts' decisions related to the release of the prisoners, which the [Egyptian] rulers refused to implement and did everything possible to obstruct justice. . . . The West would be able to gain the trust of all Arab people if it treated the Israeli occupation of Palestine in the same way in which it did the Iraqi occupation of Kuwait, and if it treated Sarajevo in the same way as Mogadishu, but the selfish interest which the West follows has made its image that of pirates and armed robbers.

Future relationships depend on the West in the first place. If they want good, then they must change their attitude from now on. If they think they can stand against the people's determination, then it is a mirage disappearing very quickly. The West will then gain more and more huge investments of enemies as a result of what its hands have done.

Finally, there may be a chance for the West. We forward this final word and call them to review their ideological attitude. We assure them that Islam is the Prophets' and Messengers' religion.

Jesus (peace upon him) preached of our prophet Mohammed (peace upon him) in which his invitation was to all peoples, and he was the last prophet and messenger. We are all very anxious that people should follow the true religion for their own welfare and safety in the day of judgement; the non-Muslim must turn immediately towards Mohammed (peace upon him) and believe in him and learn from Allah's book and follow his prophet which would benefit them in their religion and on the day of judgement.

I have no doubt that if Islam is presented to the Western people in a right manner, then a great number of them will believe in Islam, and it is here where the good and distinct preachers play their role in preaching to the followers of *The Book* and to those who are debating in good faith until the appearance of the face of truth, and sparks their understanding of the pure belief of the Unified.'

A.H. (Abbud al-Zumur)

Appendix 2

A note on Religious Fundamentalism with particular reference to Islam

Religious fundamentalism has a clear and relatively specific meaning in the West. It refers to the maintenance of traditional beliefs involving a literal acceptance of the creeds as fundamental, as well as belief in the inerrancy of the Scriptures. It is a term most readily associated with a distinct school of American protestantism, although its usage has extended to embrace a much wider context.

Perhaps the single critical quality of fundamentalism is that the believer takes religion seriously . That is to say, not only is there is a sense of truth and error in their belief systems, but in recognising truth it is the duty of the believer to follow religious prescriptions *because* they represent truth. From a psychological perspective, the significant feature of 'taking religion seriously' is that it implies not just belief, but also behaviour. A quality of the fundamentalist believer is, therefore, the expression of the particular fundamentalist priorities in behaviour of some form.

Because fundamentalism is associated with a referencing back to traditional beliefs and values, the liberal West has a tendency to view such movements as necessarily politically conservative and reactionary. In the present climate, this also tends to result in regarding fundamentalism in a negative way, in the sense of it being a reaction against modernity and a striving for a return to some earlier and (assumed) less liberal society. This assumption that the past is in some way less 'liberal' may well be erroneous when applied in Islamic contexts, however. It is also an inappropriate assumption to make about many contemporary Christian fundamentalists.

If we look at what are termed fundamentalist views on Islam, certainly its critical quality, as seen by the Western observer, is a desire to

206

return to the founding principles of Islam, and particularly those that were associated with the creation of an Islamised society at the time of The Prophet. What we cannot necessarily assume, however, is that this represents a movement 'backwards' away from what the West would regard as liberal social values and 'civilisation' towards a conservative, essentially negative, unchanging world based upon the sixth century. The renewal implied by seeking to return to the fundamentals of Islam can be seen throughout the history of Islam. What we see in the contemporary Islamic world may be better regarded in terms of cyclical religious refreshment rather than social retreat.

What constitutes 'backwards' is, of course, a matter of judgement anyway, and we must not forget the relativity such a judgement implies. Paradoxically, in the contemporary world the changes desired by the Islamic fundamentalist believer may, in many ways, be similar to those desired by the contemporary political radical, at least in terms of process. Both, for example, are searching for a new 'social formula' which requires rejection of the *status quo* and seeks profound social change. These desired changes may, in addition, also be necessarily revolutionary, resulting in the destabilisation and ultimate overthrow of an established regime. Whilst the largely secular political radical and the religious fundamentalist may ultimately desire different things, attainment of their desires might require common processes sufficient to create allegiances. We can see, therefore, why what might be thought to be contradictory terms – radical and fundamentalism – come together in some aspects of contemporary Islam. This seems to be very evident in the contemporary Islamic world, regardless of the debate about whether Islam in origin can be described as a 'political' religion.

To understand this more clearly, it is necessary to examine the aspirations of Islamic fundamentalism within the particular social context in which it occurs. A critical quality of the contemporary Islamic fundamentalist view of the world (both Shi'a and Sunni) is that all present and past Muslim society (with the possible limited exception of Shi'a Iran in some circles) are of limited significance when compared with the 38 year period from 622 to 660 (from the Hegira to the seizure of power by the Umayyad caliph Mu'awiya) which marked the 'Golden Age' of Islam of the period of the rightly guided caliphs. This referencing back to the Golden Age is not simply a response to present conditions, and indeed, for the devout (whether fundamentalist or not) needs no justification in social or economic terms. It is an imperative of belief and an essential quality of the Islamic view of the world. Given this, the transposition to the fundamentalist position of Western values such as freedom of choice, lack of certainty, and assumptions about the legitimacy of the State, can be very misleading and address the wrong frame of reference when applied to Islamic societies.

We will use here the term 'Islamic fundamentalism' to refer to the sense in which the believer does take religion seriously, where there is a sense of truth and error which manifests itself in social and political activity, and where the framework for social change lies primarily in the historical revealed word of God, rather than the present social and economic climate. We should note, however, that whilst we can identify the broad parameters of fundamentalist ideology, the social and political influences of fundamentalist thinking are much more difficult to assess. The significance of Islamic fundamentalism lies not so much in the numbers of believers who adhere strictly to the fundamentalist position, but rather that it provides the moral authority and ideological force from which significant political influence might develop. In numerical terms, the groups within Islam that might attract the term 'fundamentalist' are relatively small; their influence at the moment greatly exceeds their size.

Despite colonialism, economic limitations and political upheaval, Islam continues to command widespread general support across a broad spectrum of citizens in Islamic countries ranging from the rural and urban poor to intellectuals. It may well be that a common denominator of all the groups is a dissatisfaction with their contemporary political and economic situation. But the significance of Islamic fundamentalism lies in its capacity to influence and channel that dissatisfaction in particular directions, rather than in the total number of fundamentalist believers. Particular circumstances (such as a ruler or a war) may influence the precise qualities aspired to, and the pragmatic needs of the moment may temper the political expression of fundamentalist ideology.

The reasons for the increase in influence of fundamentalist movements within Islamic societies are very complex. They relate to both the external and internal dynamics of those societies, and analyses can be developed at a variety of levels. In contrast to this complexity for the outside observer, however, the situation from the perspective of the believer is of course much simpler. The believer would assert that his views represents the revealed word of Allah, and place any account of the resurgence of these distinctive forms of Islam within a theological context. This simplicity of belief and explanation for the believer is a significant quality of the fundamentalist view of the world.

One set of factors that can be identified from a Western social and psychological perspective lies in a general feeling of discontent expressed by many Islamic commentators with the nature of contemporary Islamic States. This discontent is one quality that seems to relate the theological to the political and which may from time to time manifest itself in overtly political activity. This may then be sometimes associated, or perhaps more accurately correlated, with left wing political movements; but it may also become evident in a theological context, and address primarily religious goals. At least in its early stages, the ferment in Algeria following the election victories of Islamic parties illustrate this. However, the all embracing social nature of Islam necessarily means that religious activity will impinge on broader socio-political issues which draws together the theological and political. Indeed, the inclusive quality of Islam presents the Western observer with great difficulties of understanding. Areas of social separation on which the West prides itself and largely takes for granted (such as the distinction between the law and due process, and social and political issues related to public wellbeing) are confounded in Islamic societies. There are surprising differences with Western legal views in assumptions about the nature of legal process, evidence and even the concept of truth, for example. Indeed, what we might characterise in the West as a retreat into theology from the problems of the world within Islam necessarily means a growing engagement with the world and an absorption of the political within the theological. This paradoxical juxtaposition of the political and theological lies at the very heart of Islamic fundamentalism.

Two broad classes of influence can be identified which seem to be associated with the general discontent in Islamic societies – those concerned with the relationship between Islamic states and the wider world, which we might characterise as external factors, and those concerned with Islam itself and its practices, which we might term internal factors. External factors tend to relate to the broad themes of Arab nationalism (at least in the Middle East), but given the social nature of Islam, the simple division of external and internal factors of course interacts in complex ways.

One significant external factor of relevance to the Islamic masses (although possibly of less relevance to the religious) is the relative failure of the Arab and Islamic states to rival Western material wealth and success. The Muslim world remains predominantly a part of the Third World, despite very considerable natural resources (in the form of oil, for example). The major Muslim countries, such as Egypt and Syria, have generally failed to achieve substantial rises in living standards for the vast majority of their citizens compared to the West, and remain with mostly poor peasant economies. In the richer countries (such as the Gulf States) economic wealth has benefited a relatively limited few, and has not been distributed to poorer Islamic countries, nor to their very large migrant communities. Indeed, despite the overt theocratic qualities of life in the Gulf states, to many devout Muslims, the effects of increased oil wealth have been to increase the influence of the West, and challenge the social basis of Islam, rather than to complement and enhance it. Similarly, the impetus to modernisation, secularism and Westernisation which from time to time characterised both Nasser's and Sadat's Egypt, for example, has clearly failed to produce much improvement in most peoples' lives. Furthermore whilst Western economic practices may have contributed relatively little to public well being, much Western investment that occurs in Islamic countries is frequently associated with multinationals, whose loyalties are seen to lie largely with the West. Indeed, such economic benefits as they may bring are often perceived as being of less significance than the negative effects of encouraging secularism and behaviour contrary to Islamic values.

A further significant factor in the current sense of unease are the repeated humiliating failures of Arab armies to defeat Israel. At the popular level, this emotive issue probably serves to polarise opinion more than anything else, and is a significant element in the appeal of Arab nationalism. This public sense of failure to achieve what are perceived to be essentially Arab (and to a lesser extent Islamic) objectives in the face of a strong West is a potent and enduring force which cannot be underestimated. Tourism and the Western media also add further to the sense of specific Islamic concern, through encouraging secularism and the adoption of hedonistic lifestyles. This results in a strange and unexpected paradox. Whilst the contemporary Western view of Islam may be one of buoyancy and concern at its advance (perhaps not without some justification), the Fundamentalist views a situation where Islam appears to be on the retreat from a growing tide of secularism and associated Western values.

Internal features of Islam complement and interact with this general sense of discontent. In the context of concern to us, relevant qualities of Islam as a religion and as a social movement that sustain fundamentalist positions can be identified. These are its claims to universal validity; its theocratic demands extending to all aspects of life; the sanctification of Islamic law and its rulings; and a general equation (at least within Sunni thinking) of the State with the implementation of Islam.

Islam claims that it is the perfect and final embodiment of God's law to the believer; it is thus necessarily the preferred, obvious and appropriate religion for all people. Conditional tolerance of other religions is strictly limited to 'people of the Book' (broadly speaking Christians and Jews) who share a common heritage, even though, from an Islamic perspective, incomplete and flawed. These religious groups can live within an Islamic state without conversion or coercion provided they accepted Muslim rule and payment of a special tax. They have the status of '*dhimmis*', and may be left in peace '. . . under conditions of discrimination, and acceptance of inferiority and humiliation'. Believers in other religions, who do not recognise the role and status of 'The Prophets' cannot be tolerated, and must be converted or killed.

This confers upon an Islamic community a sense of superiority which can draw upon a rich history of Muslim advance and military success. However, the colonial experiences of Islamic states clearly challenged this view. When Western (and largely Christian) states have confronted Islam, they have in recent times emerged victorious in all arenas of conflict. Whilst challenging to notions of Islamic superiority in the short term, this is in itself not necessarily so critical when a broader perspective is taken. There are historical examples from the time of the Prophet of the retreat of Islam, only to rise again with renewed vigour. Retreat and the development of a temporary modus vivendi with the forces of secularism can be tolerated by Islam as short-term responses to circumstances.

More problematic to contemporary Islamic believers in this context are the experiences of post-colonialism. Post-colonial Muslim aspirations to redress the wrongs of colonialism, and to re-establish the relative positions of Muslim versus Christian (from Muslim perspectives) have generally failed, yet Muslim countries have, at least ostensively, been ruled by Muslims and presumably have had the capacity to draw upon the full potential of the force of Islam. The contrast between the achievements of Islamic countries in the contemporary world and the glorious history of Muslim advance in the seventh to tenth centuries only adds to the problem. In the eyes of the Fundamentalist therefore, Islam is challenged and compromised not only by discrepancies in material wealth, but also in terms of its capacity to sustain its own moral and religious authority. Within the largely Sunni countries, such an analysis presents serious difficulties in reconciling conflicting loyalties.

Responses to these apparent challenges to the moral authority of Islam are a critical element of the fundamentalist position. Themes such as these are reflected in critical analyses of the nature of Islam, and in particular can be seen in the writings of Sayyid Qutb, who occupies an important position in the development of Islamic fundamentalist thinking. His writings provide the ideological basis on which many aspects of contemporary radical fundamentalist thinking have developed. Whilst there may be disputes within the various fundamentalist movements about the appropriateness of the solutions he offers, his ideological influence remains unchallenged. In his most influential book[1], Qutb analyses the present state of Islam with particular respect to the challenge to its moral authority. The tone of his analysis can be judged from the following extract:

> The leadership of mankind by Western man is now on the decline, not because Western culture has become poor materially or because its economic and military power has become weak. The period of the Western system has come to an end primarily because it is deprived of those life-giving values which enabled it to be the leader of mankind. It is necessary for the new leadership to preserve and develop the material fruits of the creative genius of Europe, and also to provide mankind with such high ideals and values as have so far remained undiscovered by mankind, and which will also acquaint humanity with a way of life which is harmonious with human nature, which is positive and constructive, and which is practicable.

Islam is the only system which possesses these values and this way of life.

It is interesting to note that fundamentalist analyses of the problems facing Islam never question the ideological bases of Islam. In a sense, of course, this follows from 'taking religion seriously', or at least taking seriously the original precepts upon which a religion is based. But a quality of the fundamentalist believer is that he goes beyond adherence to basic precepts, and makes no distinction between the general principles upon which Islam might be founded as viewed from the twentieth century and the pragmatic responses to life as the 7th century followers of Islam might have found it; the relationship with the contemporary world does not impinge on the analysis. Perhaps as a consequence of that, fundamentalist analyses always locate the source of any problems in their world view externally to the ideological foundations of Islam. Either the West is responsible for deflecting or distorting the inevitability of the proper progress of Islam, or Islamic leaders have failed either through being subverted (again by the West), or because they fail to follow Islamic precepts. What they perceive as the fundamental tenets of Islam are never open to question. Parallels may be drawn here with some of the psychological bases of prejudice, which will be returned to later.

That is not to say, however, that there is no criticism of different perspectives on fundamentalism from within Islam, and indeed from within the various fundamentalist positions. But such discussion is largely concerned with strategy, rather than principle. It typically identifies three themes common to fundamentalist writers – the total debilitation of the *umma* (people), the Western cause of such debilitation, and the flawed basis of any solutions to this problem other than Islam. The final theme is never questioned.

There is certainly a strong tendency amongst writers such as Qutb to stress the poor state of contemporary Islam. In this respect, the theory of modernity as the new barbarity (*Jahiliyya*), which has its origins in the writings of Maudoodi, has played a very prominent role in the fundamentalist justification for the debilitation of the *ummah*. At its simplest, the theory of the new *Jahiliyya* refers to the basic incompatibility between Islam and modernity (as represented by Western values). It echoes the struggles of the Prophet and his followers in the very beginnings of Islam, and draws on Qur'anic themes familiar to all Islamic believers. Striving against the state of *Jahiliyya* provides the focus and justification for the fundamentalist agenda, embracing both the assertion of and the reason for the debilitated *ummah*, and its remedy. Qutb expressed this theme clearly in the following:

> *Jahiliyya* (barbarity) refers to the domination (Hakimiyya) of man over man, or rather the subservience to man rather than to Allah. It denotes rejection of the divinity of God and the adulation of mortals . . . In any time and place human beings face that clear-cut choice: either observe the Law of Allah in its entirety, or to apply laws laid down by man of one sort or another. In the latter case, they are in a state of *Jahiliyya* . . . Modern-style *Jahiliyya* in the industrial societies of Europe and America is essentially similar to the old-time *Jahiliyya* in pagan and nomadic Arabia. For in both systems, man is under the dominion of man rather than Allah.

Qutb argues that Islam is forced to battle with *Jahiliyya* both to protect itself ('. . . its (Islam's) very nature demanded that *jahili* societies would attack it . . .') and as an injunction from Allah because Islam is the total and only way of life for the believer. To battle against *Jahiliyya* fulfils the requirements of *Jihad* (sacred or holy war). It may be necessary in particular circumstances to reach a temporary accommodation with the world as it exists; but restraint and tolerance is '. . . a question of strategy rather than of principle; . . . a matter pertaining to requirements of the movement and not belief'. To achieve its ends, and to fight against *Jahiliyya*, Islam '. . . has a God given right to step forward and take control of the political authority, so that it may establish the Divine system on earth. . . .'

We can see in this discussion the drawing together of the themes referred to earlier. The state of *Jahiliyya* in which the *ummah* finds itself is the fault of the West, and the remedy required of the devout is *Jihad* (holy war). The logic is compelling and attractive if the basic principles are agreed. But above all the analysis is simple, direct, non-threatening, familiar and consistent with the history of Islam. Furthermore, it has great appeal to the urban and rural poor, who have gained relatively little from the various experiments with modernity in the Islamic world. It offers a means of addressing wrongs, and by focusing on moral and spiritual issues rather than material, serves to place Islam on at least equal terms with the West.

Millenarianism

The discussion above has focused on the Islamic context to fundamentalism. These issues can also be viewed from another more general context, which both begins to place them within a broader conceptual framework and makes them more accessible to psychological analysis. Many of the features of Islamic fundamentalist thinking show strong evidence of millenarian influences. Millenarianism describes a distinctive quality of the content of an ideology. But it may also have a psychological dimension in that millenarianism can relate to the way in which ideology can influence behaviour. Millenarianism refers to expectations of the attainment of the Millennium, an expected utopian end. From a theological perspective, this may be associated with the arrival of the Messiah, or God's direct intervention on earth in some sense. From a political perspective, it may be associated with the attainment of a secular utopian state or other means of utopian social organisation. Millenarianism has played, and continues to play an important role in the development of political and religious movements and can be argued to be one of the significant factors in the development of political violence[2].

Five general qualities of millenarian ideologies can be identified:

1. An analysis of the world in terms of a real or impending catastrophe, which has an immediate effect on the individual's life;
2. A revelation that explains this state of affairs, and which offers some form of salvation or redressing of ills;
3. As part of the revelation, the possession of special knowledge by the believer that the disastrous state is the result of the action of malevolent forces (spiritual or secular) which conspire to corrupt and subvert the normal organs of society or the State. Through the possession of special knowledge, the holder has a unique and powerful capacity to fight the malevolent and corrupting forces;
4. A sense of timeliness for action, in that the forces of corruption are nearing completion of their tasks;
5. A conviction that these forces can be defeated because of the special insights, and that the defeat of the forces of evil will result in the ushering in of a new and better world.

Themes like these have recurred throughout the history of Islam. Indeed, millenarian thinking can be traced to the very beginnings of Islam, and especially within Shi'a contexts, to the martyrdom of Ali. The confident expectation of the return of Ali is a feature of many Shi'a sects, but elements of millenarian influence also remain within more orthodox Sunni thinking. More explicit Shi'a millenarian influences can be seen in the way the various Ghulat sects relate to the succession of Immans. The recurrent religious rebellions that have emerged from within Islamic communities to challenge the existing order from the very beginnings of Islam tend to be expressed in millenarian terms, with varying degrees of explicit reference to the Mahdi who would come to save his people. Whilst social and economic factors have undoubtedly played a part in these events, Islamic millenarian movements have remained essentially religious rather than secular movements.

Many of the qualities of Islamic fundamentalist thinking correspond to the qualities of millenarianism outlined above. Fundamentalist analyses of the current state of Islam strongly emphasise the catastrophic nature of contemporary life. Much of Qutb's work, for example, clearly demonstrates this, as do the content of innumerable sermons and pamphlets, based upon his and other fundamentalist thinkers work. The revelatory qualities of the Qur'an, and the role of the fundamentalists in revealing its unique capacity to redress the world's ills offer the 'special' salvation which is so much a feature of millenarian thinking. The special quality of knowledge of the cause of the disastrous present can be clearly seen in Maudoodi's concept of modernity as the new barbarity (*Jahiliyya*), where the influence of the West is very graphically presented to the Islamic masses in diabolical terms. Through returning to the basic principles of Islam, and especially the implementation of the *Shari'a* (Islamic Law), the uniquely powerful forces of Islam can be mobilised against the new *Jahiliyya*. Furthermore, a sense of timeliness and urgency is a prominent feature of fundamentalist thinking – the *ummah* must act now to avert catastrophe. All of these forces come together in the conviction that if implemented, Islam must be victorious and must defeat the forces of *Jahiliyya*. The looking back to the Golden Age of Islam necessarily heralds the dawning of a new Golden Age, if society is truly Islamised and the *Shari'a* implemented.

The assassination of Anwar Sadat in October, 1981, fits clearly into this framework. The assassins of Sadat (discussed in Chapter 6) appear to have ardently desired the foundation of an Islamic state in Egypt, and the assassination of Sadat was to be its herald. They adopted a frankly millenarian outlook where it was argued that Sadat represented the apostate, the representative of *Jahiliyya*. So much were the assassins (but not others who were involved in the plot, especially Abbud al-Zumur) influenced by the millenarian Islamic ideology that they made little or no preparation for the takeover of power after the death of Sadat. Those directly involved in the assassination appeared to have believed that once they had heeded the call to *Jihad*, and assassinated Sadat the Unjust Ruler (*Hakin Zalim*), God would intervene; their action in assassinating him was to herald the millennial event. One reason why the Faridah could be published in Egypt after the event in 1983 was that the assassination appeared not to have established God's intervention, at least in the terms envisaged by Faraj.

The themes discussed above have exercised great influence over contemporary Islamic fundamentalism. Whilst they may emerge in varying contexts, and be subject to differences in emphasis, they set the scene for the moral and psychological appeal of radical Islam. What is interesting and relevant from our point of view is the sense in which political and social issues are drawn into the theological argument. But the remedy for the problems of Islam are not simply constrained by a special world of theology; they necessarily embrace the broader society in which Islam functions and specify certain kinds of behaviour. This ideological position is very clearly developed by Faraj (whose role in the assassination of Sadat is discussed in Chapter 6). In his discussion of the theological ills of contemporary Islam in general, and Egypt in particular (very much in the style of Qutb), he accuses the existing political leadership of Islamic countries of apostasy. Whilst they were born Muslims, they do not run their States as religious Muslim States, with the use of the *Shari'a* as the basis for legislation and social intervention and planning. To Faraj, the link between theology and behaviour is the 'neglected duty', the duty of *Jihad*, the outcome from which will necessarily redress the ills of Islam.

The process of ideological control and lack of public space

There is a further perspective on this issue which we should mention here. Hannah Arendt, in her analyses of the atrocities committed by the Nazi's during The Second World War, developed the concept of lack of public space. This concept addresses the issue of how people who were in other respects normal could become involved in the appalling activities that characterised the Third Reich. Lack of public space relates to the inability of individuals to exchange and develop ideas in circumstances where extreme control is exercised over social living, most notably evident in totalitarian states. She gives to this capacity to communicate a significance in both the political and moral arena, and in particular relates the degree of social control it implies to a loss of a sense of reality and morality, making possible the atrocities of the concentration camps.

The extreme degree of social control required by fundamentalist interpretations of Islam meet the requirements for lack of public space, in Arendt's terms, and in consequence we might expect to see the lack of regard for the restraints on behaviour towards enemies emerging within Islam (although this is a subject dealt with at great length in the Qur'an, where clearly defined and explicit rules are given to regulate conduct). In behavioural terms it can be argued that lack of public space relates very clearly to the degree of control exercised by behavioural rules. Societies showing a lack of public space are characterised by both explicit articulation of rules governing behaviour, and their rigid application and enforcement. Fundamentalist Islamic aspirations readily fit this view.

In a sense, the precise detail of religious observance required is of less importance than the fact that behaviour is under close control of the religious ideology, expressed as rules. The rigidity of purpose, the insensitivity, the focusing, the intensely personalised view of the world, the tolerance of what to the non-initiate is incompatibility, the simplification of the world view and the loss of critical judgement, all seem to be qualities of the religious fundamentalist. They are also qualities which might be thought to illustrate behaviour subject to extreme rule governance, as opposed to contingency control.

Psychological approaches

There are other psychological insights that extend our understanding of these issues. One such relates to the concept of Conspiracy. As we have noted earlier, an important quality of fundamentalist thinking is the malevolence of forces opposed to Islam, which conspire to subvert its message, and undermine the allegiances of believers. Much of Qutb's analysis of the state of the World of Islam, for example, hinges upon assertions of the West's desires to subvert the rightful progress of Islam as the superior religious and social system. How else can the debilitated state of the *umma* be explained? Sometimes the conspiratorial intention is deliberate, and results from explicit acts of policy (shades of this were seen in some Islamic critiques of the Gulf War), but sometimes the West is the unknowing instrument of a diabolical power. We might note, for example, the tendency amongst the combatants in Lebanon to explain victory by reference to courage and patriotism and defeat by reference to plots. This is probably a more general process rather than one confined to the Lebanese experience, but it is particularly evident amongst the

various Lebanese parties. The defeat of Saddam Hussein in the Gulf
War has also sometimes been explained in this way, with frequent reference to 'conspiracies' of either imperialism or colonialism.

Equally, the notion of conspiracy is central to millenarianism. It is
an element of the struggle to attain the millennium, and also might
be thought to be a factor in the notion of 'timeliness' of millenarian
attainment. The central feature of conspiracy in whatever disguise it
appears, is that forces (sometimes defined, sometimes undefined)
conspire to subvert, entrap, or otherwise destroy the positive functions of society. Therefore, when millenarian Islam embraces
conspiracy theories, we might expect forces of great momentum and
power to develop.

The psychological bases of conspiracy theories are complex, but a
factor that might concern us is the sense of undeserved suffering
experienced when an individual fails to attain material or spiritual
benefits despite living a right and proper life. We can see here echoes
of the notions of psychological 'justice' referred to in Chapter 1 as an
element in the justification of terrorism. How can a devout Muslim in
a necessarily superior society and who obeys God's laws and acts in an
upright and moral way experience the defeat, humiliation, and lack
of material advance that has characterised Islamic societies this century? If you accept the premises, the believer is being subjected to an
undeserved injustice which is of fundamental importance, in that it
challenges God's order. For the devoutly religious, because his or her
way of life is ordained by God, it can only fail to deliver its promises
because it is being subverted through some conspiracy of forces
opposed to it. To admit otherwise challenges the bases of belief. This
is not to imply that conspiracy theories are inappropriate, and only
related to contrasts and inconsistencies between belief systems and
actual events. Analyses of the conduct of international affairs suggests
that sometimes, of course, there are both overt and covert conspiracies at work, and the perceptions of participants are accurate!

Leaving aside situations where there are genuine grounds for sus-
pecting conspiracy, one way of understanding the processes that
might be involved in conspiracy is to refer to Festinger's Theory of
Cognitive Dissonance. The cognitive conflict caused by the juxtaposition of firmly held beliefs about superiority, and the evident failure
to attain objectives is resolved by reference to the action of external
agencies. A related explanation refers to processes of attribution, as
a means of understanding the world as we experience it, and in particular to what has been termed actor–observer bias. This refers to
the tendency of people to attribute the causes of their own behaviour
to external factors, as opposed to qualities in themselves. In particular, a striking feature of attributional processes is that it is the world

in which we live that gives rise to our defeats, rather than the inadequacy of our own actions. Attribution of defeat to external causes that actively conspire and plot against us readily fits into this model.

However we conceptualise the issue, the notion of conspiracy is a way of making sense of a complex and confusing world, where real or imagined disadvantage occurs. The practical significance and influence of the notion of conspiracy cannot be underestimated as a factor in the Islamic perception of the world, and as a support for the structure of fundamentalism.

Other social psychological processes seem relevant to this discussion and merit some brief reference. The complex of issues discussed above with reference to conspiracy theories also have elements in common with processes of prejudice formation and stereotyping. Elements of both can be clearly seen in fundamentalism. The images of the West presented by authors such as Qutb draw upon simple stereotypes, attributing largely simplistic negative characteristics to entire communities. Indeed, in other contexts, the anti-Westernism so frequently preached in fundamentalist sermons would attract the term 'racism' and probably be seen as examples of prejudice. The psychological and cognitive bases of the refusal of the believer to question the fundamental tenets of Islam noted earlier might be thought to be related to similar processes observed in analyses of prejudice, where rigidity of view, despite evidence to the contrary, seems to characterise the prejudiced individual.

The above leads to an analysis of religious fundamentalism in terms of a framework in which particular ideological priorities might be expressed. An important implication of this is that fundamentalism is not necessarily a primary, and therefore distinctive, quality of either ideology or religious active, although it may be that it is more likely in some forms of religious expression than others. Nor need we look for particular individual qualities that allow for the expression of fundamentalist views. Rather, fundamentalism can be seen as an instrumental quality of ideology, its incidence being determined by the interaction of ideology as contingency rules, the particular content of ideology, local and immediate behavioural contingencies and situational factors. Indeed, under some circumstances, what we regard as fundamentalism may simply be a rather minor element linked with, and subsidiary to, other more powerful controlling contingencies. The broader consequences of fundamentalism may, of course, be profound for the recipient, or the society in which it occurs. But as far as the individual is concerned, it may well be an incidental element in the broader contingencies controlling behaviour.

The behaviour of the religious fundamentalist can be thought of as having qualities similar to those of normal people, differing along a continuum of some kind rather than differing in absolute terms. Perhaps one way of characterising that continuum is in terms of the extent to which the fundamentalist's behaviour is closely controlled by a limited set of rules which are relatively constrained in extent and closely interrelated. This contrasts with the relative multiplicity of rules that might control normal behaviour, and the extent of control exercised by immediate circumstances.

If we express this difference in such a way, this is not simply a tautology, nor is it an elaborate version of mentalistic accounts. An individual can be 'fanatical' (for this is another way of describing the qualities that we are concerned with) about a variety of things – he might fanatically follow a sport or become wholly absorbed and involved in an aspect of work. All are examples of the control exercised by behavioural rules. The nature of the particular rule following behaviour will clearly determine the focus. The distinctive quality of fanatical religious behaviour (which might be an appropriate term for fundamentalism) is the extent of control which is itself a reflection of the all embracing qualities of religion, in contrast to the limited scope of sport related rules, for example. In describing ideologically controlled behaviour in this way, and in particular by relating it to the behaviour of the religious fundamentalist, we are not therefore only describing the nature of behavioural control, but also describing the processes whereby such control develops.

We can identify a number of important qualities of religious ideology that can now be brought within a broader framework. In particular, distinctions may be made between the content of ideology (the particular kind of religion, the specific nature of religious rules), and the process of ideology, implied and influenced by an ideology's particular content. At least three principal factors can be identified:

1. The specific content of an ideology (in terms of militancy, injunctions at a micro-level, etc.);
2. A more diffuse and higher level aspect of content, particularly as it relates to millenarianism;
3. The process implied by extreme ideological control, which can been characterised as 'lack of public space', as discussed above.

Other factors may of course be relevant, and this area needs further exploration. In the following, we will examine 1. and 2. above in more detail.

If we examine the notion of specific ideological content, the precise day to day injunctions of a religion are clearly one important element in determining religious behaviour. The prescriptions to prayer, for example, or the performance of fasting during ramadan are examples of the control of day to day religious life. The five 'pillars' of Islam can be seen in this light, as an example of specific ideological content. Allied to this level of specificity are more general injunctions, perhaps even directly related to violence. Nazi ideology was replete with reference to the Jews as negative objects, and it urged discrimination and violence upon them in a very explicit way. The extent to which an ideology explicitly rejects a group, and expresses that rejection in militant terms, is clearly one aspect of the potential for violence within an ideology.

Fundamentalist Islam quite clearly develops as part of the content of its ideological prescriptions militancy against Western life and Western culture. Islam contains many qualities which can be used to sustain a militant approach, the most notable of which is the concept of *Jihad*. '*Jihad* in Islam is simply a name for striving to make this system of life dominant in the world', (Qutb) expresses clearly the combative nature of Islam, at least as seen by Qutb. If it is accepted that Western life is *jahili*, that the state of *Jahiliyya* is by definition opposing Islam, and that it is the righteous duty of the believer to fight and defeat *Jahiliyya*, Islam must necessarily be in a state of *Jihad* against the West. Strategic considerations may limit the extent and nature of warfare and short term accommodations may be made; but ultimately, war must be engaged (an important rider to this is the conviction that victory is certain).

This ideological imperative for *Jihad* need not in any way diminish the peaceful aspirations of Islam seen from the perspective of the believer. A fundamental requirement of Islam is that a Muslim is required to establish the sovereignty of God on earth. *Jihad* is a means of establishing this – '*Jihad*, then, is a means to achieve a universal change by establishing peace of conscience, domestic peace, national peace and international peace' (Qutb). Because, for the believer, Islam is necessarily the only possible way to attain God's dominion on the earth, the establishment of an Islamic world must produce God's peace and justice. Islam might be termed a self-contained religion – it contains within itself all that is necessary for the believer to attain salvation and God's peace. Not to accept this obvious and unchallengeable logic can only be the result of malevolent influences, which are working to oppose the establishment of God's law (an issue related to conspiracy theories discussed earlier). Qutb argues at considerable length the tolerant nature of Islam, but the tolerance only extends to those who accept the logic. Enemies of Islam are offered three choices – to adopt Islam, to pay the tribute (as an acknowledgement that the non-believer will not impede the progress of

Islam), or to fight (because they 'obdurately stand between men and Islam's righteous and peaceful principles'). Given these views, what might be termed the militant logic of radical and fundamentalist Islam will inevitably establish confrontation between Islam and the West.

In behavioural terms, what we might characterise as the logic of Islam is no more than an expression of behavioural rules, that specify relationships between long term ends and immediate behaviour. The rules have their origin in the bases of Islam and the *Shari'a*, (the Qur'an, etc.) and the more detailed relationships are made explicit (and given a distinctive emphasis) by authors such as Qutb. They are further refined by various commentaries and at the local level by weekly sermons in the Mosques, etc.

A more explicit example of behavioural rules is of course the concept of *Shari'a*. Islam equates the laws of human nature with the laws of the universe (what we might term physical laws). Both are aspects of God's Will, both are immutable qualities of life, and both must be obeyed. This extends as much to voluntary as involuntary behaviour -- but for the former, God especially prescribed the *Shari'a* to ensure that man's '. . . life is in harmony with his own nature' (Qutb). *Shari'a* is the divine expression of God's law, and is found in the Qur'an, the Sunna and the Hadiths (the precise weighting and form given to each element of the Holy writings relates to particular emphases and traditions within Islam).

The refinement process in the development of religious behavioural rules can be seen in the relationship between *Shari'a* and the sources of Islamic law. The only source of authoritative written law in Islam is the Qur'an. 'It is the exact spoken word of God as reduced to writing by the Prophet . . .' Whilst the Qur'an contains direct guidance, it is often expressed at a level of general principle, from which detailed judgements have to be derived. The Sunna were recorded after the Prophet's death, and constitute more substantive forms of guidance. The other sources of law (analogical reasoning or, *qiya*, and the notion of consensus or *ijma*) allow more detailed working out of general propositions related to the particular social circumstances of the time. It is of some significance that the contemporary role of *qiya* and *ijma* in the determination of *Shari'a* constitutes one of the watersheds that divide fundamentalist thinking from other emphases within Islam. However, *Shari'a* serves to establish a common bond between all Muslims, and its divine origin places it in a unique position with respect to human affairs. Its application is an element of faith for the devout, as the clear, unambiguous and detailed expression of God's will.

The *Shari'a* specifies behaviours appropriate to situations at a variety of levels. In the West, we tend to be most aware of *Shari'a* when applied within the context of criminal law, and more specifically in terms of the system of punishments specified for theft (amputation) and adultery (stoning). But *Shari'a* extends far beyond these limited confines, and embraces all aspects of jurisprudence, social living, the relationship between people in business and commercial enterprises, and indeed the relationship between states. The self-contained nature of Islam is apparent in this area as in others – 'One cannot enforce a part of Islamic law and neglect another for then it would not be Islam' (Qutb).

The detail of what is precisely meant by *Shari'a* is itself a matter of some debate, and as we noted earlier, its exact meaning and referencing to the Qur'an, Sunna and Hadiths represents one of the watersheds along which approaches to Islam divide. No matter what particular approach is taken, however, an essential social expression of the necessary fundamental and total change desired by the fundamentalist believer is a demand to implement the *Shari'a*. This is generally regardless of the broader social contexts and religious allegiances of those subjected to it. It is this demand that embodies in many respects the particular ideological qualities of social control within contemporary radical Islam. Because most Muslim States do not apply *Shari'a*, the issue has become a tangible social aspiration which brings together both fundamentalist politics and theology. 'Thus the *Shari'a* which God has given to man to organise his life is also a universal law. . . obedience to the *Shari'a* becomes a necessity for human beings so that their lives may become harmonious and in tune with the rest of the universe' (Qutb).

For the Islamic fundamentalist, the *Shari'a* is essentially an expression of behavioural rules. We should note that it is expressed at a behavioural level, and sets out clearly and unambiguously (subject to whatever interpretation authority places upon it) what an individual should and must do in given situations. If the fundamentalist does take religion seriously, (as we noted earlier), and acts upon what religion requires, he implements and adheres to these rules in his everyday life. It is difficult to imagine a clearer example of behavioural rule-following than the fundamentalist believer.

Two other aspects of the 'content' of Islam merit attention in this context. These are the concepts of *bai'a* and *taqiia*. Both address issues related to the relationship between behaviour and Islam. *Bai'a* relates to the notion of allegiance and homage of the faithful to their leader. In Sunni terms, precedents for its significance lie in the succession of Abu Bakr to the Caliphate, which was made legitimate by the concept of *bai'a*, where those present also pledged the absent. The concept extends beyond simple allegiance in any Western sense, however, and draws upon the relationship between the Caliph (or leader) and Allah. *Bai'a* implies, therefore, a bond of absolute allegiance, which may ultimately be to death if necessary. Faraj extends this issue, however, by distinguishing between the Oath of Allegiance to the Caliph, and the Oath of Allegiance till death. The significance of this is that the strength and moral demands of the Oath relates to the Caliph as the representative of Allah.

The requirement of *bai'a* can at times conflict with the duty which both Qutb and Faraj stress of the appropriateness of *Jihad* under some conditions against the rulers of Islamic states. The conflict is resolved, however, if the ruler does not follow the principles of Islam, and is therefore either an apostate or *Jahili*. In this case, the devout are required to kill him, despite claims from the ruler of *bai'a*.

The essentially Shi'a concept of *taqiia* relates to piousness that requires deception. The Qur'an contains detailed accounts of how Muslims must behave, both to other Muslims and to non-believers, which generally stress propriety and respect for others. In conditions of *Jihad*, however, there are circumstances where the injunctions against such things as deceit may be waived to enable some eventual achievement. Qutb discusses this, but a clearer account is given by Faraj where he discusses the appropriateness of lying to the enemy. Faraj asserts that it is quite permissible to lie in the course of *Jihad*.

The actions of the group to which Faraj belonged illustrated both the limits on *bai'a* and the notion of *taqiia*. The assassins of Sadat were army officers, who remained as a clandestine group until the assassination itself. Whilst Sadat, as leader of the Egyptian State, could command *bai'a*, his position as analysed by Faraj placed him in the realms of *Jihad*, where *taqiia* and breaking *bai'a* was appropriate. In one sense, *bai'a* clearly relates to the strength of rule control, and the behaviour of the conspirators associated with Faraj clearly demonstrate this. But the ideological bases of fundamentalist thinking can also result in a shift of control, expressed as a limitation on the concept of *bai'a* with respect to particular rules, and an extension of the concept to embrace the supra-ordinate demands of *bai'a* to Allah. Deception and *taqiia* then become appropriate.

The significance of this for analyses of fundamentalist behaviour should not be underestimated. In the capacity of Islam to sustain the suicide bombers, for example, we can see at one level evidence of the strength of *bai'a*. Similarly, we can see that what might appear to be duplicity on the part of participants in some negotiation is entirely appropriate and moral from their perspective where it involves *Jihad*. There is another sense in which this is significant, however. Both *bai'a* and *taqiia* are concepts more readily associated with *Shi'a* thinking rather than that of Sunni. The stress Sunni fundamentalist authors (such as Qutb) place on these concepts, marks the introduction of a significant new factor into Sunni ideology through a re-examination and re-emphasis of these concepts. These are clearly articulated aspects of fundamentalist ideology, and in the terms of the analysis presented here, because they are clearly articulated we would expect them to play a part in determining the behaviour of believers. It follows, therefore, that the actions of Faraj and his co-conspirators should not be seen as isolated aberrations within Sunni thinking, but as markers of its radicalisation, or even, as some commentators have suggested, its Shi'atisation. If we are to take the content of ideology seriously, as is argued above, then the following comments by Qutb encompass the fundamentalist agenda: 'The foremost duty of Islam in this world is to depose *Jahiliyya* from the leadership of man, and to take the leadership into its own hands . . .' (Qutb). The grounding of fundamentalist Islam in its classical history, and the historical strength of the Muslim empire provides a rich source for very worrying analogies with the present day.

Ideology can be seen as affecting behaviour at a variety of levels. An example of this can be seen in the earlier discussion, where reference was made to the millenarian qualities of militant Islam. These qualities can also be located within a general framework emphasising behavioural rules. But of particular relevance to our discussion are the relationships in millenarian ideology between the expected end state and human agency, in bringing about the desired state. Many, if not all, religions are millenarian, in the sense that they allow the believer to look forward to a better, happier and probably more just life after death. The particular quality that brings millenarianism within our explanatory framework is the sense of imminence of millenarian attainment. It is also this quality that relates millenarianism to violence.

Whether imminence is a variable affecting the positive consequences of behavioural rules, or whether it relates to notions of 'easy to follow' and 'hard to follow' rules, or indeed other factors, is unclear. There are, however, cogent arguments to support the notion that the timeliness of action, which is so much a feature of millenarian activity, relates to the imminent attainment of the millennium, and that such a sense of timeliness is a significant factor in the development of violence and an associated sense of personal agency .

Millenarianism is at one level an aspect of the content of ideology, but at another level of analysis it has certain features that relate to more general processes. As we have seen in our earlier discussion, fundamentalist thinkers strongly emphasise the timeliness of action for the believer, given the apocalyptic features of the present, and the profoundly positive consequences of engagement with the apocalyptic forces. Consistent with the above discussion, we might note that the focus of the negative effects on the world is secularism, embodied by Western values and economic power. Thus we see a further behavioural pressure towards fundamentalist confrontation with the West, which we can conceptualise within the context of behavioural rules.

The nature of Islamic fundamentalism is little understood by most citizens of the Western world. They would do well to study it and come to realise that it is a force of vast potential. As the North/South divide deepens in the years ahead, so will the threat of a devastating confrontation between Islam and the West, and so of *jihad* increase. Unlike Communism, Islam does not contain the seeds of its own defeat.

Chapter Notes

Chapter 1: Introduction
1 Taylor M, *The Terrorist* (Brassey's, London 1988). Taylor M, *The Fanatics* (Brassey's, London 1991)

Chapter 2: Becoming and Remaining Involved
1 A more extensive discussion of the various paramilitary organisations in Northern Ireland is presented in Chapter 3.
2 Arendt, Hannah, *Eichmann in Jerusalem* (Penguin Books, Harmondsworth, 1987)
3 The events leading to the arrest of Wackernagel and Schneider and a discussion of the Red Army Faction, to which they belonged, is presented in Chapter 5.
4 Pig: Saracen Armoured Personnel Carrier, widely used by the British Army in Northern Ireland.
5 For further details of this phase in the development of the UDA, see Chapter 3.
6 For a discussion of the UDF and its relationship with the UDA, see Chapter 3.
7 For further discussion of Alberto Franceschini and the Italian Red Brigades, see Chapter 5.
8 Initials are used to obscure the identity of the man concerned.
9 Nelson's activities are described in detail in Chapter 3
10 For details of the contents of *The Green Book*, see Chapter 4.
11 IO: Intelligence Officer

Chapter 3: Terrorist Organisations in Ireland

1 See, for example, Adamson I, *Cruthin. The Ancient Kindred* (Pretain Press, Belfast 1978) and Adamson I, *The Identity of Ulster. The land, the language and the people* (Baird, Belfast, 1982). These views are developed further at a more popular level in political literature associated with the UDA, such as the magazine *Ulster* and *The New Ulster Defender*, the magazine of the Ulster Information Service. For example, in the Vol I, No. 6 issue of the latter, under the title 'A sense of belonging can take us beyond the religious divide', there is a four page account of the defence of Ulster against the invasions of the Gaels by the early inhabitants.

Chapter 4: Two Crazed Peoples

1 See discussion in Chapter 3
2 OC: Officer Commanding
3 IO: Intelligence Officer
4 Cumann: organisation, committee, society
5 SDLP: Social Democratic and Labour Party – the major constitutional nationalist political party holding seats in the British Parliament.
6 The six counties: term used to describe The Province of Northern Ireland, which is made up of the counties of Fermanagh, Armagh, Tyrone, Antrim, Londonderry and Down.

Chapter 5: Action and Engagement

1 The interview was conducted in Italian and the recording translated into English.
2 The *Collettivo Politico Operai Studenti* (CPOS) was popularly known as the 'Apartment Group' (after its meeting place). It was the fusion of this group with similar groups from Milan in 1970 that led to the formation of the Red Brigades.
3 A bomb exploded in the Piazza Fontana in Milan causing 17 deaths and injuring 88 people. Although the Government placed the blame for the bomb on left wing groups initially, a more likely explanation is that it was the work of right wing extremists.
4 A founder member of the Milanese group, *Colletivo Politico Metropolitano*, one of the Apartment Group to produce the Red Brigades.

Chapter 6: The Ends Justify the Means

1 *The Times*, London, 25 October 1986.
2 This document is reproduced in translation as Appendix 1 on page 202.

3 See Taylor M, *The Fanatics: A Behavioural Approach to Political Violence* (Brassey's, London 1991) for a full discussion of Millenarianism.

Appendix 2: A Note on Religious Fundamentalism with particular reference to Islam

1 Qutb S, *Milestones* (Holy Koran Publishing House, Beirut and Damascus, 1978)
2 For a more detailed discussion, see Taylor M, *The Fanatics: A Behavioural Approach to Political Violence* (Brassey's, London 1991)

Index